BALLET CHRONICLE

B. H. HAGGIN

BALLET CHRONICLE

715648

HORIZON PRESS • New York

FOREWORD

Early in 1935 I ended a Sunday article in *The Brooklyn Eagle* with a passage which began:

Ballet is not my field; but I think I may speak, without presuming, of aspects of George Balanchine's work that have delighted me in *Pastorale*, *The Prodigal Son* and *The Ball*, which I saw performed by the Diaghilev company; in *Concurrence* and *Cotillon*, which were done last year by the Monte Carlo company; and now in the various productions of the American Ballet.

By ballet not being my field I meant that I hadn't had the professional training in ballet that I had had in music, and therefore didn't see what the dancer's eye could see. But I wrote nevertheless in the belief that even a report of what my non-dancer's eye could see would have some interest and value for the reader. (I might add that in the last Diaghilev season of 1929 I had seen also Balanchine's *La Chatte*, his version of Act 2 of *Swan Lake*, which became the one danced by other companies thereafter, and Fokine's *Petrushka* with Karsavina; that in the 1928 season I had seen one of the first performances of Balanchine's *Apollo*, which had baffled me completely with its originality of movement and metaphor; that in New York in 1916 I had seen the Diaghilev company with Nijinsky in *Petrushka*, *The Specter of the Rose*, *Scheherazade*, *Les Sylphides*, *Carnaval* and *Afternoon of a Faun;* and that a couple of years earlier I had seen Pavlova and her company in a few performances, including one of *Giselle*. (I still retain the image of Nijinsky, in *Scheherazade*, at the feet of the Sultana, his hands moving avidly all over her body but not touching it, his eyes looking up to where I sat in the first row on the extreme left side of the Family Circle in the Metropolitan Opera House.)

Even my non-dancer's eye had learned to see more of what it looked at by the time I wrote my next piece on the subject, in *The Nation* in December 1940. It brought me a letter from Lincoln Kirstein, to whose *Hound & Horn* I had, in 1933 and 1934, contributed several music chronicles, and who wrote now that Balanchine would like to thank me for the article, and would I come to the School of American Ballet, where I could watch him teach a class and then go somewhere with them for lunch. Actually I had already seen and been introduced to Balanchine a few times in his first years at the school, but as one of many people whom he had no reason to remember five minutes later. This time I was the only observer at the class, and there were only the three of us at lunch.

On the way to the restaurant I said to Balanchine I wasn't sure I had any business writing on a subject about which I had no technical knowledge; and he replied: "Oh no: you look; you see; you write what you see; and that's good." And he went on to speak of the critics in Europe: "Each time I made a new ballet they said it was a deterioration from the good one I made the last time; but they said the same thing about *that* one when it was new."

Still on the way to the restaurant I mentioned the pleasure I had had from seeing *Cotillon* again, performed by the de Basil company, which was then in New York. And when Balanchine answered that with the passing of time and changes of dancers the choreography *of Cotillon* had become very inaccurate, I begged him to restore it to accuracy. He looked pleased by my feeling about the work, but said nothing.

Later, in conversation at lunch, Kirstein asked Balanchine how the rehearsals of the new ballet he was doing for the de Basil company were going. "Oh, all right," said Balanchine. "You must know what you are doing; because the dancers can tell if you know or you don't know. If you know, they will do whatever you say. If you say, 'Take off all your clothes,' they will do it. If you say, 'Lift both your legs and stay in the air,' they will do it." When he left the table to make a telephone call I asked Kirstein if there was any possibility of my watching the rehearsals of the new ballet. "Ask him," said Kirstein; and when I did ask, Balanchine's answer was "Certainly."

So I began to attend, day after day, the rehearsals of *Balustrade*, where I observed Balanchine inventing, phrase by phrase, the connected movements of the new ballet* and demonstrating them to the dancers, and discovered that although the movements were devised to suit the particular body and individual style of each dancer, they invariably were more exciting when Balanchine did them. And not just *Balustrade*: to my surprise and delight Balanchine held two rehearsals of *Cotillon*, at which, as he taught the dancers the correct movements, he made me aware of details I would have missed at the subsequent performances—the last in New York of this unforgettable ballet. Nor only *Balustrade* and *Cotillon*: my observation of Balanchine's rehearsals continued in the years that followed, and continues today.

Morever, at the same time as I was learning to see some things by watching him invent the

movements of *Concerto Barocco* and *Ballet Imperial* for the American Ballet's 1941 South American tour, I was learning to see other things by repeatedly watching Markova dance in the Ballet Theater performances of *Giselle*, *Les Sylphides*, *Swan Lake* and Tudor's *Romeo and Juliet*. When Balanchine, in 1944, began to work with the Ballet Russe de Monte Carlo, and I watched him produce *Danses Concertantes*, *Le Baiser de la Fée*, *Night Shadow* (now called *La Sonnambula*), *Mozartiana* and *Raymonda* with Danilova and Franklin, I began my learning from Danilova (on one occasion from a rehearsal of *Swan Lake* in which she showed a new partner the mechanics of her performance). With the advent of the New York City Ballet I learned, at rehearsals and performances, from LeClercq, Moncion, Kent, Verdy, and recently Mimi Paul and Farrell. And of course I learned from the occasional performances here of Fonteyn, Bruhn, Ulanova, Kolpakova, Sizova, Nureyev.

What I saw and learned I reported in *The Nation* until 1957, and from 1958 in *The Hudson Review*; and this book offers a number of those reports of happenings in ballet here in the years since the collection of Edwin Denby's reviews and articles, *Looking at the Dance*, reissued in 1968, was first published in 1948. Since I don't have the dancer's eye Denby has, my reports don't include things he would have described; but I offer them, in spite of my awareness of their limitations, in the belief that even what my non-dancer's eye saw can have interest and value for the reader. Morever, to what I saw the book adds what is to be seen in the photographs.

Not everything discussed in the text is documented with photographs. For one thing, since the number I could include was not unlimited I couldn't use all I wanted to use even of important ballets, and therefore omitted those of unimportant ones. And I found myself unable to provide some of the photographs I wanted of important works and performances: they simply didn't exist. I did manage to obtain from Lazovsky himself the old photograph of him in *Petrushka* I wanted; but even Danilova didn't have photographs of her perform-

*At one of these rehearsals he said to me: "In Massine's ballets the dancers make some movements here; then they walk to another place and make some movements there. In my ballets the movements are all connected from beginning to end."

ances in *Night Shadow* and *Mozartiana*. Nor could I find photographs of the extraordinary opening solo in the *Phlegmatic Variation* of Balanchine's *The Four Temperaments* that was done for ten years by Todd Bolender (a photographer who had photographed the New York City Ballet those ten years but had no photographs of Boldender's solo said: "He moved his wrists up and down; who would want a photograph of that?"). In some such instances I had to use photographs of later performances by other dancers; in some instances I preferred to use them; and in some I provided both.

One thing to point out is that the still photographs catch impressive moments but cannot give the connections from one such caught moment to the next that are so exciting in Balanchine's choreography and Verdy's dancing. Thus the three successive moments caught in the photographs of Verdy's supported adagio with Ludlow in *Emeralds* are strikingly beautiful in themselves; but the photographs cannot show them in the breathtaking progression in which they are seen on the stage — the progression in which the dancers' fascinating exchanges of hands make possible the leverages for the turns and other movements that take Verdy from the moment in the first photograph to the one in the second, and from this to the one in the third. Only a motion picture can show this; and I was fortunate in being able to reproduce from films of Verdy and Villella in *Giselle* and Balanchine's Tchaikovsky *Pas de Deux* a number of frames which give one an idea of what happens in a few of the sequences of movement.

Finally an explanatory note on one feature of the text. Writing my reports at intervals of months I felt free to repeat a useful phrase like Otis Ferguson's "as fresh and glistening as creation itself" or an actor-director friend's evaluation of Balanchine as a creator in the theater. And bringing them together in this book I decided against eliminating such repetitions.

BALLET CHRONICLE

1947   *12 July 1947* The Monte Carlo Ballet Russe, which began its season in New York last September insufficiently rehearsed, returned to the City Center for its spring season in a state of exhaustion which made the opening performance of *Danses Concertantes* as agonizing for the spectator as it appeared to be for the dancers. One learned that a wreck on the New Haven had kept them in the Bridgeport station until four o'clock that morning; but this didn't account for the fatigue that continued evident the rest of the first week. The third week Alexandra Danilova was out several days with a blister; the last week Maria Tallchief left, Danilova was out again with a sinus attack, and Ruthanna Boris with an injured ankle. Even with the company intact there aren't enough first-rank dancers for all the parts that require them, or for alternation in those parts—so that one gets *Swan Lake, The Nutcracker* and *Ballet Imperial* with Nicholas Magallanes in parts in which he is embarrassingly incapable of the brilliance they are intended to exhibit; *Ballet Imperial* with Natalie Krassovska in a part which requires dazzling speed and sharpness that she lacks; Krassovska also as Danilova's alternate in *Night Shadow*, in which she is incapable of Danilova's sustained intensity; Krassovska and Leon Danielian as the inadequate alternates—without the wit and grandeur —of Danilova and Franklin in *Mozartiana*; Herbert Bliss in the Franklin part in *Rodeo*, for which he hasn't the brilliance and personal force. And when things go wrong the company has no replacements: there was, last spring, more of Krassovska in place of Danilova; there

were Gertrude Tyven, coquettish but unimpassioned, in Tallchief's role in *Night Shadow*, and Vida Brown, without Tallchief's sinister force, as the Fairy in *Le Baiser de la Fée*.

With luck—which I didn't always have—one got the occasional great performances of some of the greatest works in the present-day ballet repertory — *Le Baiser, Danses Concertantes, Mozartiana, Night Shadow, Le Bourgeois Gentilhomme, Coppélia, The Nutcracker*. Without luck one got the less effective performances of these works and of other great works—*Ballet Imperial, Concerto Barocco, Serenade*. If one was lucky one got, with these, at least a Danilova performance in *Swan Lake* or *Gaîté Parisienne* or *Raymonda*; if not, one got an evening without Danilova in anything at all. And with no luck one got, in addition, *The Bells* or *Snow Maiden* or *Comedia Balletica* or *Scheherazade* or *Le Spectre de la Rose* with Danielian. *(112–113)*[*]

As for the new ballets, with good luck one saw Antonia Cobos's little dance suite, *Madroños*, not all of it as good as the very funny opening scene and some of Miss Cobos's own amusingly light and sharp Spanish-style dancing at the première. With poor luck one saw Valerie Bettis's *Virginia Sampler*, a long and dull piece by a modern dancer unable, working with more richly equipped ballet dancers, to transcend the limitations of her vocabulary and the ideas based on it.

[*]Throughout the text, such numbers in parenthesis refer to the pages on which photographs illustrating the text will be found.

19 July 1947 Going to the opening of Ballet Theater's spring season at New York's City Center with high expectations, after last fall's performances, I was shocked by a performance of *Les Sylphides* in which the soloists jabbed and flung themselves in all directions with exhibitionistic violence, distorting the piece and destroying its poetic quality. And this was only the first of the performances which provided the clearest, most forceful illustration of the tendencies Edwin Denby warned against repeatedly in his *Herald Tribune* reviews.

As far back as 1943 he spoke of Ballet Theater's stress of obvious dramatic expression in dancing, and of how the need of getting specific points across to the audience encouraged the dancer to focus attention on himself and got him to think this was the only kind of dancing that was important; whereas, said Denby, there were old and new ballets with poetic rather than dramatic intention, which was realized by delicate finish in the execution of movements with dance meaning rather than dramatic meaning. Ballet Theater's dancers had, then, developed a fine verve in dancing, but not "the sensitive articulation of movement which people call elegance"; they "got across to the audience boldly," but overdid their parts and tried "to top each other till the effect has been silly and vulgar." He therefore welcomed their new interest in the classics which he thought the best corrective for those faults. "For though the classics need dance verve and stage presence to bring them to life, they also need dance elegance and personal reticence: a classic dancer doesn't spill his personal glamor all over the stage as a dancer in a character part is sometimes tempted to do." But what Ballet Theater's dancers did recently was to carry the faults of their character dancing into their classical dancing.

In this the company followed the lead of Alicia Alonso, illustrating Denby's observation that in classical ballet the ballerina sets the style for the company. Alonso's own tendency is toward brilliance in *allegro,* with "high extensions . . . quick balance . . . bold, clear speed"; in competition with Alicia Markova she acquired a considerable measure of quiet and reticence;

with Markova gone from the company Alonso feels free—and privileged by her new status as ballerina of the company—to do again what comes naturally.

In the two performances of Balanchine's *Apollo* Igor Youskevitch knew his part even less well than last fall—from which one got an idea of how many performances of *Apollo* he had danced in since then, and how *Apollo* was regarded by the artistic directors of the company, and what sort of artistic brains and conscience were to receive the high-powered support of the newly formed Ballet Theater Foundation.

3 January 1948 If Alicia Alonso is capable of 1948 gratitude—and perhaps I should say first if she is capable of realizing what Balanchine has done for her in his new piece for Ballet Theater, *Theme and Variations*—she will sell her earrings,* if necessary, to buy him a suitably expensive present.

After the violence that I had found disturbing in her work last spring, its quiet in the opening *Les Sylphides* of Ballet Theater's recent season at City Center was an agreeable surprise—the more agreeable since it resulted in similar quiet in the work of the other dancers. It was an enjoyable performance, in which Alonso danced with the impressive technical assurance, the cool grace and clarity, the ease and elegance of the first-rate dancer she has developed into—though without the powers of personal, emotional projection of the great ballerina, which would have irradiated the *Sylphides* performance and made it an excitingly great one. This lack of projection was one reason for the difference in the effect of Alonso's beautiful dancing in the second act of *Giselle* as compared with Alicia Markova's—another being her lack of Markova's subtlety of rhythm and phrasing. And what Balanchine did for her in *Theme and Variations* was not merely to use everything she does best as a dancer—her sharp attacks, her secure feats of point-balance, for

---

*"They're from Woolworth's!" Balanchine exclaimed in pretended indignation.

example—but to use them in a style that made her glamorous and radiant. After seeing an early rehearsal of her *pas de deux* with Igor Youskevitch Edwin Denby had written me that Balanchine had invented another new character; but what he also invented was a new personality for Alonso. (This enabled John Martin, an admirer of Alonso, for the first time to enjoy a work of Balanchine—his way of putting it being that Balanchine for the first time had produced a good ballet.* It also led Walter Terry to call *Theme and Variations* the greatest classical ballet of our time, when in fact it is a lovely work but Balanchine has done far greater ones —*Concerto Barocco, Danses Concertantes, The Four Temperaments.*)

In *Theme and Variations* Balanchine also used to best effect the things Youskevitch does well in his elegant classical style. These, unfortunately, are not the things he is required to do in Balanchine's *Apollo*; and what he is required to do there he does even less well than a year ago—the infrequent performances having caused him to forget much of what he barely learned. I am glad Ballet Theater is adding works of Balanchine to its repertory; but I would be gladder still if it treated the works as though it really valued them—by rehearsing and performing them sufficiently to keep them from deteriorating like *Apollo*, or being forgotten entirely like *Waltz Academy. (116–118)*

15 May 1948 The works of Balanchine that Ballet Society presented during the past season were new manifestations of the powers which make him, for me, the greatest living creative artist. Most obviously, of course, the powers in his own medium, which astound and delight one in each new work with their further transformation and enriching elaboration of the familiar elements of his distinctive vocabulary, their inexhaustibly inventive use of that vocabulary, their strokes of fantasy and wit. But

*Martin's writing about Balanchine's work for many years was that of someone with an unerring eye for greatness and an unrelenting hatred for it.

in addition, as one tries to account for what is new in each work one realizes that it is related to what is different in the vocabulary, the style, the texture, the rhythmic flow, the emotional connotations of the particular piece of music by Mozart *(Symphonie Concertante)* or Bizet *(Symphony in C)* or Haieff *(Divertimento)* or Hindemith *(The Four Temperaments)*—in other words, that it represents the operation of extraordinary powers in relation to music. And when one comes to works like *The Triumph of Bacchus and Ariadne* (with music by Rieti and scenery and costumes by Cagli) or *Orpheus* (with music by Stravinsky and scenery and costumes by Noguchi) one recognizes the operation of equal powers in drama and its realization in the theater. In the case of *Orpheus* I would say that Balanchine's powers are such as to enable him not only to profit by one of Stravinsky's most masterly dramatic scores but to overcome the handicap of an intrusively alien extremism and preciousness in the scenery and costumes. *(118–125)*

The works showed another power of Balanchine—his ability to use the personal style of each dancer and what the dancer does best, whether it is Maria Tallchief's dazzling speed, accuracy and clarity, or Tanaquil LeClerq's exquisite suppleness and delicacy, or Francisco Moncion's superb presence and style and gift for pantomime, or Herbert Bliss's sensitiveness. These were outstanding members of the company which included such excellent dancers as Beatrice Tompkins, Gisella Caccialanza and Elise Reiman, among the female soloists, and Todd Bolender, among the male. What the company lacked was a brilliant male virtuoso as a partner for Tallchief: Magallanes performed the difficult feats he was given to do, but not with brilliance. His one impressive performance was his Orpheus.

26 June 1948 The Monte Carlo Ballet Russe has been greatly strengthened by the addition of Mary Ellen Moylan, whose clarity and supple ease, based on extraordinarily strong and secure technique, brought new beauty to *Con-*

certo Barocco and who showed at the beginning of a performance of *Danses Concertantes* (before she became intent on remembering the difficult steps) a gaiety and wit something like Danilova's. What the company needs is similar strengthening by a male dancer of comparable powers; for outside of a pair of dazzling legs Danielian has only what wrecks every performance one has the misfortune to see him in — not only the faults of appearance, movement and personality that spoil his own dancing, but the clumsiness as a partner that knocks Krassovska off balance, stops Danilova dead in a spin, and so on.

Ruth Page's *Billy Sunday* was worth seeing for — and only for — Danilova's *tour de force* of comic grotesquerie as the seducing Mrs. Potiphar with a Russian accent ("Wottah hendsome young men! So tull; so strung! Weel you heve tea weeth me?"). One enjoyed Danilova having fun; but that extraordinary theater sense would have been better employed in *Le Baiser de la Fée* and *Mozartiana*, two of the Balanchine masterpieces that were not given, or in *Night Shadow.*

10 July 1948 The first pleasure of Ballet Theater's spring season at the Metropolitan Opera House was to see ballet properly placed and framed once more — though the Metropolitan's technical inadequacies showed up in the poor lighting of the wonderful Berman fore-curtains and second-act back-drop for *Giselle.* A second pleasure was the revival of *Billy the Kid*: Copland's finest score as lovely, Eugene Loring's imaginative choreography as fresh and touching, as ever (but the opening and closing processionals more questionable than ever); the performance newly perfected, with John Kriza an even stronger Billy than Loring but not as amusing in the first scene, and Alonso exquisite in the waltz. *(131)*

That brings me to the next pleasure: Alonso's dancing. Edwin Denby once wrote that "in all the severity of exact classicism Danilova's dancing rhythm fills the time quantities of the music to the full; it does not, like the rhythm of lesser dancers, jab at a stress and then leave a gap till the music catches up." As late as a year ago I was criticizing just such jabbing by Alonso; but in these recent performances she filled out the time quantities with a continuous flow of movement of the utmost elegance. This elegance in quietly secure and superbly assured brilliance of both Alonso and Youskevitch was a delight in the *Black Swan pas de deux* and Balanchine's *Theme and Variations. (116)*

But the season didn't provide only pleasures. For one thing — as against Alonso's quiet and elegance in *Swan Lake* — there was Nana Gollner's violently hammed-up performance. For another there were the new ballets: first, Antony Tudor's *Shadow of the Wind*, its astonishingly feeble and padded choreography as unrelated to the music and words of Mahler's *Lied von der Erde (Er stieg vom Pferd herab,"* the contralto sang mournfully while Gollner and Muriel Bentley rose and whipped themselves around on one point) as the drably "modern" movements of Tudor's *Dark Elegies* were to the music and words of Mahler's *Kindertotenlieder.* Then Agnes de Mille's *Fall River Legend*, more completely derived from Tudor's *Pillar of Fire* than her *Rodeo* was from Loring's *Billy the Kid* — which is to say, with almost nothing this time of her own style that made *Rodeo* a real creation even with its borrowings — and Morton Gould's serious dramatic music sounding even more pretentious and empty than his smart-Alec humorous stuff.

Also — as against the well-rehearsed, accurate performances of these and other works of Tudor and de Mille and of *Billy the Kid* — there was the increased dilapidation of Balanchine's *Apollo.* The piece is so infrequently performed — to say nothing of rehearsed — that the first time Youskevitch forgot the gestures with which Apollo parts Terpsichore from the other muses in their *pas d'action*, and merely stood watching interestedly as they parted by themselves; the second time he forgot to place his knees for Alonso to sit down on; both times his performance throughout was something only approximately remembered and unprecisely timed, with occasional filling in of his own or mere waiting out what he had forgotten entirely; and both times the sequence of leg gestures by the three muses at their first entrance was spoiled by incorrect timing. Even the blacking out of the first scene for Youskevitch to run off stage and change his costume was again, as at City Center last year, forgotten —from which you can get an idea of the complete lack of care with which the piece is kicked onto the stage when it *is* given. A representative of the company explained that Balanchine had been asked to rehearse the work but had been too busy with Ballet Society; but Balanchine informed me he had been offered one hour for what needed several days.

The company's representative also explained the cancellation of Balanchine's *Six Waltzes* (formerly *Waltz Academy*) by Alonso's inability to add to her heavy burden of rehearsal. But Balanchine worked several days last fall to bring the work to the point where it could be finished and performed in Chicago; and evidently it was not finished and performed there. What all this reveals is an attitude toward a great artist's work with which Tudor, the company's artistic director, and Lucia Chase and Oliver Smith, its administrative directors, do themselves great discredit.

Postscript 1970 A year later there was occasion for me to write this letter to Lucia Chase:

Can't I persuade you to change the order of the ballets on April 27? *Pillar of Fire* is scheduled for three performances, all in second place; *La Fille mal Gardée* for six performances, four of them in second or last place. Can't I, therefore, persuade you to put either of these two ballets in first place on April 27, so that *Apollo*, which is being given only once, will not this time be damaged by latecomers?

The company's press representative answered for Miss Chase that she couldn't put *Apollo* second on April 27 because *Pillar of Fire* [in which Miss Chase had an important role] would then have to come first, which would be ruinous to its mood; and this was the season's first *Pillar*, which would be seen by the press.

Nor could *La Fille mal Gardée* be put first, *Apollo* second and *Pillar* third, because the critics of *The Times* and *The Herald Tribune* wouldn't be able to stay for all of *Pillar*. This caused me to write to Miss Chase:

... Why no concern about the ruin to the more fragile mood of *Apollo* when *it* is put first—at not only its first but its only performance, whereas *Pillar* would have two additional performances, both in second position. I am by no means indifferent to the welfare of *Pillar*; you are concerned with nothing but the welfare of *Pillar*—to the point of being completely indifferent to the welfare of *Apollo*: and that I find shocking.... You might put *Apollo* third ...

This time Miss Chase wrote herself to deny that she was indifferent to the welfare of *Apollo*, citing the fact that she had had Balanchine rehearse it with great care and with the best cast one could find anywhere; to disagree with my contention that *Apollo* was damaged by being put first; and to say it couldn't be put third because the critics of the morning papers would be unable to stay for it, and she felt it was important for them to see it. In reply I expressed my appreciation of her taking time out to write to me; then I pointed out that she couldn't say putting *Pillar* first would be ruinous to its mood and then deny that putting *Apollo* first would do similar damage to this ballet; and "obviously when you make sure that *Pillar* is undamaged in second position for all three of its performances, and for this allow *Apollo* to be damaged in first position for its single performance, you show concern for the welfare of *Pillar* and indifference to the welfare of *Apollo*."

A footnote on what Miss Chase considered the best cast one could find anywhere: In *The Nation* of 4 June 1949 I reported:

The single performance of Balanchine's *Apollo* was rehearsed enough for Tallchief, Kaye and Adams to dance their parts beautifully, but not enough to keep Youskevitch from forgetting an important detail in the *pas d'action*. The fact is ... that he cannot learn it, and doesn't even look and move like a young god disporting himself with the muses, but is always a mature Ballet Russe *danseur noble*.

16 October 1948 One must regret the loss this year of the concerts of the New York City Symphony with Leonard Bernstein at the City Center; but it has made possible an event of far greater artistic importance. The Monday and Tuesday nights have been taken over by Ballet Society, which under the name of the New York City Ballet will present in October and November the best of the repertory it has offered its subscription audiences during the past two years. And among the year's artistic events of first magnitude one must include this series of ballet evenings, which will place on view for the general public a number of works by Balanchine.

All of these works delight and amaze one with their beauty and unending variety; each provides a fascinatingly new example of Balanchine's constant enriching elaboration of the distinctive vocabulary that he has made out of the elements of classical ballet and that he uses with inexhaustible inventive imagination in one work after another. One of them, *The Four Temperaments*, outstanding in its power, weight, density and impact, provides the most striking example of that development of vocabulary. Hindemith's music is a series of variations on a set of three themes; the ballet, then, is a series of variations incorporating and elaborating in new contexts certain of the movements that are first seen in the three themes danced by three couples at the beginning; and it is in these themes, from the first movement of the first couple, that one sees the process I have spoken of: the basic elements of classical ballet being altered, transformed, combined with movements newly invented by Balanchine's fantasy and wit, producing in the First Theme details like the girl's enveloping leaps around the boy, the split position in which she is carried off at the end; in the Second Theme the boy's and girl's upward-downward pivoting of their forearms as they leave the stage; in the Third Theme the girl's slides into a sitting position on her points, on which the supporting boy pivots her now to left, now to right.

The slow movement of *Concerto Barocco*— one of Balanchine's earlier works that will be given with the Ballet Society repertory—provides one of the clearest illustrations of the relation of movement to music in his ballets: the movement doesn't express or interpret the music, but like a line of counterpoint completes the music and gives it additional significance. And it is in such slow movements that Balanchine achieves some of his most exciting invention—one outstanding example being the slow movement of *Symphonie Concertante*, where the boy supports two girls in their fascinating maneuvers, with background comments and interpolations by the *corps;* and another being that of *Symphony in C*, where the ballerina and her partner involve two subsidiary couples and the *corps* in intricate interweaving of movement. *(126–130)*

Palais de Cristal, which the Paris Opera Ballet presented during its recent visit, is Balanchine's first version of *Symphony in C*; and it was interesting to see what he had done differently the first time, especially in the slow movement, and how much more strikingly beautiful solutions he had achieved in the second try. In this movement of *Palais* Mlle. Vaussard's arms were stiff and angular; but in the first and third movements Mlles. Moreau and Bardin were lovely, and Mm. Kalioujny and Renault were more brilliantly agile than Magallanes and Bliss of Ballet Society; and there was a spectacular finale. These dancers are very good (though Renault needs to be brought under control), and Mlle. Chauviré, the leading ballerina, has the presence, style and technique of a great dancer. The company as a whole seemed to me excellent; but it was fatally handicapped by the dreadful works it appeared in. Most of these were Lifar's; but his also were the two good works outside of *Palais de Cristal*. They were the ones in which Lifar didn't attempt philosophy or dramatic fantasy, but merely, as a dancer, contrived dance movements that would be effective for dancers: *Suite en Blanc* was a series of choreographic études; *Divertissement,* an ingenious reworking of the material of what we have seen as *Princess Aurora*, was much the same thing in costume. They were pieces skillfully and tastefully contrived to show off a company which achieved their purpose brilliantly.

The International Dance Festival which presented the Paris Opera Ballet also presented

Ram Gopal and his company of Hindu dancers and musicians, whose exquisitely subtle and finished performances were a refreshing delight.

19 February 1949 Jerome Robbins, who has produced brilliant comedy in *Fancy Free*, the Mack Sennett ballet of *High Button Shoes*, and the sleepwalking ballet of last year's *Look, Ma, I'm Dancin'*, seems to want to show he can deal with serious matters too. His latest demonstration is *The Guests*, produced in January by the New York City Ballet, with music by Marc Blitzstein, who I suspect also provided the idea.

The scene is a vast ballroom, in which we see first the host whose wealth and social class are demonstrated by a brightly luminous little disc on his forehead. Several couples with similar discs on their foreheads enter: they are the guests whom he expects, and whom he welcomes grandly. Suddenly three other couples without the discs on their foreheads enter; the host and his guests stare at these uninvited strangers; then he inclines his head slightly in cold greeting and turns from them; and in the dancing that follows they are ignored and crowded aside by the invited guests. All this apparently to show the snobbery of the rich, who, if they were to barge uninvited into a social gathering of the poor in a railroad-flat parlor, would of course be warmly welcomed and made to feel at ease.

The rest is more of same. The host distributes masks to his invited guests, and one of the uninvited couples picks up and puts on a pair of masks that he has dropped—whereupon, with the foreheads covered, he cannot tell the poor from the rich among the masked couples. A masked boy and girl dance together; and when the masks are removed it turns out that the boy has a disc on his forehead but the girl has not. He is dragged away by his group, she is pushed over to hers; they break away to embrace and are brutally parted by the host; but in the end they hold fast.

Of the music to carry the dance detail in which the ideas are worked out one can say that Blitzstein is never at a loss. As for that detail, it includes a *pas de deux* with some lovely movements, beautifully danced by Tallchief and Magallanes; but the invention for the large groups is uninteresting.

Another new work presented by the company was Tudor's *Time Table*, which he did in 1941 for the South American tour of the American Ballet. Except for a dance by three marines that is like some of the three sailors' dancing in Robbins's *Fancy Free*, it is the usual Tudor movements expressing the usual Tudor frustrations that give false meanings to some of Copland's *Music for the Theater*.

As for *The Seasons*, originally presented by Ballet Society, nothing in it—not the music of John Cage, nor the scenery and costumes of Noguchi, nor the choreography of Merce Cunningham—makes sense to me.

22 October 1949 The ballets of Roland Petit presented by Les Ballets de Paris at the Winter Garden turned out to be described with remarkable accuracy by a phrase of Edwin Denby about Petit—"the Orson Welles of French ballet." It is accurate both in its recognition of Petit's powers, and in its characterization of his use of them. The powers are an arrestingly individual style, a flow and variety of invention for every purpose of a wide-ranging imagination, and a lightness and wit that one thinks of as French; the use of them is free-wheeling, sometimes flamboyant, sensational. The individual style is interesting even in something as banal in idea as *Le Rendez-vous*; the lightness and wit make the farcical *L'Oeuf à la Cocque* a delight; the instances of sensational erotic realism in *Carmen* provide a few shocks in a work of remarkable dramatic imagination and theater sense. Moreover, in addition to the dance style I mentioned a moment ago there is, as with Welles, an over-all style which carries Petit's intelligence and personality into everything in the work. Scenery, costumes, the precise and finished dancing of the talented young members of the company—all appear as expressions of the one creative mind.

The fourth work of the program, William

Dollar's *Le Combat*, offers an agreeable surprise in the freshly and ingeniously contrived dance style in which the idea of the piece is worked out.

29 October 1949 Up to now I have seen only one program of the Sadler's Wells Ballet: Ninette de Valois's *The Rake's Progress*, Frederick Ashton's *Symphonic Variations* and *Façade*, and Robert Helpmann's *Hamlet*. The first piece tells its story in terms which have no interest as dance movements; the last is a lurid, tasteless mimed hash of elements of Shakespeare's play; the Ashton pieces are works of a very distinguished art. *Symphonic Variations* is an abstract setting of Franck's music such as we have had from Balanchine; and though its classical ballet movements aren't as astoundingly complex and original as Balanchine's, they have a freshness and sweetness which are in part the qualities of Ashton's imagination and in part the style of the dancers they are contrived for. The assured technique which a Russian or American ballerina would use for outgoing brilliance Margot Fonteyn uses for an exquisite quiet elegance in which she is followed by the other dancers; and Brian Shaw's display of virtuosity is not the less impressive for being done with good manners. All this, with a remarkably beautiful and effective abstract décor by Sophie Fedorovitch, adds up to a quietly lovely piece. And *Façade* gives us a progression of Ashton's wit and fun—very quiet at first in the deft movements of the Scotch number, but getting broader in the succeeding episodes, and reaching a side-splitting climax in the Tango danced by Ashton himself with Moira Shearer.

Postscript 1969 Twenty years later I found the movements of Ashton's *Symphonic Variations* "feeble, inane and boring."

5 November 1949 In the Sadler's Wells Ballet *Cinderella* we have Ashton's gifts for dance and comedy invention operating on a three-act scale, and operating again, nevertheless, with unforced projection, even in the passages of farcical miming: the second Ugly Sister, wrote Edwin Denby after the London première, "is the shyest, the happiest, most innocent of Monsters," who "wins everybody's heart," and who is played by Ashton himself "reticently, with the perfect timing, the apparently tentative gesture, the absorption and the sweetness of a great clown."

Denby foresaw that this evenness of quiet tone might make the piece invisible to an American audience; but the New York audience seemed to be delighted with the clowning of the Ugly Sisters played by Robert Helpmann and Ashton; with the fantastic and spectacular leaps and spins of the Jester, which I thought the most impressively imaginative dance invention of the piece, and which were brilliantly done by Alexander Grant; and even with the passages of classical dance—the solos of the four seasons, the *pas de deux* of Cinderella and the Prince—whose quietly ingenious and lovely details might have passed unnoticed by eyes that had seen Balanchine's dazzling achievements. In these passages Moira Shearer danced with secure elegance and Michael Somes contributed a princely handsomeness and manner, if not a brilliant agility.

A word, finally, about Prokofiev's sometimes sugary and most of the time acidulously sardonic and brashly vigorous music—that is, about its incongruity with what one saw on the stage.

Postscript 1970 Years later I found this work uninteresting.

26 November 1949 Of the additional modern ballets presented by the Sadler's Wells Ballet, I found Helpmann's *Miracle in the Gorbals* as bad as his *Hamlet,* and de Valois's *Job* impossible to sit through; but her *Checkmate* offered some interestingly individual dance invention; and Ashton's *A Wedding Bouquet* was another of his masterpieces of dance comedy, this one with its effect heightened by the blandly innocent music of Lord Berners and even more by the words of Gertrude Stein spoken by an orator seated at a table off at one side of the stage. The words much of the time accompany the witty dancing as a half-heard counterpoint of amusing irrelevancy, with every now and then a hilarious moment when the dancing is contrived to throw a particular irrelevant statement into high-lighted prominence (as Virgil Thomson's music does in *Four Saints in Three Acts*) and one hears with sudden clarity, apropos of nothing, that "she has no plans for the summer," and, as the roar of laughter is dying down, that "she has no plans for the winter."

In addition to the pleasure from Ashton's choreographic wit the company's visit offered the various pleasures of its productions of *The Sleeping Beauty* and *Swan Lake*—the pleasures, that is, of seeing these famous works and hearing their Tchaikovsky scores virtually in their entirety; of having them presented to the eye and ear so completely and so brilliantly achieved; of seeing the company, in the process, presented so effectively. That is, the effect of splendor and opulence which these works were intended to produce was achieved in large measure by the sheer profusion of dancers on the stage, the profusion of talent all the way from the dazzling virtuosity of the prima ballerina, Margot Fonteyn, to the secure competence of the well-trained and rehearsed *corps de ballet* (the one inadequacy which marred the perfection of the performances was that of Alexis Rassine in the *Blue Bird pas de deux* of *The Sleeping Beauty* and the first-act *pas de trois* of *Swan Lake*—his lack of disciplined elegance in the one, of mere physical endurance in the other), the harmony in the deployment of all these dancers and display of their talents. *(131)*

1950 *21 January 1950* Balanchine's new version of *Firebird*, with Chagall's scenery and costumes, gave the New York City Ballet its first box-office success with the public, and pleased John Martin, who contended that Balanchine

had "never been more freshly inventive nor used his perhaps not so fresh devices from other ballets with more aptness." To which I would say that *Firebird* is certainly a fine work, but that among such dramatic ballets of Balanchine *Le Baiser de la Fée* is a work of far greater stature and power; that the invention for the *pas de deux* of the Prince and the captured bird is fresh and imaginative in the way it is related to the dramatic situation, but no more so than the invention for the two *pas de deux* in *Le Baiser* in which the Fairy possesses the Boy, or for the wonderful episode of the Boy and Bride looking for each other and their playful and tender *pas de deux* when they find each other; and that such invention occurs constantly throughout *Le Baiser* in a richer profusion than in *Firebird*. *(132–133, 142–143)*

I might add that a few details of *Firebird* seem to me open to question. The sensational climax of the *pas de deux*, in which the bird is swung at arm's length by the Prince in large circles, has a violence which seems to me excessive in a dance that until then expresses the Prince's gentleness and courtesy with the bird he has captured. In the infernal dance Kastchei is not the terrifying figure he should be; and dramatic confusion and weakness result from the Prince's leaving the stage and returning to it repeatedly, especially after he has waved the feather: once attacked by the Monsters, it seems to me, he should be involved with them until his final victory. At this point, the program says, "the secret of Kastchei's power is discovered and broken"—a reference to the breaking of the huge egg in the Fokine version, an effective detail which I think it was a mistake for Balanchine to omit. And I think a conclusion as glamorous and grandiose as Fokine's—and as Stravinsky's—is called for, rather than the quiet simplicities of a few peasants.

Mr. Martin also made known his decision that on the basis of her dancing in *Firebird* Maria Tallchief was now to be "admitted, formally, as it were, to the ranks of the real ballerinas"—to which I would say that the clarity, elegance and brilliance of Tallchief that are exciting in *Firebird* have been evident and exciting for some time in *Symphonie Concertante, Sym-*

phony in C, *The Four Temperaments* and other works. He said nothing about Moncion; but Edwin Denby said it all after Ballet International's season five years ago, when he described Moncion as "the most gifted American character dancer (if one may use the term for dramatic characterization in ballet)," and added: "Moncion, well trained as a classic dancer, strong and manly, is like a modern dancer in the freedom with which he can use torso, arms, and neck. But his exceptional gift is his intense imaginative sincerity. He creates a character completely. . . ." What I am aware of, in addition, is that Moncion, on the stage, is a powerful presence in the way that great dancers are and that no other male dancer in the New York City Ballet is.

Bourrée Fantasque, also a popular success, has in its first scene some of Balanchine's most hilariously witty and amusing invention since *The Ball* and the early scenes of *Cotillon*—the rest being as good as even a hurried product of resourceful craftsmanship will be when the craftsman is a Balanchine. And the stars of that first scene are Tanaquil LeClercq, who has revealed her comic gift before, and Jerome Robbins, a delightful comic as far back as *Three Virgins and a Devil. (141)*

18 March 1950 Jerome Robbins's *Age of Anxiety,* produced by the New York City Ballet, is again a ballet about lonely people—four this time, as against *Facsimile's* three; and much of the Martha-Grahamesque movement in which they define their loneliness is again like an exhibition of personal privacies that one is embarrassed to look at. But this time the four get involved with a lot of other people; and it is in some of these episodes that Robbins's powers of observation and imaginative invention achieve exciting images and large-scale orchestrations of movement. One of these is the frenetic close of the first part; but the best, I think, is the Masque in which the four "attempt to become or to appear carefree"—an episode danced to what I think is also the best music of Bernstein's score, the section of piano jazz

(with percussion). It is another example of what happens when Robbins's sharp eye and satiric sense concern themselves with American lowbrow dancing; and it makes one wish that if he feels that as a serious artist he must deal with serious subjects he would deal with them in comedy, of which he is so brilliant a master. Oliver Smith's scenery, finally, seems to me the best he has done.

Another new ballet presented by the New York City Ballet, Ashton's *Illuminations,* is an extraordinarily beautiful work of his distinguished art—an art as masterfully sure in touch in the delicate and subtle details as in the powerful ones. It is helped in achieving the fantastic atmosphere of the piece by the scenery and costumes of Cecil Beaton; Britten's music for the Rimbaud words I am—at this moment several days after the one performance I saw—unable to recall anything about.

In contrast with these two works, which were handsomely mounted and danced with precision, Balanchine's *Prodigal Son* was given with insufficient preparation which blurred its powerful dramatic images, and with some indeterminate makeshift scenery and sleazy costumes as the disturbingly inadequate replacements for the magnificent Rouault scenery and costumes of the original 1929 Diaghilev production. In addition, even make-up wasn't used as it might have been: nothing was done with Robbins of the kind that was done with Tallchief, or that was done with Lifar in the 1929 photograph I have before me—with the result that this was a ballet about a clean-cut American boy in fancy dress who gets involved in some peculiar goings-on.

Postscript 1970 In later years I found *Illuminations* less impressive.

22 July 1950 For its tenth anniversary season at the Center Theater Ballet Theater added four new works to its older repertory: Tudor's *Nimbus* (music by Louis Gruenberg, scenery by Oliver Smith, costumes by Saul Bolasni); William Dollar's *Jeux* (music by Debussy, scenery and costumes by David Ffolkes); John Taras's *Designs with Strings* (music by Tchaikovsky, setting by Irene Sharaff); and Herbert Ross's *Caprichos* (music by Bartók, costumes by Helen Pons).

Taras's designs had no imaginative life in them; and the lovely, infinitely ingenious variation movement of Tchaikovsky's Piano Trio made one recall longingly its previous choreographic setting by Massine—the second scene of *Aleko*, with Chagall's scenery and the unforgettable dancing of Markova, Hugh Laing, Yurek Lazovsky, Rosella Hightower and the rest. Dollar's piece was more interestingly inventive in its danced tennis play at the beginning, its flirtation and love-making later, but didn't remain interesting and clear in expressive point all the way to the end. Tudor's— longer and more elaborate, and set to a bad piece of music—was unusual for him in having a story idea that was slight and simple and light in tone and that was worked out almost entirely in dancing rather than miming, and in dancing for the entertainment of the spectator, I would say, rather than for tearing at his heart: long dance sequences in all dance styles— classical ballet, polite ballroom, rowdy nightclub, smart musical-show, humorous caricature, Tudor-romantic-love, etc. And as entertainment it entertained, mildly.

But *Caprichos* struck with impact. The impact, for one thing, of the horribleness—frightening, fascinating, even funny in a grim way that should have frozen the audience's laughter —of the four episodes elaborating Goya's commentaries on certain of his *Caprichos* series. And the impact also of the astonishingly developed and assured powers, in so young a choreographer, that produced all this with such individuality of imagination and style, such completeness and precision.

New works aside, there was pleasure in seeing again Balanchine's *Theme and Variations*, for me the most excitingly beautiful and distinguished piece in the company's repertory; Loring's masterpiece, *Billy the Kid*; Robbins's *Fancy Free* (which he ought to clean up). Walking out on Gollner's hammed-up *Swan Lake* performance one mourned the company's loss

of Alonso just when she had begun to dance with beautiful quiet and serenity; but for the rest there was only pleasure in watching the similar quiet and elegance of Youskevitch (he should be persuaded to wear a wig in the old classical ballets and *pas de deux*), in noting what superb dancers Nora Kaye and John Kriza had developed into in those ten years, what a superb dancer Laing, in his special style, continued to be, the security Diana Adams had achieved in her cool, clear, lovely style.

As for the Ballet Russe de Monte Carlo, of its great Balanchine repertory only *Ballet Imperial* and the third act of *Raymonda* were presented at the Metropolitan last April. *Le Baiser de la Fée, Mozartiana, Night Shadow* and *Le Bourgeois Gentilhomme* were no longer even included in the repertory listed in the souvenir program; and though *Danses Concertantes* was listed I doubt that it will be performed again. They have been replaced by trivialities and guests stars. The company's glory is still Danilova, who in New York did occasionally exhibit the surviving splendors of her *Coppélia* and *Nutcracker* performances, but elsewhere—even in Boston—is seen mostly in the trivialities (Boston may have seen *Danses Concertantes* in 1944-45, but hasn't seen it since then. The work was announced, but invariably replaced—on one occasion by *Frankie and Johnny*, I believe).

The new edition of Karsavina's *Theater Street* (Dutton) has a new chapter about Diaghilev. This dreamily fragmentary account needs to be filled in with other accounts—those of Nicolas Nabokov in recent issues of the *Atlantic Monthly*, of Lifar in his books. Nabokov gave a fascinating description of Diaghilev's creative powers in action; and with all his obvious extravagance and probable inaccuracy Lifar is valuable on the personality, for he writes with adoration and yet the picture comes through clearly of a complicated and tormented man who tormented others, a monster who made the company the collection of monsters it was described as to me by someone* who observed it at close range for a number of years.

*Glenway Wescott.

25 November 1950 Of the new works presented by the Sadler's Wells Ballet this year Ashton's *Les Patineurs* made much the same impression as when it was done by Ballet Theater: that the subject limited the style of the movement, and the banal and short-breathed Meyerbeer music held it down further, the result being choppiness and, in the end, monotony in the repetition of what was amusingly ingenious at first. The movements of de Valois's *Don Quixote* had no point beyond the literal one of the story; and a couple of scenes were all I could sit through. Ashton's *Dante Sonata* I did not see.

The enriching experiences were therefore the repetitions of some of last year's offerings. On the one hand Ashton's comedy masterpieces: *Façade*, with its heavily underlined caricatures; and the subtler and more elaborated *Wedding Bouquet*, so wittily contrived in relation to the blandly innocent music of Lord Berners and the Gertrude Stein irrelevancies issuing explosively from a mind seemingly preoccupied and apart. And on the other hand *The Sleeping Beauty* and *Swan Lake*. The public that has seen only fragments of these old classics is enormously indebted to the Sadler's Wells Ballet for the opportunity to experience them in their entirety and with such splendor of scenery, costumes, music and dancing.

An additional pleasure again was the special style of the company—its precision achieved with unostentatious assured competence, its personal sweetness and good manners. And the greatest pleasure of this sort was provided by the company's leading ballerina, Margot Fonteyn, who epitomizes its style in the elegance of carriage and movement with which she goes through the dazzling technical feats in those old ballets.

As for the Marquis de Cuevas's Grand Ballet, the artistic intelligence and taste directing its operations hit one in the eye right from the start with a piece called *Divertissement*, which turned out to be an assemblage of some of the fragments of *The Sleeping Beauty* we have seen in *Princess Aurora* and *Aurora's Wedding*—with the costumes in a hideous modern style that clashed with the luxuriant style of music

and movement, the music badly conducted, the movement badly danced, and the piece blasted apart by the interpolated *Black Swan pas de deux*. In this there was the beautiful dancing of André Eglevsky (but also his walking about with upturned wrists) and the technical security and brilliance of Hightower (but also her hamming of the ballerina grand style). There were, then, occasional enjoyable experiences— Balanchine's *Night Shadow* and *Concerto Barocco*, however imperfectly done, his amusing *Pas de Trois Classique*, Ana Ricarda's *Del Amor y de la Muerte*; the dancing of Eglevsky and Hightower in classical *pas de deux*; the impassioned elegance of George Skibine and beautiful dancing of Marjorie Tallchief in *Night Shadow* and *Del Amor*; the dancing of Ricarda in her own piece. But with them there was much more that was unattractive.

23 December 1950 The New York City Ballet presented no new works during the first week of its recent season at City Center; but some of the old ones had a new beauty that made them appear "as fresh and glistening as creation itself." What struck the eye first, in *Symphony in C*, was the spectacular effect of the lighting and the new richly colored costumes of the men; but then one became aware of something more important—the assured ease of the company and the smooth running of the performance, which were the results of the many weeks of continuous rehearsal and performance of the English tour. The performances now gave the impression of something completely achieved; and this effect of complete achievement was greatest in *Prodigal Son*, where there were not only the clarification and tightening of the choreography that had been blurred and slack last spring, but the superb performances of the new leading dancers—Moncion, with his powerful presence and dramatic intensity; Yvonne Mounsey, with her long-legged sinuous body— and the Rouault scenery and costumes to give the work the force and stature it had not had. Balanchine himself, in early performances, also contributed to the effect of the work with his brief appearances as the Father—with the fascinating stylized movements of hands and arms in his appeal to the Son at the beginning, but especially at the end, with the expressive power of each slow step toward the prostrate Son and of his immobility as the Son dragged himself over the ground and up his body into his arms and enfolding cloak. *(141)*

The company's improved functioning was also evident, the second week, in the smoothly-running performances of the major new work, a revival of Balanchine's *Le Baiser de la Fée*, in which, as in *Prodigal Son*, his remarkable dramatic and theater sense produces wonderfully imagined invention. Comparable with details in *Prodigal Son* like the Companions' crossing their hands before their faces or squatting and scurrying back to back, are in *Le Baiser* details like the Fairy pointing ahead and pushing the Boy off the stage at the end of the village scene or the Boy and his Bride looking for each other in the mill scene; and they occur in even greater profusion and richer contexts in the later work. Balanchine attempted this time to achieve choreographic continuity by filling in the musical interludes between scenes with movement; but I found that after the Fairy had pushed the Boy off the stage and followed him off with arm pointing ahead, the effect of this stroke of *fantaisie Balanchine* was weakened by their reappearance and movements before the curtain, and similarly that the effect of her dragging him off at the end of the mill scene was weakened by the appearance of the Bride before the curtain in search of him. I also found myself questioning the epilogue in which the Boy who was last seen being dragged off by the Fairy is now seen climbing upward in an attempt to reach her—this apart from the fact that it doesn't come off clearly on the City Center stage and must be invisible to part of the audience. On the other hand the newly introduced premonitory reappearance of the Fairy's shadow in the mill scene is excellent, since it makes visible the source of the shadow that falls on the Bride's playfulness.

The role of the Fairy calls for precisely the physical intensity in dancing and the dark dramatic power that Tallchief has; and her per-formance of it is, I think, still the best thing she has done. Magallanes as the Boy again shows himself to be a good character dancer; Patricia Wilde does the two solos of the opening of the mill scene with the clarity and speed they require. But standing out from everything else here, as in every ballet she appears in, is LeClercq's performance as the Bride, with its exquisite deployment of bodily configuration, its amazing range of expressiveness, its power of presence and projection that gives an extra animation and radiance to her quietest movement.

In addition Balanchine produced two new short pieces. One was a grand *pas de deux* to music from Delibes's *Sylvia*, which had Tallchief not only displaying her virtuosity but dancing, in the languorous introduction, with a new supple delicacy. It also included passages which exposed the company's weakness—that it has no male dancers comparable in technical virtuosity and brilliance of style with Tallchief, LeClercq, Melissa Hayden and Janet Reed, among others; and that consequently a Magallanes or Bliss must struggle embarrassingly with what calls for a Youskevitch or Skibine.

The other new piece, the Mazurka from Glinka's *A Life for the Tsar*, was exciting for its exhibition of the beautifully finished style of Balanchine's own dancing; and for me there was the additional exciting experience of seeing Lazovsky dance again with his extraordinary lightness and ease and continuity in flow of movement. This great dancer's inactivity has been a saddening loss; and now that Balanchine has been able to get him to dance in this one piece, I hope he will try to persuade him to do more with the company. Balanchine cannot produce *Petrushka*, in which Lazovsky's performance was the definitive one of our time; but he can revive *Mozartiana*, among whose unforgettable moments were Lazovsky's pose as the curtain went up, and his wonderfully subtle performance of the intricate opening dance.

And not just *Mozartiana*. An experienced and intelligent actor and director I know remarked after *Prodigal Son*: "The fact is, the important things happening in the theater nowadays are being done right here"—which was a way of describing the fact that at long last the greatest living creative artist has a theater and a company for a repertory of his own ballets and any others he finds worth producing. And what he must do is bring into that repertory the masterpieces he created for companies which no longer perform them—*Danses Concertantes, Ballet Imperial, Le Bourgeois Gentilhomme, Waltz Academy, Cotillon.*

1951   *24 March 1951* In 1937, when *Card Game* was first produced, and as late as 1941, when it was done by the Monte Carlo Ballet Russe, I was blind as well as deaf, finding in the Balanchine choreography "thinness and brittleness" which I accounted for by the fact that "its point of departure is one of the worst of· Stravinsky's pieces of synthetic music." The recent revival by the New York City Ballet provided me with an opportunity to perceive at last what a masterpiece Balanchine had created—what a profusion of delightful details he had contrived with dance movement in which his basic classical ballet idiom was enriched not only with amusing conceits derived from the cards and game but even more with the American musical comedy style that his eye, in 1937, had been observing for three or four years. And I was able to perceive also how intimately the movement was related to the Stravinsky music—each completing, enlarging, and intensifying the other's meaning and effect—which is to say that I could now appreciate what a fascinating score Stravinsky had produced. Also contributing to the delightful effect are Irene Sharaff's costumes and set. And then the indispensable contribution: the beautifully clear, precise and sharp dancing of the company, the charming performances of Janet Reed, Bliss and some of the other soloists, the outstanding performance of Todd Bolender as the Joker, which is in a class with his *Phlegmatic Variation* in *The Four Temperaments.*

But if I was wrong in 1941 about Stravinsky I don't think I am wrong today about the sheer nothingness of Ravel's *Valses Nobles* and *La Valse*—the nothingness for Balanchine's creative imagination to respond to, which may be why he produced what seemed to me a mere filling in of time and space. Except when there were LeClercq's amazing gifts to stimulate his imagination, and we got her strangely perverse dance with Magallanes, her sinister encounter and dance of death with Moncion (one recalls her death-like face as she begins the dance). What Balanchine did was to bring into operation his powers as a theater artist, and to create with the color of costumes in a play of darkness and light the excitement there would not be in the movement alone.

Balanchine's *Pas de Trois* was added for Eglevsky, only a guest (one hopes) with the company, who also appeared in the *Sylvia pas de deux,* and who exhibited shocking faults of deportment, style and even technique—e.g. the beats that were, as Hightower once tactfully described Dolin's, "something special." *Pas de Trois* also provided a role for Nora Kaye, who was reported to have joined the company permanently, and who looked better in the last performance of the piece than she had done in the first and in her early performances in *Symphony in C.*

Tudor's new *Lady of the Camellias* was put on for Diana Adams and Hugh Laing—to give Laing a role in the special personal style of his roles in the Tudor repertory of Ballet Theater. The Tudor public cheered; and John Martin—for whom criticism is a matter largely of taking and maintaining public positions about dancers and choreographers—wrote that the work "may well touch the highest level of sheer artistry of any of the Tudor repertory"; but for me it provided one of the most painful experiences anyone can have—that of watching someone go through the motions of creating artistic life with powers that no longer can achieve it. What Adams was given to do she did exquisitely; but the feeble borrowings from *Romeo and Juliet* that Laing was given to do he did without his former intensity and projective force.

2 June 1951 "A fantastic operation" was my

guest's comment as we left the Metropolitan after Ballet Theater performances of Balanchine's *Theme and Variations*, Herbert Ross's new *Thief Who Loved a Ghost*, and Roland Petit's new *Le Jeune Homme et la Mort.* "You get," he continued, "a distinguished work of art as a curtain-raiser for a piece of the most unutterable balderdash ever seen on the stage, and for a Grand Guignol shocker" (we had left in time to miss Tudor's *Gala Performance*). And other programs I saw could have been characterized in the same way.

Theme and Variations continued to be used as a curtain-raiser—twice for de Mille's worst work, *Fall River Legend*, once for her *Rodeo*, of which I now find the portions concerned with the story tiresome and embarrassing, and only the few moments of straight dancing still enjoyable. And in addition to *The Thief Who Loved a Ghost* (a shocking disappointment of the expectations aroused by *Caprichos*) new works were presented which, if they weren't the most unutterable balderdash, were not of much, or of any, consequence. That holds for *Le Jeune Homme et la Mort*, a characteristic Petit product in its combination of sex and brutality, its shock-after-shock method, which acquired importance only from the fact that it employed, and was the means of revealing, the extraordinary powers of the dancer Jean Babilée. More obvious were the powers in violence which produced the spectacular spins and leaps, the no less spectacular acrobatic feats in slow motion; more extraordinary were the powers in quiet—the power of personal projection and compulsion that he exercised in a quiet movement of his extended arm, or when he was not moving at all. The most impressive moment in his own ballet *L'Amour et son Amour*, and one which has remained most vividly in my memory, was the one in which he stood, spotlighted on the dark stage, with arms circling slowly in a series of *ports de bras*.

But most impressive of all was his performance in the *Blue Bird pas de deux*; for this was a standard piece in which one had seen brilliant dancers more suited to it in physical appearance and style—Youskevitch, for one—and one could appreciate the new and special thing Babilée made of it with his own and special resources. He hasn't Youskevitch's slimness and elegance, but is short and chunky; he either hasn't, or chose not to try for, the exciting elevation of Youskevitch and other dancers in the first leaps; but he has the extraordinary power of personal projection and compulsion I have mentioned; and what was exciting in his performance was the operation of this power without interruption. There were none of the usual passive moments—of waiting to begin, or of withdrawal for the ballerina to do her series of *pirouettes*; instead, from the moment the curtain rose until it fell—whether he was dancing, or preparing to dance, or moving behind Ruth Ann Koesun as she danced (very beautifully)—he was active continuously, powerfully, in a way that placed the performance among the things one is glad to have been alive to see.

8 August 1951 Of the new works presented by the New York City Ballet in June, Ruthanna Boris's *Cakewalk*, to music by Gottschalk with scenery and superb costumes by Robert Drew, was an ingenious and amusing dance paraphrase of its subject. Janet Reed again (I say "again," recalling her Queen of Hearts in *Card Game*) demonstrated her powers in comedy; and there were fine performances by the other soloists.

Jerome Robbins's *The Cage*, to Stravinsky's Concerto in D—suggested by the practices of certain insects whose females devour the males—presented, in something like a hive, a group of females whose costumes (by Ruth Sobotka of the company) and movements (the rubbing of hands like feelers) suggested insects, and one of whom (Nora Kaye) killed two male intruders—the first (Michael Maule) at once, the second (Magallanes) after courtship (*pas de deux*) and copulation. A progression from the unpleasant to the shocking and horrible; but my objection was not to that; it was to the fact that the piece was nothing more than that: the movements achieved nothing beyond their unpleasant or shocking explicit meaning. This in contrast to, say, the Fairy's taking possession of the Boy in *Le Baiser de la Fée,* or the seduction in *Prodigal Son,* in which the movements are not literally meaningful but a transmutation of the literal meaning into powerfully and excitingly imaginative dance metaphors.

27 October 1951 Of the two new works presented by the New York City Ballet in September, Balanchine's *A la Françaix,* to an engaging score by Jean Françaix, was a small-scale piece with charming dance invention for the gaiety of the scenes with Janet Reed, and a bit of the kind of dead-pan comic invention that Balanchine gave us at greater length in the *Scheherazade* burlesque of *On Your Toes.* The piece was danced to perfection by Reed, Eglevsky, Tallchief, Frank Hobi and Roy Tobias; but in one of the performances Hayden's powers of dead-pan comedy proved to be less than Tallchief's.

As for Bolender's *The Miraculous Mandarin,* except for a few lovely details in the *pas de deux* its movements achieved only the literal telling of the gruesome story, with help from the hideous Bartók score; and that made it another example of the kind of ballet which interests a lot of other people more than it does me.

3 November 1951 Of the two new works presented by Ballet Theater, Babilée's *Til Eulenspiegel,* to Strauss's tone-poem, was made notable not only by Babilée's central performance — with its compulsion of mere presence, its powerful projection of a distinctive personality and style in its miming and dancing — but by the further projection of that personality and style into all the movement surrounding his, which produced an extraordinarily integrated piece as well as a delightful one. Notable too were the setting by Tom Keogh and costumes by Helene Pons.

Bronislava Nijinska's *Schumann Concerto* turned out to be still another of her equivalents of a pianist coming out on the stage of Town

Hall to perform finger exercises for a half-hour — incredible and painful to anyone who saw *Les Noces* and knows what creative powers she once operated with.

1 December 1951 Balanchine's *Apollo* as it is performed by the New York City Ballet is like a great painting after it has been cleaned — the accumulated obscuring grime removed, the original splendors revealed. The grime on the *Apollo* presented by Ballet Theater in recent years was, to begin with, the excessively fast tempos of the Stravinsky music that provides the foundation for the dancing, the consequent hurrying and cramping of the movements, and the inaccuracies of dancers who forgot between the infrequent performances what they had barely learned in the insufficient rehearsals; and at City Center now one hears the music played well and sees the movements executed accurately. One can merely consider the work that is presented to ear and eye — the beautiful, imaginative and touching details of movement into which the poetic ideas are transmuted. But one may in addition reflect that what is so beautiful and touching was also amazingly original in 1928, and that while still in his twenties Balanchine produced a wonderfully beautiful and great work of art which defined a new personal classical style that he had made out of the traditional idiom of classical ballet and was to elaborate in the great works that followed.

I have looked up Edwin Denby's review of Ballet Theater's 1945 production and found my recollection of Eglevsky's performance confirmed by the terms "magnificently powerful" and "sweep" that Denby applied to it. This time, however, one sees no Apollo with god-like power, magnificence and sweep — only an Eglevsky with a hugely muscular body but no strength in the quiet movements in which he steps delicately with wrists upturned, no vital energy even in his leaps. It is the muses — Tallchief's Terpsichore, LeClercq's Polyhymnia, Adams's Calliope — who have this strength and energy; and in addition — contradicting a casual Balanchine observation that "the muses were not intelligent"—Polyhymnia is irradiated by LeClercq's joyous intelligence. And it is their beautiful and brilliant dancing that achieves what Denby described as "the melodious lines and lyric or forceful climaxes...which are effects of dance continuity, dance rhythm, and dance architecture," and in the end the impression of "effortless and limpid grandeur." *(134–140)*

29 December 1951 The original conclusion of Balanchine's *Le Baiser de la Fée* has never worked at City Center; and Balanchine's experiments with substitutes continued until the very last of the recent performances, where he achieved what seemed to me exactly right: the room from which the Fairy has dragged the Boy remains empty; the Bride returns in bewildered, anguished search of him, recalls moments of her earlier happiness there with him, and slowly sinks to the ground; then the room disappears and the triumphant Fairy is seen with the Boy for a moment before the curtain falls. Or at least it seemed right with LeClercq on the stage to communicate the Bride's tragic desolation, as earlier she had communicated her sweetness and gaiety, with a force of presence and projection and a range of expressive power that amaze one anew in her every performance.

Of Balanchine's two new works, *Tyl Ulenspiegel* is a product almost entirely of his theater sense—a spectacle with magnificent scenery and costumes by Esteban Francés, an action piece with amusing incidents which are made effective by Robbins's gifts as a comedian, but almost no dancing. It is, then, a good work of its kind (and for its purpose of drawing people to the box office); but the kind—since it doesn't employ the most important of Balanchine's powers—keeps it from being a work of much consequence; and I doubt that it had much interest for him.

On the other hand I doubt that he has ever done anything he cared more about than his new version of Act 2 of *Swan Lake*, which engaged all his powers, and which is one of the most beautiful and most consequential of their achievements. It engaged, first of all, his remarkable powers as a musician: what he talked most about was Tchaikovsky's music—the fact that it had been put together with a mastery of musical construction like Stravinsky's; that it had always been played and danced to in a way which had destroyed its subtleties of accentuation and phrase-construction; and that these would now be heard in the music and seen in the dancing. Those musical powers are evident in the two pieces of music he has introduced from Act 3 and the dances he has invented for them—a brilliant *pas de trois*, superbly danced by Wilde with Edwina Fontaine and Jillana; and a *pas de neuf* which is the most enchantingly beautiful number in the entire ballet, exquisitely danced by Mounsey and the *corps*. His dramatic powers are evident not only in the revisions which create a clear line of dramatic meaning in the first encounter and last scene of the Swan Queen and the Prince, but above all in his invention for the Swans—their wonderfully animated entrance and first waltz, their groupings when threatened by the hunters, their hair-raising swirling and rushing at the end. And no doubt his theater sense had something to do with the magnificent scenery by Beaton. *(143–145)*

Tallchief dances the Swan Queen not only with her technical perfection and brilliance but with the lovely delicacy that she has acquired in the last couple of years, and with dramatic expressiveness. The one thing her performance lacks is the projected personal presence and force that made Danilova's and Markova's the great performances they were. As for Eglevsky, he is less damaging to this work than to *Apollo* only because there is less of him.

The Pied Piper of Robbins's new ballet of that title is the solo clarinetist of the performance of Copland's Clarinet Concerto, who sits in a corner in the front of the bare stage, and whose playing, we are asked to believe, lures onto that stage dancers in practice clothes and impels them to dance. As it happens, the music, to my ears, is something contrived by an efficient technique out of no ideas; and so there is, for me, no lyricism in the slow first movement to produce the soaring lifts and other lyrical movements of the first pair of dancers. Neither am I able to believe in the make-believe of the violent compulsive effects of the fragmentary jazz figures of the cadenza and the second movement; and most of the resulting movements that the audiences have found terribly funny I find terribly and embarrassingly cute and corny. Nor, finally, can I believe in the climactic compulsive effect of the music at the end, which is to drive the dancers frantic, and which I suspect represents a Serious Idea, this time about the Jazz Age. There were no Serious Ideas in *Fancy Free* and the wonderful ballets of *High Button Shoes* and *Look Ma, I'm Dancin';* if there had been they probably would have been no better than *Age of Anxiety* and *The Pied Piper*—to say nothing of *Facsimile* and *The Cage.*

In Tudor's *Lilac Garden*, in which Kaye and Laing danced their old roles very well, LeClercq's distinction and force created, for me, the only moments of the "amplitude of meaning" that art—and dancing, like any other art—can give.

Postscript 1970 Reminiscing during a rehearsal in 1968, Balanchine described how he had made for Diaghilev the version of Act 2 in which I saw Spessiva-Spessivtseva in 1929; which was taken over by the post-Diaghilev companies, including the Monte Carlo Ballet Russe and Ballet Theater; and which Balanchine replaced with his new version in 1951.

1952   *12 January 1952* The New York City Ballet is now a superb company; and its great Balanchine ballets are enough to make its repertory quite the most distinguished in the world. The company is a superb one even without a Youskevitch, a Lazovsky, a Kriza whom it needs, and even with Laing whom it doesn't need and Eglevsky whom it would be better off without; the repertory is a distinguished one even with the inferior ballets of other choreographers than Balanchine. So far from objecting to the inferior

ballets, I contend that these other choreographers must be represented in the repertory, and by what they produce. Not only that, but if keeping the Balanchine works on view for the small public which appreciates "poetic suggestion through dancing" depends on attracting to the box office the larger public which goes for literal representation of private neuroses and *crimes passionels* and for corny cuteness and comedy, I think the company is right to attract the larger public in that way. And I recognize a similar justification for the engagement of popular dancers like Eglevsky and Laing, but contend only that the proper way to use them is not to fit them into Balanchine ballets which they spoil but to present them in their specialties—Eglevsky in virtuoso *pas de deux*, Laing in a succession of *Lilac Gardens.*

If such tactics with the general public are necessary it is because there is nobody writing for it today as Edwin Denby wrote several years ago—nobody to explain, for example, that "to recognize poetic suggestion through dancing one has to be susceptible to poetic values and susceptible to dance values as well . . . I find that a number of people are, and that several dancers, for example Miss Danilova and Miss Markova, are quite often able to give them the sense of an amplitude in meaning which is the token of emotion in art." Instead there are, among others, writers like the one in *Theater Arts*—one of those for whom modern dance expresses emotions whereas classical ballet is merely beautiful to the eye, and who credited Balanchine only with superb craftsmanship, not with artistic creativeness. There are, that is, writers who themselves lack the susceptibility to poetic values and to dance values that would enable them to recognize poetic suggestion through dancing.

The others include John Martin of the *Times*, whose new line with Balanchine is that of an admirer and friend who can understand Balanchine's affection for *Apollo*, a "historical milestone," but must point out that it is "a very young and dated effort" which will never be a popular ballet; or who regrets having to counsel Balanchine to consign the wonderful invention of *The Four Temperaments* to oblivion for lack of the right music to carry it, and to return as beautiful a work as *The Fairy's Kiss* to the storehouse until its technical problems are solved; or who, conceding the beauty of *Swan Lake,* must nevertheless admonish Balanchine sternly not to concern himself again with such old chestnuts—which is as though a theater director were admonished not to concern himself with Shakespeare or Tchekhov. "As a friend, and for your own good," says Mr. Martin to Balanchine, "I urge you to cut your throat."

26 April 1952 Ashton's *Picnic at Tintagel* for the New York City Ballet is a work that I found uninteresting in invention except for a few details—the movements of the Caretaker (Robert Barnett), the exquisite first part of the *pas de deux* of the lovers (Adams and Jacques d'Amboise), before Ashton yields to his compulsion to daring explicitness. As for Tudor's *La Gloire,* if even John Martin found it "impossible to report very happily upon it," I can dispense with comment altogether.

8 November 1952 It was in 1946 that Markova's dancing first showed a reduced intensity —most strikingly in *Giselle,* in which she merely sketched in the early scenes and saved her strength for the big solo of the first act and the taxing second act. Nevertheless a *Swan Lake* performance at that time had, in addition to its continuous flow of exquisite movement, a dramatic force I had never experienced in her previous performances of the work. As it happened, *Swan Lake* was the first of her performances with Ballet Theater that I saw recently; and the saving of lessened strength this time produced an exquisite flow, but of movement done on the smallest possible scale—some of it in fact only half-done (the leg trailing when it should have been raised high), and some not done at all but faked (an easier movement substituted for a taxing one)—and without the slightest projective force. And in the *Nutcracker pas de deux* the lessened doing was concealed

by a lot of twitterings of hands and lovely arms.

On the other hand her performance in *Les Sylphides* was made as breathtakingly beautiful as ever by that unique "instinct for the melody of movement as it deploys and subsides in the silence of time" (as Edwin Denby once described it)—not only in the supported dances but in the Prelude which she danced alone, and in which there were the additional "refined rhythmic delights" of her movement around, rather than on, the accents of the music. And even with the things she could no longer do in *Giselle* her performance had those enchanting subtleties of phrasing, with in addition a distinction of style, of mere carriage and appearance, which lifted it to a level of grandeur, of compelling dramatic credibility: as one acute observer put it, you believed Markova was someone who would die of the hurt of having been deceived, which you couldn't believe of Alonso. *(146)*

But though it lacked this distinction Alonso's performance in *Giselle* offered dancing of extraordinary brilliance and loveliness. So with Youskevitch: the observer I have mentioned could point out that his dancing near the end conveyed increasing exhaustion, when it should have conveyed increasing exaltation; but most of the time it offered the brilliance achieved with elegance that we get from no one else.

De Mille's new ballet, *The Harvest According,* is another of those birth-life-death affairs that leaves *Tally-Ho* still the last good piece she has done. The other new ballet, Caton's *Triptych,* is a pleasantly inventive series of classroom exercises in costume.

6 December 1952 Balanchine's first new piece, *Scotch Symphony,* is danced to the scherzo, slow movement and finale of Mendelssohn's symphony. The long slow movement seems to have provided Balanchine with stimulation for nothing more than a resourcefully spun-out supported adagio in which Tallchief, who used to dazzle one with her spectacular energetic brilliance, takes one's breath away with the unobtrusively achieved perfection and loveliness of a continuous quiet flow of exquisitely contoured movement. But to go with the scherzo and finale Balanchine has produced delightful dances for the *corps*, and solos which show off Wilde's brilliance, make Tallchief utterly charming, and keep Eglevsky too busy to do any damage (such as he does at his first entrance in *Swan Lake* with a great gesture and smile of greeting to the audience). The setting by Horace Armistead I find less distinguished than the girls' costumes by Karinska and the boys' costumes by David Ffolkes.

Balanchine's other new piece, *Metamorphoses*, which was to have been presented the third week, was not ready; but I can speak of one completed section that I saw at rehearsals—the latest in the series of his great supported adagios, one of the odd kind that he is stimulated to produce by contemporary music (the score is Hindemith's Symphonic Metamorphoses on Themes of Weber), but contrived also for the elegance and distinction, the force of presence and projection, that are LeClercq's.

I might remark at this point that Bolender's Tennis Player in *A la Françaix* and Bliss's King of Hearts in *Card Game* are examples of the performance that not only is good in itself but enables one to see how much less good another performance is. The outstanding example of this the last two years has been Moncion's *Prodigal Son*, particularly the last two scenes. Watching Robbins and Laing in these scenes one sees what they were given to do by Balanchine: in the first, for example, the Son, left clinging to the upended table, sinks to the ground, pulls himself up again, becomes aware of his nakedness, sees water which he kneels to drink, and after a terrified look back to the place of his despoilment drags himself off the stage. Watching Moncion one sees what he has made of what he was given to do: the single long progression—in which in one action the movement of one part of the body flows into the movement of the rest, and each action flows into the next—with sustained continuity, tension and expressive force. This not only is tremendously effective itself, but enables one to see how much less effective the sequence of

one separate, jerky action after another in Laing's or Robbins's performance is. And the same is true of what Moncion does with the Son's return to the arms of the Father.

6 June 1953 Though Lincoln Kirstein thought it advisable to step before the curtain and justify the presentation of Lew Christensen's *Filling Station* by the interest he hoped it would have for the audience as a document in the early history of what became the New York City Ballet, the audience knew better than he and responded to the piece not with an interest in it as history but with delight in its moment-to-moment operation as a work of art. *Filling Station* takes its place with Loring's *Billy the Kid* and Robbins's *Fancy Free* as one of the enduring works, one of the classics of American ballet—brilliant in its observation, its dance invention, its organization. So brilliant and so completely successful that, as in the case of *Billy the Kid*, one wonders why the eye and mind that produced it did not produce anything as good after it.

I was going to say as in the case of *Fancy Free* too; but Robbins produced several brilliant ballets for musical shows; and now he has given us *Afternoon of a Faun*, with its keen perception about the people of the world bounded by the walls and mirrors of the dance studio: a movement which begins as personal involvement ends with the two dancers turning to see how they look in the mirror.

In *Filling Station* young d'Amboise's brilliant dancing is exciting not only in itself but for what it promises; Reed again demonstrates her superb gift for comedy; and there are excellent performances by Maule, Barnett and the others. And among the good things about *Afternoon of a Faun* is how well it uses the special gifts of LeClercq and Moncion—how much it profits by the way each establishes her or himself as a powerful presence on a stage. *(147)*

Postscript 1970 For years, enjoying Robbins's low-key realization of his perception, I failed to notice something that was pointed out to me recently by a great dancer: that "this little point about dancers' narcissism" had no relation to, and was incommensurate with, Debussy's music. Nor had the Nijinsky version, this dancer added, been any better in this respect. I could answer only that what Nijinsky, and now Robbins, had put together on the stage, misusing Debussy's piece as a mere sound-track, had been effective in and for itself.

27 June 1953 Con Amore, the new Lew Christensen piece presented by the New York City Ballet, begins pleasantly and amusingly; but apparently it is easier to begin something than to continue it and bring it to a conclusion in a clear line of development, as Christensen did so brilliantly in *Filling Station*, and as he doesn't do in *Con Amore*. Heading the cast were Sally Bailey and Nancy Johnson of Christensen's San Francisco Ballet, which first produced the piece last March; and Bailey's dancing in the opening scene was very lovely. And d'Amboise had another opportunity to display his dazzling spins and leaps.

Most of Robbins's *Fanfare* represents nothing beyond a professional resourcefulness in filling the stage with movement; but in this setting of Britten's *The Young Person's Guide to the Orchestra* Robbins contrives three episodes of brilliant comedy for the bassoons, the trombones and tuba, and the percussion.

29 August 1953 At the very least public performers have the traits of personality and character of any other human beings—traits conditioned, developed, and distorted by the ordinary experiences with family, friends, enemies, teachers, employers. There is, then, that reason for their behavior to be no better than the behavior of other people; but as it happens there are additional reasons why it is often worse. Public performers are subjected to the additional distorting strains of their intensive training and their careers; and some of them begin with the unbalance that makes possible a fanatical dedication and concentration during long years of training and then during the years of artistic achievement. The result is often irrational, unreasonable, outrageous behavior—though also the capacity to continue, day after day, to endure, cope with, and survive the circumstances of their careers that would deprive a balanced, rational person of his reason.

I speak of this because of people's attitudes toward such behavior. I have heard them condemn Toscanini vehemently for his unreasonableness, his inconsistency, and above all of course his explosions of rage at rehearsals, demanding in effect that in addition to being a great musician he should be rational, patient, just, fond of children, kind to animals, and what not—which they would not demand of a businessman or an engineer. For my part, I am content to settle for the great musician; and I know that the unreasonableness and rages are not, as these people think, mere self-indulgence by a man who could be reasonable and patient if he didn't feel privileged to be unreasonable and impatient. Toscanini is, in his relation to music, a man obsessed and possessed; and such a man is not rational and reasonable—not in music nor in anything else. Many years ago that remarkable critic, W. J. Turner, wrote that as he had sat watching Toscanini he "was suddenly reminded of Berlioz's remark, 'Do you think I make music for my pleasure?' I am certain that it is not a pleasure for Toscanini to conduct, but rather that he suffers. It is because of his extreme musical sensibility and intense concentration. Here lies the essence of his superiority." Not self-indulgence, but extreme musical sensibility, intense concentration, suffering (which Toscanini has in fact said conducting is for him)—these are the causes of the rages; and it follows that they are reasons for forgiving him, as intelligent orchestral players do. Moreover, Turner's perceptive observation teaches us something else —not merely about Toscanini but about all great artists: that we owe them gratitude not only for the experiences they give us but for what they have endured and continue to endure to make those experiences possible, and what we are unaware of as we watch or listen to them perform.

We have to learn of it from other sources; and it is from Anton Dolin's *Alicia Markova: Her Life and Art* (Hermitage) that we learn with horror of the childhood and the first years in the Diaghilev company (she joined it at fourteen) in which her existence resembled that of the hen that nowadays is kept in a cage and allowed to do nothing but lay eggs. The damage of such an existence to the personal life of the hen we don't know; the inevitable damage to the personal life of Markova is something we do *not* learn from Dolin's book. But it is known by those in the ballet world; and Agnes de Mille, who had numerous contacts with her, revealed a little in an article in the *Atlantic Monthly* last fall in which, writing that Markova had sacrificed every interest in life to the one objective of dancing better and better and better, and citing the fact that "Alicia has never married — never, as far as I know, even been engaged," she went on to say that "outraged nature must have backed up on her from time to time and taken blackmail payments . . . Whether . . . [the sacrifice] was necessary is a question she has probably asked herself . . . at lonely moments." And again in her brilliant review of the Dolin book in *The Times*, in which she spoke of its omissions: "There is no hint of the terrible melancholies [Markova] is known to sustain." De Mille ascribed the omissions to Dolin's gallantry; but I think the major reason is the one responsible for her own such omissions even in what I have quoted — the reason being that one cannot write with complete candor about the personal lives of the living.

Nor does one find in Dolin's book anything about the lessened intensity and reduced scale that began to be evident in Markova's dancing around 1946, and the omissions and substitutions and prettified faking this had come to by last fall. For this one reason is undoubtedly Dolin's gallantry — another being the way Dolin operates as a dancer himself. But what de Mille's reason was for writing last fall that "she is dancing better than ever . . . Instead of slacking off with the years she seems to be reaching greater and greater physical and emotional strengths" — I can't imagine.

12 September 1953 One thing true of Dolin's book about Markova is true also of Anatole Chujoy's *The New York City Ballet*. Mr. Chujoy acknowledges his indebtedness to Lincoln Kirstein, who "submitted to unending questioning . . . and gave me frank and forthright answers to literally hundreds of questions, some of which must have been embarrassing to him . . . opened his private correspondence files to me, let me read memoranda that had the character of personal diaries. . . ." And all this certainly is evident in the book: reading it I have learned many things I didn't know about the succession of Kirstein ventures initiated by the founding of the School of American Ballet in 1934 even though I was in contact with Kirstein from the beginning. But my own knowledge has enabled me to perceive that here something is missing or there something is told differently from the way I believe it happened — from which inevitably I assume there must be other instances that I am unable to perceive. It may be that Mr. Chujoy found out a great deal but didn't find out everything, or — what I think more probable — that he doesn't feel free to tell some things. On page 163, for example, he describes how personal friendships caused Kirstein to include on the second program of Ballet Society a modern dancer and a Javanese group that had no place on the program; but this is the only time he mentions this important factor in Kirstein's decisions and actions. I would say, therefore that the difficulty in writing about living persons that was evident in the Dolin book is evident in this one, and the book tells a large part of the story, but not "the full story" the jacket says it tells.

Moreover, in addition to the bare facts of this or that ballet having been produced on a certain date the story has to include an evaluation of the work and the performance. And there we encounter another of Mr. Chujoy's difficulties: that one may have almost everything—love of the art, experience of it, knowledge about it—that a critic needs to write about it, and lack the one thing that is essential, namely critical perception. It isn't a matter of Mr. Chujoy liking something I dislike, or vice-versa; it is a matter of what he finds to say about something we both like or dislike, which makes it clear that he has nothing to say. And this is true of most of the writers he quotes—the fact being that many write about the arts but few are critics who should be writing. On the other hand the extensive quotations from John Martin's writings have the special value of spreading his performance on the record.

What I said earlier about Kirstein was not meant as disparagement. It would be fine if we got not only ballet but everything else from people who operated with rational minds and clear purposes unaffected by personal loves and hates and other such impure elements; but the fact is that we don't get good things always for good reasons and don't reject them even when they come to us for bad reasons. And one has to recognize that amid the general Kirstein confusion there has been the particular holding fast to Balanchine which, implemented by Kirstein's willingness to spend every penny of his own for the purpose, has resulted in the creation of some of the greatest works of art of our time.

31 October 1953 The few Sadler's Wells Ballet performances I saw offered again the pleasure of richly mounted and carefully prepared productions in which the large well-rehearsed company danced with unostentatious assurance and precision and engaging sweetness and good manners. This was in fact the only pleasure from the new works I saw—Ashton's *Sylvia, Don Juan* and *Daphnis and Chloë*; and it was mixed with the pain of the dull, empty works themselves. Perhaps because Ashton's earlier *Les Patineurs* followed *Don Juan* and *Daphnis*, and certainly because it was danced so well by Brian Shaw and the others, I enjoyed it this time much more than ever before.

As for other older works, I had no opportunity to see again the company's most beautiful production, *The Sleeping Beauty*, but did see *Swan Lake* with Leslie Hurry's new scenery and costumes and de Valois's revision of the Sergeyev production. I couldn't tell whether it was the deadening choreographic hand of de Valois that made the groupings and movements of the *corps* unimpressive, and even some of the movements of Odette unattractive, this time, or whether they seemed so after what Balanchine had contrived in his version of Act 2. However, the brilliance and elegance of Fonteyn's dancing imparted distinction to the performance I saw; and Act 3 suddenly came to life with a Neapolitan dance which turned out to have been contributed by Ashton, and which was danced superbly by the company's finest male dancer, Alexander Grant, with Julia Farron.

6 February 1954 Balanchine's *Opus 34*, the first new piece presented by the New York City Ballet this year, is in two parts, danced to two successive performances of Schönberg's *Music to Accompany a Motion Picture*; and the first part is Balanchine's most extraordinary piece of dance invention since *Danses Concertantes*. What one saw in that work—the "changes from staccato movements to continuous ones, from rapid leaps and displacements to standing still, from one dancer solo to several all at once"; the "spurts, stops, and clipped stalkings"°—all these were a special use of elements of the ballet vocabulary in a special style; and it is another such special use of a special style that one sees in the first part of *Opus 34*. This one uses something of modern dance (in the way other Balanchine pieces have used elements of the American musical-show idiom); and the result is, among other things, a demonstration

°Edwin Denby.

of how much more effectively Balanchine can use it than the modern dancers themselves. The modern element works in with the occasional distortion—the twisted distortion, for example, in the movements of the *pas de deux*—to make the intricate involvements of the piece austere and grim to the point of frightening. And this brings us to the relation of the dancing and the music: both are frightening, but one by the way its progression of distorted musical elements makes no coherent musical sense, the other by the powerfully coherent dance sense made by its progression of occasionally distorted movements.

For the second performance of Schönberg's piece Balanchine exercises his powers of theatrical invention; and we get, with the music that is horrible in its incoherent distortion, the gripping horror achieved on the stage by masterly use of all the resources of the theater: action, costumes, props, scenery, lighting. Here Balanchine has assistance from Esteban Francés, who designed the costumes, and Jean Rosenthal, who did the décor and lighting, that is even more spectacular than their striking contributions to the first part. At the première he also had the assistance of the dancers headed by Adams, Wilde, Magallanes and Moncion who performed the difficult first part with dedication as well as perfection; and of LeClercq and Bliss who were superb in the second part. And finally he had the assistance of the accomplished orchestra and Leon Barzin who performed the difficult music as though it were as easy as Stravinsky's *Sacre du Printemps*.

27 February 1954 "The fact is," an actor and director I know remarked once after the City Center curtain had fallen on a Balanchine ballet, "the important things happening in the theater nowadays are being done right here." Balanchine has continued to demonstrate the truth of that observation—most recently in his production of *The Nutcracker* for the New York City Ballet. It is an exciting work of theater art, offering not only the characteristic invention of Balanchine the choreographer in the second

act—notably the freshly imagined supported adagio of the Sugar Plum Fairy and her Cavalier, with its quiet and delicate beginning, its crescendo of impassioned brilliance; her solo, with its almost casual rhythmic intricacy; *Marzipan Shepherdesses*, with its rhythmic counterpoint of the soloist and her companions—but the invention of Balanchine the theater artist, with its details that warm and touch one, in the Christmas party of the first act. What is especially touching is the feeling for a child's world, a child's imagination, which one also hears in Tchaikovsky's music—for example the music at the end of Act 1, and the introduction to Act 2. And Balanchine is helped by Horace Armistead's scenery, Karinska's costumes, Jean Rosenthal's lighting, the brilliant performances —Tallchief's Sugar Plum Fairy, LeClercq's Dewdrop, Reed in *Marzipan Shepherdesses*, Barnett in *Candy Canes*, William Dollar's characterization of the at once sinister and benign Herr Drosselmeyer. *(148)*

13 March 1954 Most of us get nothing out of Japanese music; but Japanese painting and sculpture make exciting sense to us, even if not the sense they must make to the Japanese; and this is true also of the highly formalized and ritualized dances presented by the Azuma Kabuki Dancers who are here for a tour sponsored by Prince Takamatsu and the Japanese Foreign Ministry. The mask-like make-ups and sculptured magnificence of costume contribute to the powerful effect of the stylized movements in some of the dances; and in others the movements of Tokuho Azuma exercise a no less compelling power with their exact delicacy—e.g., the delicacy of the movements of her feet—and controlled fluidity. Something of a surprise after this high art are the engaging folk dances, executed with the same precision, and with a humor that needs no translation.

13 November 1954 What the Balanchine eye sees—whether it is American musical-show dancing or Scotch dances or modern dance—turns up in his ballets; and in the delightful new *Western Symphony,* which the New York City Ballet presented in September, it is Western American square dancing. The steps are those of classical ballet; but they are done by groups whose striding about and falling into formations and ducking in and out of these formations are those of the square dancing, done to the succession of American folk tunes of Hershy Kay's engaging score (whose four movements may make it a symphony to his ears but don't to mine). The detailed invention is ample, genial, gay, funny—with some quiet little Balanchine jokes in the slow movement, as well as the more vigorous fun of the fast movements. As for performance, the slow movement employs Reed's dead-pan comic gift; the earlier fast movements are danced engagingly by Adams, Wilde, Bliss and Bolender or Eglevsky; and LeClercq and d'Amboise—the one in an amusing elegantly slangy American style, the other with his brilliance—lead the company in an increasingly exciting finale.

In Balanchine's other new work, *Ivesiana*—so called because its musical basis is several pieces by Charles Ives—one thing to say is that like last year's *Opus 34* it offers evidence of Balanchine's having seen modern dance and demonstrates how much better he can do it than the modern dancers themselves. Which amounts to saying how much greater powers operate in his use of the modern idiom than in theirs, and brings us to the important fact about *Ivesiana*—that it is another remarkable manifestation of his creative power and originality, in the particular line of development which revealed itself in *Opus 34,* and in that line because of a musical basis similar to that of *Opus 34.* That is, except for the jazz that breaks in for a few moments, Ives's *Central Park in the Dark* is in a modern idiom that makes no more coherent musical sense to me than the Schönberg piece used in *Opus 34;* and like that piece it provides Balanchine with a suitable sound-track—this time for the powerful metaphors of an episode of sexual brutality, the powerful comments of the *corps.* Ives's *The Unanswered Question* performs a similar function

for the most strikingly original episode in the ballet—the latest in Balanchine's series of extraordinary supported adagios: one in which, this time, the man crawls after, reaches up for, and never succeeds in making contact with, the girl who enters supported aloft and erect by four other men who move and swing her down and up and around and eventually carry her out. And on the other hand the distorted jazz of *In the Inn* is directly and obviously related to Balanchine's grotesque caricatures of popular dances. LeClercq and Bolender in this episode, Reed and Moncion in *Central Park,* Allegra Kent and Bolender in *The Unanswered Question,* Wilde, Adams, d'Amboise and Bliss in the other episodes that I don't remember as clearly—all contribute to a superb performance of this extraordinary work.

On the other hand, in the revival of the Rodgers-Hart-Balanchine *On Your Toes* Balanchine demonstrates—in the routines for the excellent Bobby Van, and in the big ensemble numbers for *Quiet Night* and *On Your Toes*—that he can use the American musical-show idiom as effectively as any American; and in the *On Your Toes* number he begins with this idiom, then has one of the repetitions of the song danced in his classical-ballet idiom, and then combines the two, with first only one couple jitterbugging around a couple doing a classical-ballet adagio, and then the entire company joining in one of his brilliant final crescendos. All this in addition to the famous *Slaughter on Tenth Avenue* and the hilariously funny *Princess Zenobia* burlesque of *Scheherazade.* (200)

8 January 1955 With Mounsey and Tallchief 1955 absent I saw Adams not only in *Scotch Symphony,* in which she danced with a beautiful lyricism, but in *Prodigal Son,* in which she achieved what my actor-director friend characterized as "the most antiseptic siren ever seen on the American stage". But for John Martin, for whom a ballet comes to life when it is danced in by a former member of Ballet Theater, Adams's Siren made this the outstanding per-

formance of *Prodigal Son* in many a season—one in which Moncion could be credited with a newly acquired effectiveness, whereas actually his performance was less controlled and contained this time than on other occasions.

And seeing Jillana and d'Amboise in *Afternoon of a Faun*, I discovered how many overtones of presence and expressive point LeClercq and Moncion had enriched the piece with.

26 March 1955 Each new work of Balanchine exhibits an extended and enriched vocabulary and new groupings and formations that are amazing evidence of his continuing creative power. One line of development is seen in the powerful modern-style movements and distortions of *Opus 34* and *Ivesiana*; another in the delicate intricacy that is one of the enchanting features of his new piece, *Roma*. Enchanting too is a new counterpoint of slow against fast: the music, at one point in the first movement, continuing fast while two groups of boys and one of girls suddenly drop into a slow saunter as they look each other over; the boys continuing slow while the girls become increasingly animated; LeClercq, in the final tarantella, performing intricate fast steps while the boys' arms make an enormous slow circling movement; and other things of the sort. Bizet's unfamiliar and charming music adds to the effectiveness of the piece; Eugene Berman's costumes, unattractive in design and color, diminish it: LeClercq's movements are contrived to make exquisite use of her long silhouette, which the costume chops in two, with the result that the loveliness of her dancing isn't fully revealed. Eglevsky is luckier in having nothing to obscure his brilliant performance of the delicate intricacies that keep him too busy to get in more than an occasional Eglevskyism.

Last fall's *Ivesiana* was given this time with the *Hallowe'en* episode replaced by one called *Arguments*, in which—to the music of a quartet movement by Ives in which the four string voices scream at each other—a couple of youngsters who alternate between quarreling and making love are disturbed by three female busybodies with whom they get into a wrangle in the amusingly visible form of a Balanchine labyrinth of intertwining bodies violently stepping over and under locked arms. Also, last fall's *Western Symphony*, which was effective and funny without costumes, was made twice as effective and funny with marvelous costumes by Karinska which pointed up the movements and jokes. LeClercq's hat—to say nothing of the way she wore it—was alone worth the price of admission.

4 June 1955 For its recent New York engagement Ballet Theater had the idea of reviving some of its earlier productions with former members of the company in guest appearances in their original roles. And this worked out well in some performances I saw, but poorly in some others.

In the Tudor *Romeo and Juliet* with Markova and Laing it worked out poorly. As early as 1946 Markova had begun to exhibit the reduced intensity which by now had reached the point where her dancing was completely without the projected animation and force that once made her quick darting movements in the early scenes of *Romeo* and her lyrical lifts in the bedroom and vault scenes breathtaking. It was Alonso's dancing in a later performance that now was breathtaking in this way; and it was Youskevitch, in this performance, who exhibited not only the security in sustained balances and slow turns that Laing no longer has, but the fluidity of subtly inflected movements that Laing never had. *(115)*

The part of Taglioni in Dolin's *Pas de Quatre* lent itself better to Markova's miniature-scale operation, in which the configurations of her body as it moved through the air or came to rest in a pose were exquisite. But Moylan, in a later performance, reminded us of the exciting leaps which Markova's present itsy-bitsy hops are reduced from. *(114)*

Of Tudor's *Lilac Garden* also the performance with Viola Essen back in the role of the Bride and Tudor as the Bridegroom was much less effective than the one with Nora Kaye and Job Sanders in these roles. And other performances of Lichine's *Graduation Ball* must have been more effective than the one I saw with Lichine himself as a portly forty-year-old who somehow had strayed in among the cadets of the military school.

On the other hand de Mille's *Three Virgins and a Devil* with de Mille, Chase, Annabelle Lyon and Lazovsky in their old roles came off delightfully. It would have achieved sheer perfection if Robbins had also been there to do the Youth's saunter across the stage with an economy in its jauntiness that Kriza might emulate. And Lazovsky's *Petrushka* retained its power—though in a performance in which the carnival scenes were a shambles. *(115)*

The program that began with the Markova-Laing *Romeo* ended with Balanchine's *Theme and Variations*—previously one of the company's most distinguished achievements—which shocked me this time with the evidence of diminishing powers in the classical dancing of Alonso and Youskevitch, and with the company's lack of the sharp clarity and animation I had become used to seeing in the dancing of the New York City Ballet. The Ballet Theater *corps* exhibited the same lethargy and blurring in a shabby performance of *Swan Lake* in which Alonso returned to her old practice of doing too much too hard; and here again Youskevitch had to have the tempo slowed down in part of his solo. Kaye also required this in the opening section of the *Black Swan pas de deux*; but her young partner Erik Bruhn executed his brilliant leaps and turns with the ease, elegance and noble style of a superb classical dancer. And I might add here that in the revival of Massine's *Aleko* with Alonso and Kriza in the Markova and Laing roles, it was Bruhn in the Skibine role who, with his elegant sustained style, contributed the only impressive moments in all the Massine clutter.

It was good to see Muriel Bentley again in Robbins's *Fancy Free*; and it would have been even better if Robbins himself had returned not only to dance his original part but to clean up the production. Even in its hammed-up state this piece and its performance were one of the best things Ballet Theater offered—the others I saw being Loring's *Billy the Kid*, the second scene of de Mille's *Rodeo* (I don't like the first scene), and Ross's *Caprichos*. In them Kriza, though a little less secure in his dancing, remained an outstanding performer.

It seems to me that Ballet Theater would do well to stop thinking up spectacular ideas like this one of revivals with guest appearances by former members of the company, and settle down instead to the urgent task of building up a stable company for a stable repertory. And in this it would be wise to disregard the flattering suggestion by its doting admirer John Martin. The New York City Ballet's excitingly beautiful production of even one act of *Swan Lake* with a ballerina and *corps* superbly equipped for the purpose brought from Mr. Martin only a stern rebuke to the company for messing around with such old chestnuts; but in the Ballet Theater performances of this act with Kaye Mr. Martin's eyes recently saw the company and the "ideal ballerina for a full-length 'Swan Lake.'"

5 November 1955 Each time the Sadler's Wells Ballet has appeared in New York I have had great pleasure from the richly mounted and carefully prepared productions. But seeing the productions with eyes increasingly accustomed to Balanchine's use of the classical idiom and to the sharply defined execution of his choreography by the dancers of the New York City Ballet, I have been increasingly aware of the softness, amounting almost to flabbiness, of the general dancing style of the Sadler's Wells company—though not of certain of its soloists—in the execution of classical ballet movements less distinguished and impressive than Balanchine's. I was aware of this a few weeks ago even in the Sadler's Wells company's most beautiful achievement—its production of *The Sleeping Beauty*, with the scenery and costumes of Oliver Messel and, at the performance I saw, the elegant precision of Fonteyn.

To its revivals of this work and *Swan Lake* the company this year added productions of another old classic, *Coppélia*, and two classics of the Diaghilev repertory, Fokine's *Les Sylphides* and *Firebird*. In Sergeyev's version of *Coppélia* I saw a lovely and charming performance in the title role by Svetlana Beriosova, but a mazurka that betrayed the English nationality of its participants. *Les Sylphides* was revised by Serge Grigoriev and Liubov Tchernicheva of the Diaghilev company, whose changes of detail merely, in effect, added another variant of the piece to those we have seen; and the piece is one in which the company's soft style worked well in the context that set off the stronger dancing of Fonteyn.

On the other hand Grigoriev's and Tchernicheva's restoration of the original Fokine choreography for *Firebird* to the luxuriant original version of Stravinsky's score was very different from the streamlined Balanchine version to Stravinsky's reduced score that we have seen in recent years. The general effect of greater amplitude—in music, in story line, and from the use of a larger company in the dance of Kastchei's subjects and in the finale—was one thing I liked; another was the *pas de deux* of the captured Firebird struggling in the arms of Ivan Tsarevitch, which seemed to me as original and imaginative and effective today as when I first saw it forty years ago. And as for the movements in the big dances that are ineffective today, I accepted them as less effective parts of a great work, with the further thought that they might be revised by someone with skill and taste like Ashton. Fonteyn's performance in the title role, in which she was coached by Karsavina who created it originally, was superb, and revealed to my eyes no reason for the controversy it aroused in England.

I saw this time Ashton's *Homage to the Queen*, which I missed the last time, and which had been described as Ashton's *Four Temperaments*. It turned out to be as rich in invention as this praise implied, but invention in which I was conscious always of artful contrivance, as against the naturalness and inevitability of Balanchine. But Ashton's *Façade* I again found to be a masterpiece; and recalling his *Wedding Bouquet* and his performance as one of the Ugly Sisters in *Cinderella* I will risk the generalization that he is strongest in all forms of comedy.

7 January 1956 The *Pas de Dix* that Balanchine contributed to the New York City Ballet's recent season not only uses some of Glazunov's engaging music for the *divertissements* in the last act of the ballet *Raymonda*, but includes at least two of the dances Balanchine devised for this act when he staged *Raymonda* for the Monte Carlo Ballet Russe ten years ago. One is the Orientale danced then by Danilova, which is now Tallchief's solo; the other is the dance of the four boys. To these Balanchine has added solos for the four girls and for Eglevsky, and a brilliant conclusion; but most impressive are the opening dance in which the four couples provide a context for the entrance of Tallchief and Eglevsky, and their supported adagio filled with fascinatingly intricate invention, which Tallchief executes with her beautiful clarity and elegance.

In another new ballet, *Jeux d'Enfants*, most of the toys come to life—to the charming music of Bizet, and in the ingenious costumes of Esteban Francés—in dances devised by Barbara Milberg and Francisco Moncion which are, with one exception, pleasantly inconsequential. The exception is Moncion's *Music Box*, an arresting interlude with its three figures in magnificent Spanish costumes whose jerky, repetitive movements, amusing at first, are seen to be enacting a love triangle which ends with the husband stabbing the lover. And later on Balanchine imparts astonishingly fresh life and humor to the operations of the toy soldier and the doll, danced brilliantly by Tobias and Hayden.

The other new work presented by the company was Bolender's *Souvenirs*, in which he employs very effectively the gift for comedy that he has exhibited on occasion in his dancing—for example in Balanchine's *A la Françaix*. *Souvenirs* is concerned with the goings-on in a resort hotel in 1914, and with characters whose appearance, clothes and movements are caricatures of what Bolender and Rouben Ter-Arutunian, who designed the scenery and costumes, have seen in photographs and films of the period. Bolender himself dances a man about town in a hallway episode which develops into a Mack Sennett chase in and out of a series of bedroom doors; Irene Larsson and John Mandia burlesque an impassioned scene in a vampire-type film; and on the other hand Jillana carries off marvelously what I consider the most brilliant thing in the piece — the acutely observed pantomime of a young woman in a quarrel with her escort, which is of all time. Barber's music, whose dissonances caricature musical styles evocative of the period, is an effective sound-track.

24 March 1956 At the first performances of its spring season the New York City Ballet has exhibited its clear, beautiful and brilliant dancing, and has presented the first of three new works, Balanchine's *Allegro Brillante,* a setting of the one completed movement of Tchaikovsky's Piano Concerto No. 3. This piece, composed in the last year of Tchaikovsky's life, begins magnificently and excitingly with some of his most arresting ideas, and continues with effective writing to the end of the exposition, but becomes aimless and diffuse in the development. And it is interesting that in Balanchine's piece it is the beginning too — the placing of the dancers on the stage, the establishing of the style of their dancing — that is most impressive. After that what is interesting is the resourceful ingenuity that keeps things going with coherence even to music which is diffuse and aimless, and that makes beautiful use of the individual capacities of the dancers — in particular Tallchief's capacity for movement of marvelous delicacy in quiet.

28 April 1956 Jerome Robbins's contribution to the New York City Ballet's recent season was *The Concert,* described in the program as a charade, and actually a series of revue sketches representing the reveries induced in a group of people as they listen to Nicolas Kopeikine playing a number of piano pieces by Chopin. Robbins gave us one such sketch in the *Percussion* episode of *Fanfare*; and in *The Concert* his comic gift operates with equally amusing effect. In some instances, the effect is achieved with dancing; in a few it is not. On the one hand we get LeClercq's high-stepping entrance on points as a romantic young lady who then sits gazing soulfully at Kopeikine; or her frenzied *pas de deux* with terrified little Richard Thomas; or her joining Bolender and four boys in a burlesque mazurka; or a group of girls wrecking a Balanchine-style ensemble piece with their mistakes. On the other hand we get these girls being carried in and carted about and set down — now here, now there — like inanimate props; or LeClercq trying on ridiculous hats and choosing one joyfully, only to be crushed by a meeting with someone else wearing the same hat; or Mounsey making one attempt after another to do away with her husband and managing each time to do away with herself instead. In addition there is a serious interlude — a lyrical solo beautifully devised for LeClercq's lovely style. In the other sketches she and Bolender exhibit their superb gifts for comedy, with assists from Mounsey, Barnett and the rest of the accomplished cast.

As a choreographer Bolender, besides making last fall's *Souvenirs* even funnier, turned serious in *The Still Point,* in which Hayden repelled sex as personified by Tobias and Mandia, to the first movement of Debussy's String Quartet, took to it sluttishly, to the second movement, and was redeemed by pure love in the person of d'Amboise, to the third movement. All very embarrassing to watch, except for a few effective details — like Hayden's wild spin with frantic flings of her arms at the climax of the second movement. By now Hayden has become a specialist in the dancing of Profane Love, and she did it as well in this new piece as in Ashton's *Illuminations*; but d'Amboise's appearance is suited to innocence only when it is gay, not when it is solemn.

I might add that not enough thought seems to be given to what roles certain dancers are and are not suited for — to the fact that d'Amboise's face makes him convincing as the Sugar Plum Fairy's Cavalier in *The Nutcracker* but not as the Prince in *Swan Lake.* Or that Adams can replace Tallchief in *Scotch Symphony* but not Mounsey in *The Prodigal Son.*

2 June 1956 At the Ballet Theater's recent New York engagement one important new feature was the performances of Rosella Hightower and Erik Bruhn in the roles that used to be danced by Alonso and Youskevitch. Bruhn, executing his leaps and turns with disciplined elegance and noble style, was in every instance a satisfying and impressive replacement; Hightower's normal operation was an exuberant virtuosity punctuated by grand-ballerina-style poses, instead of the sustained continuity in plastic movement in which such poses are moments of emphasis and climax. Moreover, in the second act of *Giselle* the configurations of head, arms, torso and legs in the poses didn't always look right; and surprisingly enough there was a lack of the kind of projective force that would have made Giselle's exhibition dance in the first act the exciting thing it should be. The most effective dancing by Hightower that I saw was in the *Nutcracker pas de deux*, with its large-scale spectacular effects, and on the other hand in Balanchine's *Theme and Variations*, where she was held to the tightly continuous Balanchine invention.

The restoration of the Tudor repertory, begun a year ago with the return of Kaye and Laing to the company, continued with revivals of *Dim Luster* and *Undertow*, which I didn't see. But I can report that in *Romeo and Juliet* Kaye's lightness and quickness in the darting movements of the early scenes, her lyrical lifts in the bedroom and vault scenes, her dramatic projection throughout added up to a completely and beautifully achieved performance, and that Laing's greater security in the sustained balances and slow turns of his role contributed to a much more effective performance of the work than last year's. Tudor's invention for the two leading characters is what I find imaginatively distinguished and interesting to see repeatedly in this piece—not those many details so ingeniously contrived for their pantomimic significance.

The restoration of the de Mille repertory continued with a revival of *Tally-Ho*, which may be unconvincing in story line and a little long and repetitious but contains much that is amusing in the de Mille manner. Kriza and Bentley were as funny as ever in their old roles; and Sono Osato, in a guest appearance as the Wife, was charming. In addition *Three Virgins and a Devil* was highly enjoyable as danced by de Mille herself, Lucia Chase, Barbara Lloyd and Enrique Martinez; but I continue to wish Kriza would not exaggerate the jauntiness of the Youth's saunter, which used to be done with such effective economy by Robbins.

De Mille also contributed one of the two new ballets, *Rib of Eve*, described as a morality play, which tells about a woman who alternates between her craving for the shallow involvements with the crowds of people who invade her home at her parties, and her revulsions against them, and who in the process exhausts the patience of the husband whose love isn't enough for her. The telling is done in choreographic terms which include some enjoyable dancing by large groups, a lovely *pas de deux* of the wife and husband, some amusing details in one of their arguments. The Hostess is a role tailored for Kaye, which she acted and danced effectively; and James Mitchell gave an engaging performance as the Husband. Noisy music by Morton Gould; efficient scenic constructions by Oliver Smith; striking costumes by Irene Sharaff.

On the other hand Kaye was miscast as the captivating Operetta Star in the other new ballet, Tudor's *Offenbach in the Underworld*, the feebleness of which extended even to his choice of music, but not to René Bouché's set and Koesun's dancing as the Debutante. (And though I didn't see Kaye in *Giselle* one perceptive and reliable spectator informed me that her first-act Giselle suggested some of the characteristics of her role in *The Cage*—which is certainly a remarkable achievement by "the foremost actress-dancer of our day," but one I am content not to have seen.)

23 June 1956 The American Shakespeare Festival Theatre at Stratford, Connecticut, put on what it described as the first of a series of annual music festivals—this one devoted to Mozart. It included on the one hand a convocation, with Virgil Thomson as chairman, which discussed the subject *What Mozart Means to Modern Music*, and on the other hand two ballets which demonstrated in living art what Mozart's music means to the man I have come to regard as the greatest creative artist of our day, George Balanchine. One, *A Musical Joke*, danced to Mozart's piece with that title, was entirely new; the other, *Divertimento*, danced to the Divertimento K.287, was a largely new version of *Caracole*, which the New York City Ballet presented briefly a few years ago.

Divertimento, like *Caracole*, is one of what have been described as Balanchine's "concentrated essays . . . in extended classic vocabulary"—which is to say the classical-ballet vocabulary as extended by Balanchine in invention of increasing intricacy and unending originality. That invention delights the eye with its brilliance in the Allegro and Minuet of *Divertimento*; but its high points are the variation and adagio movements. In the first, Mozart's own elaboration of his musical theme in the series of variations elicits from Balanchine a succession of richly diverse, fascinatingly complex and marvelously beautiful solos; for the long aria in the second Balanchine produces one of his great supported adagios. As against the singing of the aria by one instrumental voice, there is the shifting from one supported dancer to the next; but this is less disturbing than in *Caracole* because Balanchine gives each couple a longer stretch to do and thus reduces the number of breaks. *(149)*

A Musical Joke, characterized as a "ballet-burlesque," is another such essay, but with special features related to the special character of the music. Mozart begins with the banalities a group of village amateurs would play; he includes obvious jokes in the form of the occasional dissonant disasters of their performance, and subtle ones concerned with tonality for the eighteenth-century ears that could appreciate them; but in a slow movement apparently he cannot be anything but serious—that is, write anything but music that is characteristically lovely and affecting, except for a burlesque cadenza at the end. And in response to all this Balanchine too begins with banalities,

contrives details that are obviously funny to anyone and subtler "mistakes" that dancers will smile at, but produces for the slow movement another of his great supported adagios, with a few jokes in the cadenza, but until then holding one spellbound with the sustained beauty and grandeur of its development, the new things which the Balanchine imagination contrives for the dancers to do.

The pieces make enormous demands on the dancers; and their effectiveness at the Stratford performance I attended resulted from the way those demands were satisfied by Adams and Bliss, LeClercq and Magallanes, Wilde and Moncion in *A Musical Joke*; Adams, Hayden, Kent, LeClercq, Wilde, Bliss, Magallanes, Tobias and a small group of girls in *Divertimento*. It is for his female dancers that Balanchine produces his most brilliant invention; and each of the soloists was, in her own way, dazzling. But LeClercq's movements—her unfolding *arabesques* in the long supported adagio of *A Musical Joke*, for example—were made breath-takingly beautiful by the aura of personal radiance that gives an added dimension to her dancing.

Karinska contributed enchanting costumes for *A Musical Joke*, and charming new ones for *Divertimento*. There was no scenery for the first piece; and I think none would have been better for the second than the backdrop from *Symphonie Concertante*.

20 October 1956 The Royal Danish Ballet, like the Sadler's Wells, offers the pleasure of seeing a permanent subsidized company dance in richly mounted and carefully prepared productions with the assurance and precision achieved by years of study and rehearsal and performance together. Like the English dancers, too, the Danes charm one with their sweetness and good manners, but with this difference —that whereas the general dancing style of the English company exhibits a softness amounting almost to flabbiness, the Danes dance with an engaging alertness and spirit. Their female soloists include no one with the dazzling technique, glamorous presence, and power of projection of Fonteyn; but Margrethe Schanne, Mona Vangsaa, Inge Sand and Kirsten Petersen are accomplished and lovely dancers. And the Danish company is strong in its male soloists, among them the technically brilliant Fredbjorn Bjornsson and, most impressive of all, the poetic Henning Kronstam.

An additional feature of interest is the company's repertory. Since it has a continuous existence and tradition which extend back to the opening of the Royal Theater in Copenhagen in 1748, it offers works of the eighteenth and nineteenth centuries—Galeotti's *The Whims of Cupid* (1786), Bournonville's famous *La Sylphide* (1836) and his *Napoli* (1842)—which have been kept in the repertory since their premières. It is impossible to believe that they have been preserved intact in the process of being handed down by one generation of dancers to the next; but they are interesting to see even in their altered state. To these the company, in its New York season, added its own version of one of the ballet classics, *Coppélia*; its productions of two twentieth-century classics, Fokine's *Les Sylphides* under the title *Chopiniana* and his *Petrushka*; its productions of two modern works, Lichine's *Graduation Ball* and Balanchine's *Night Shadow* under the title *La Sonnambula;* and the *Romeo and Juliet* that Ashton created for the company to Prokofiev's score.

Of the three museum pieces I enjoyed most *The Whims of Cupid,* in which the dances of the several couples and the ensemble dance in which Cupid mischievously rearranges them, were charming. *La Sylphide,* the first of the Romantic ballets concerned with the involvements of human and supernatural beings, had some beautiful sequences in which Margrethe Schanne danced with exquisite delicacy and lightness suitable for the incorporeal Sylphide. In *Napoli,* on the other hand, I found not only the long stretches of miming in the first two acts but the dance invention less interesting; but a comedy bit by a street singer and his drummer was done superbly.

Most of the dances in the *Coppélia* were as effective as those in the version that used to be danced by the Ballet Russe de Monte Carlo;

and the piece as a whole was performed by the Danish company with a precision and verve which the Monte Carlo performances didn't have. One missed certain details of the ear-of-wheat *pas de deux* in the first act and the entire third-act *pas de deux* that Danilova used to make into some of the great moments of the work; but Inge Sand, though in her own way a charming and effective Swanilda, doesn't have the resources that would have enabled her to make of these passages what Danilova made of them.

In John Taras's staging of the version of *Night Shadow* that Balanchine created for the de Cuevas company one was aware of occasional changes and losses; but the piece was unmistakably Balanchine's, and was exciting to see again. The production had distinguished scenery by André Delfau and costumes by him that I liked better than the horrible ones of the Monte Carlo company's production; and it gained by Henning Kronstam's performance of the Poet. But the climactic *pas de deux* of the Poet's encounter with the Somnambulist—one of the most extraordinarily imaginative strokes of *fantaisie Balanchine*—lost by Margrethe Schanne's lack of the concentration and intensity with which Danilova gave it terrific impact in the Monte Carlo performances.

As for *Romeo and Juliet,* Prokofiev and Ashton both were able to contrive music and movement for the scenes of spectacle, brawling, dueling and violent death, but not for the poetry of the scenes of the two lovers. A dance of Juliet with Paris was lovely to hear and see; an episode of the Nurse and her Page was amusing; the rest I found increasingly uninteresting.

2 February 1957 The New York City Ballet 1957 began its season with a week of repertory, which was followed by Christmas-week performances of *The Nutcracker.* During the opening week it offered the first new ballet—the *Divertimento No. 15* to Mozart's Divertimento K.287 that Balanchine produced for the Stratford Festival last May. With the additional performances the piece has had in Europe since then it now has a greater clarity of outline and articulation that increases its effectiveness—in particular the effectiveness of the series of fascinatingly complex and marvelously beautiful solos of the variation movement and the great supported adagio of the slow movement. The piece was performed brilliantly by the Stratford group with a few replacements: Wilde, Hayden, Adams (dancing LeClercq's part because of her illness), Mounsey (in Adams's part), Barbara Milberg (substituting for the temporarily absent Kent), Magallanes, Tobias and Jonathan Watts (substituting for the temporarily absent Bliss). And it was interesting to see Adams executing the movements evidently devised for LeClercq's body and style, Mounsey giving a similar quasi-impersonation of Adams, and Milberg giving one of Kent. The impersonations were good, but not as good as the originals: Adams could not give off the personal radiance and wit of LeClercq; nor could Milberg produce the exquisitely modulated bodily configurations and movements of Kent.

The company managed to give excellent performances not only without LeClercq and Kent but, much of the time, without Tallchief, who acted the *prima ballerina assoluta* Maria Tallchieva by appearing in one performance of Balanchine's *Pas de Dix* and one of his *Allegro Brillante* and nothing else—not one performance of *The Nutcracker*, not *Swan Lake*, not even the second performance of *Pas de Dix*. In this one it was Wilde who played the Russian *prima ballerina* in legitimate and impressive fashion with dancing that not only was technically dazzling but had a beautiful fluidity, suppleness, delicacy and continuity which lent themselves to the nobility and elegance of the evocation of Petersburg grand style.

In the third and fourth weeks Tallchief made an occasional appearance in *Firebird*, *Swan Lake* and *Sylvia pas de deux*, while Kent assumed roles in *Pas de Dix*, *Concerto Barocco* and other works in which she exhibited a brilliant technique, a loveliness and a spirit that establish her as one of the company's finest dancers. And in the second *Prodigal Son* Moncion gave one of his most distinguished performances of the title role—a performance richly filled out with dramatically meaningful detail, the vigorous

dances of the opening scenes contained and precise, the slow movement of the scenes after the despoiling made impressive by its continuity of flow and tension and by Moncion's powers of presence and projection. The performance as a whole was better in important respects: the companions were attentive and involved during the Siren's dance; and Barnett and Mandia made the servants' obscene dance sharp and clear. But Barnett's deprecatory gesture in the direction of the garrulous Father in the opening scene is one I think he should omit.

23 March 1957 Ballet Theater, at its single appearance in New York, presented a new piece, *Winter's Eve*, by the young English choreographer Kenneth MacMillan. The reports about his work for the Sadler's Wells companies had created interest and expectations which were disappointed by this piece created expressly for Ballet Theater. Set to Britten's *Variations on a Theme of Frank Bridge*, with striking scenery and costumes by Nicholas Georgiadis, it is concerned with a blind girl's involvement with a young man from whom she conceals her blindness, her distress when he discovers it, her accidental blinding of him in their struggle, their being separated by the crowd and being unable to find each other. And as the story is contrived and unplausible, so the dance and mime movements in which it is told are forced and unconvincing when they are freshly inventive, which they are only part of the time. The one exception is the spectacular effect of fluttering birds produced with the white-clothed arms of dancers in black against a black back-drop. The piece provides Kaye with the type of dramatic part that she does so well; and one noted again how much better she looks in this company than in the New York City Ballet.

30 March 1957 Of the New York City Ballet's additional new works the first, Bolender's *The Masquers*, offers poor Hayden in still another distressing sexual misadventure, this time one that ends with her murder; and d'Amboise, who in *The Still Point* was the youth whose pure love redeemed her, this time is the brute who mistreats and finally kills her. The important thing is not the unpleasant story but the uninteresting dance movements in which it is realized on the stage. Bolender has given us delightful invention for comedy in *Souvenirs,* but nothing comparable in his serious ballets. The music was an inconsequential piece by Poulenc; David Hays designed the costumes and scenery which included a movable gateway, the significance of whose changed positions was not clear.

Moncion, who contributed the arresting *Music Box* episode to *Jeux d'Enfants* last year, offered his first full-length ballet in *Pastorale,* which is about a blind youth's encounter with a blindfolded girl who has strayed away from her fiancé and companions, and the distressing situation when they find her. Again the important thing is the dance movements in which the incident is realized; and for me the piece comes alive when Moncion begins to move in his encounter with the girl, and what precedes and follows this dance of their involvement is only competent use of familiar materials. The effectiveness of the central encounter is heightened by Moncion's force of presence and projection as a dancer, and by the similar contribution of Kent in the part of the girl. The luxuriantly nostalgic music is by Charles Turner; the scenery, mostly a striking tree, by David Hays; the costumes by Ruth Sobotka.

It was not only in *Pastorale* that Kent was impressive: in her every appearance—and most notably in *Divertimento No. 15* and *The Four Temperaments*—she compelled fascinated attention with her exquisite modulation of bodily configurations and movements, her clarity and exactness, her fluidity and grace, her projection of personal radiance and force. All these made her advent to the first rank of soloists more eventful than the new ballets.

1958   Winter 1958 The Royal (formerly the Sadler's Wells) Ballet, when it first came here in 1949,

placed us in its debt with its richly mounted productions of Nicholas Sergeyev's authentic reconstructions of two great classics of Russian imperial ballet, *The Sleeping Beauty* and *Swan Lake* (however, in 1953 the *Swan Lake* exhibited the damage done by de Valois's deadening choreographic hand). Two years ago it placed us further in its debt with similar productions of two great Diaghilev classics, *Les Sylphides* and *Firebird,* with the Fokine choreography restored by Lubov Tchernicheva, one of the principal dancers of the Diaghilev company, and Serge Grigoriev, its *régisseur.* And this year we got their restoration of *Petrushka.* In it the crowd milled about in the opening scene very much as always; but the first dance of the three puppets gave me an impression of clarification and, in some details, of freshness and newness that I continued to get from the scenes in Petrushka's and the Blackamoor's rooms and the succession of dances in the final scene. The performance I saw had an excellent Blackamoor, Gary Burne, and Showman, Franklin White, but a Petrushka, Brian Shaw, and a Ballerina, Maryon Lane, who were humans with puppet-like characteristics rather than puppets with intimations of human emotions; and it did not therefore produce the effect of the less accurate performances years ago with Lazovsky as Petrushka. But it did show what happened in the piece and what would be effective and moving if done by dancers like Lazovsky and Danilova—which made it a satisfying experience. And the group dances of the Nursemaids and Coachmen in the final scene were excellent, with brilliant moments contributed by the two Stable Boys, Ray Powell and Basil Thompson.

The company also has presented similar richly mounted and carefully prepared productions of works by living choreographers—more accurately, living British choreographers (it hasn't performed here the one Balanchine ballet in its repertory, *Ballet Imperial*). The most distinguished of these is Ashton; and the most distinguished of his achievements remain the two masterpieces of dance comedy that the company offered in its first visits: *Façade,* to the music of William Walton, and *A Wedding Bou-*

quet, to the music of Lord Berners and the words of Gertrude Stein. The other works of Ashton that we have seen here have included pieces as dull as *Daphnis and Chloë* and *Sylvia* or as downright trashy as this year's *La Péri*, and abstract classical ballets like *Homage to the Queen* that have exhibited no more than the ingenuities of a resourceful craftsman; but in this year's *Birthday Offering* the invention had the life and the effect of art.

In its first seasons here the company performed the ballets of de Valois, which more recently it has spared us; this year it presented new works by its younger choreographers John Cranko and Kenneth MacMillan. I can report only on MacMillan's *Noctambules*, which exhibited imaginative dance invention in the carrying out of its dramatic idea of a theater hypnotist who hypnotizes his audience and falls under his own spell. The piece had striking scenery and costumes by Nicholas Georgiadis and pointlessly ugly music by Humphrey Searle.

Spring 1958 The movement in Balanchine's *Agon*, fitting among, around and across the notes of Stravinsky's music like an additional counterpoint, gives it an additional significance—the significance imparted, for example, to a crabbed-sounding musical motif or phrase by visually exciting changes in an anything-but-crabbed-looking configuration of a girl's body or a larger configuration of several such bodies. And much of this imparted significance is humorous. The movements in the two *Pas de Trois* are—in ways that are difficult to convey, since they are often matters of no more than the movements' angularity, energy, brevity, abrupt cessation, or their canonic imitation, or their exaggeration of charming or noble attitudes—amusing to see; they make the music amusing to hear; and Balanchine says he had this implicit humorous character of the music in mind when he created the movements; nevertheless the music is not enjoyable by itself, and what delights one is what Balanchine adds to it. So with the climactic *Pas de Deux* to which all this fun leads: "expressive" phrases of the music are in an idiom which is not a medium of expressive communication for me; and their expressiveness is therefore, for me, mere manner without reality; but they provide a sound-track for the successive involvements of the two dancers that hold one spellbound. It has always seemed to me that Balanchine's imagination operated at its highest potential in his invention for ballerina and supporting male dancer—the seduction in *The Prodigal Son*, the ominous *Hand of Fate* episode in *Cotillon*, the tender and playful *pas de deux* of the Boy and Bride, the violent one in which the Fairy possesses the Boy, in *Le Baiser de la Fée*, the Poet's encounter with the Somnambulist in *The Night Shadow*, the dance of Apollo and Terpsichore in *Apollo*, the Andante in *Concerto Barocco*, the Third Theme in *The Four Temperaments*. If one saw only one of these and nothing else of Balanchine's one would know him to be a great master; seeing one after the other and marveling at what he contrived, one has felt certain each time that his imagination could go no further; and then it has gone still further in the next. So now with the *Pas de Deux* in *Agon*, which takes its place with the great examples I have mentioned: it involves the bodies of the two dancers in astounding new intricacies which would appear to be the utmost the human mind could conceive of, but which are probably not the last conceived of by the mind of Balanchine.

The difficult piece was danced superbly; its two *Pas de Trois* in particular were delightfully executed by Todd Bolender, Barbara Milberg and Barbara Walczak, and Melissa Hayden, Jonathan Watts and Tobias; and the *Pas de Deux*, with its unimpassioned intensity, had as performed by Diana Adams and Arthur Mitchell in their cool, good-humored manner—overwhelming impact. The girl's part is perfectly suited to Adams's long-limbed body and her quiet temperament; and her performance was her most impressive achievement in my experience. *(150–151)*

Agon got the most attention because it was a new work and a setting of a new Stravinsky score. But equally important was the revival of *Apollo*, a setting of Stravinsky's *Apollon Musagète* which Balanchine produced for Diaghilev in 1928. *Agon* amazes one with what Balanchine's imagination continues to produce after so many years; *Apollo* amazes one with what it produced at the beginning—the visually exciting and touching dance and pantomime metaphors that express Apollo's growing consciousness of his powers and describe his involvement with the three muses: the leaps around them that express his wonder and delight; the leaps that frighten them in the coda; the turns with which, fascinated, he follows Terpsichore's playful little hops; the exquisite episode in which he and Terpsichore sink to their knees facing each other, he holds out his open hands, she rests her elbows on them and opens her hands, and he lays his cheek on them. Those large-spanned, soaring leaps of d'Amboise around the muses had exciting effect; and his performance gained in continuity of flow at each repetition. His was of course the crucial performance; but the muses also were danced effectively—Terpsichore by Tallchief or Adams, Polyhymnia by Wilde, Calliope by Hayden. *(136)*

In another new work, *Gounod Symphony*, the first and last movements of Gounod's Symphony No. 1 seemed to me too small in scale and consequence for Balanchine's manipulation of large groups; but the second movement lent itself to a *pas de deux* of elegance and charm, and the third movement to an engaging minuet. As for *Stars and Stripes*, it is another illustration of the fact that what the Balanchine eye happens to see—whether it is American musical-show dancing or Scotch dances or modern dance—turns up in his ballets; and what turns up in this new piece is American parades and marches—the striding about, the falling into formations, the costumes (skillfully adapted by Karinska), the Sousa music (crudely arranged by Hershy Kay). The piece is one of Balanchine's brilliant and enjoyable "applause machines" (the term is his), and was danced brilliantly by Hayden, Kent, Adams, d'Amboise, Barnett and the *corps.*

In an earlier "applause machine," *Western Symphony*, to an arrangement of American folk songs, one saw the formations and the ducking in and out of formations of the American square

dance; and this year Balanchine used them again in the enchanting ensembles that he fitted to the lovely music of Vivaldi and Corelli in *Square Dance.* Unfortunately, not content to use the dance style, Balanchine had the idea of putting the little group of string-players on a platform on the stage, and having a square-dance caller call out what the dancers did; "otherwise," he said, "it will be only another ballet, with Vivaldi music." And so the movements of great elegance were done to an accompaniment of appalling jingling words ("Now watch her feet go wickety-wack") blared out by loud-speakers and forced on ear and mind to a degree that made it impossible to hear the music and see the movements. What little I saw enables me to report that Patricia Wilde danced with exquisite delicacy and grace and that the ensembles were executed brilliantly by the *corps.*

Balanchine not only has created a great repertory; he also has created a great company to perform it. Under his guidance Tallchief, in the past ten years, has changed from the dancer whose physical strength appeared to direct itself downward at the floor in leg movements like thunderbolts, to the dancer whose strength goes into achieving the appearance of effortlessness in slow turns and quiet movements of breath-taking plastic beauty; Wilde's dancing, a high-powered operation a few years ago, has acquired delicacy, suppleness and elegance; the other soloists have blossomed less spectacularly; the girls of the *corps* have acquired technical brilliance and a distinctively and excitingly clear and sharp style; and this year's changes in the boys' group gave it too the brilliance it had lacked.

The company was, then, a pleasure to watch this year; and there was special pleasure in watching the progress of the younger soloists. Kent, for example, continued to compel fascinated attention with her exquisite modulation of bodily configuration, her clarity and exactness, her force of projection, with which she gave tremendous impact to the Third Theme in *The Four Temperaments*, and, on a less important but interesting occasion, quietly held her own in a performance of the Minkus *Pas de Trois* with higher-powered Tallchief and André Eglevsky. And Barnett, whose special style of acrobatic brilliance combined with delicacy makes *Candy Canes* one of the most exciting things in *The Nutcracker,* was able to exhibit his spectacular gifts at length in *Stars and Stripes.*

But for some older spectators there was an aching feeling of loss over the absence of LeClercq from the works in which they had watched the development of her extraordinary powers as a dancer and a stage personality.

1959   *Winter 1959* The New York ballet season was opened early in September by the New York City Ballet's four-week presentation of works from last year's repertory—except for one new *pas de deux*—with changes in personnel that brought interesting new performances in old roles, and consequent changes in the character and effectiveness of the ballets. In particular, in the temporary absence of Tallchief and Adams for the entire period, and of Hayden for a few days, some of their roles were taken over by Kent. In her first *Swan Lake* her dancing in the big adagio didn't flow with the clear and continuous definition it had in her next performance; and what remained for it to acquire through repetition was an amplitude in the filling out of time with movement that would give the performance an additional largeness and grandeur of style. On the other hand, literal physical largeness was what the movements of the *Pas de Deux* of *Agon,* created for long-limbed Adams, did not have when they were executed by Kent who is very small; and the effect was that of an impressively accomplished doing of the enormously difficult movements, as against the cool disposing of them by Adams. The largeness and grandeur of style I referred to were something Kent also needed to acquire in the series of *arabesques* in the second movement of *Symphony in C*; but the opening and closing sections of the movement call for precisely the lyrical flow that she made so lovely.

And most impressive was her Terpsichore in *Apollo,* with its every exquisite bodily configuration in pose and movement completely and enchantingly achieved. *(143, 137)*

Kent was not the only young dancer whom it was exciting to watch in new roles. The departure of Barnett resulted in the moving up of the outstandingly gifted Edward Villella into Barnett's roles in the third movements of *Symphony in C* and *Western Symphony* and the second "campaign" of *Stars and Stripes.* In these he didn't exhibit Barnett's personal spectacular style, but he did leap, spin and soar with his own technical precision and brilliance, fluent grace and superb elevation. In *The Four Temperaments,* on the other hand, the *Melancholic Variation,* with Bliss gone, was danced by Richard Rapp, who didn't, these first times, fill it out with the expansiveness and weight of Bliss's movements. *(123)*

I recall the security and stability of American Ballet Theater's early years, when it presented the classical repertory with Markova, operating in full exercise of her powers, as the prima ballerina who set style and tone for the company, and when it had Tudor watching over the works he contributed to the modern repertory; I also recall a measure of such security and stability in the later years when Alonso and Youskevitch were the company's first classical dancers. Since their departure it has had the outstanding classical *danseur noble* of today, young Erik Bruhn; but the moments of splendor he has contributed haven't effaced the general impression of confusion and deterioration: in September, for example, the second *Giselle* had, with Bruhn, Markova in a guest appearance in the title role; but the first *Giselle* had the dancer who, incredibly, ranks at present as the company's prima ballerina and dances the title role regularly—Nora Kaye. A *Nutcracker pas de deux* that I saw had Bruhn dancing with the highly accomplished, if somewhat flashy, Violette Verdy; but a *Black Swan pas de deux* had him dancing with Kaye. And the two performances of Balanchine's *Theme and Variations* I saw had not Bruhn but the less brilliant

Royes Fernandez, and not Verdy but Lupe Serrano, who danced with bold strength but no fluidity and grace—the result being that the piece which used to be dazzling was now drab.

Deterioration was evident in some other fine ballets of the company's repertory. In Loring's *Billy the Kid* Kriza exhibited lessened technical security and precision; and Robbins's *Fancy Free* now made its points with a sledge-hammer. In Dolin's *Pas de Quatre* too, the little strokes of delicate humor were now magnified and heavy; and Markova, who made one of her guest appearances in this piece, contributed to the overemphasis with the exaggerated primness of her Mme. Taglioni.

This was only part of the change in Markova's dancing since 1946, when, after her year in a Billy Rose show, it began to exhibit a reduction in physical scale and intensity. As this economizing in effort continued, her performances gradually were reduced to miniatures of what they had been; and in her prim little leaps in *Pas de Quatre* this time her feet barely left the floor. However there still were moments— when, for example, she came to rest in an arabesque—which took one's breath away with the deployment and configuration of her body in movement and pose. *(114)*

In *Giselle* too, this time, her dancing in the early scenes—e.g. the skips about the stage which were as short in trajectory and as close to the floor as they could be made—exhibited a saving of effort for the big movements later that could not be reduced—in particular those of the second act, which again were breathtaking in their unique beauty, produced by what Edwin Denby once described as her control of "the full continuity of a motion from the center to the extremities" and her "instinct for the melody of movement as it deploys and subsides in the silence of time." With Markova's dancing; with dancing by Bruhn that was sensational in its unstraining technical brilliance and its elegance; with Berman's distinguished setting and costumes—the black tulle over white and the green showing underneath, of the Wilis' costumes—this second act of *Giselle* was the one instance in which the company attained greatness.

As for the four new ballets I saw (of the six that were presented), two, *Concerto* and *Paean,* were by Herbert Ross, who several years ago gave the company a stunning piece, *Caprichos,* but since then has produced nothing of value or interest. *Concerto,* to Tchaikovsky's Violin Concerto, carried its boring imitation of Russian-peasant ballets to excruciating lengths; whereas *Paean,* to Chausson's Concerto for Violin, Piano and Strings, bored one with its straining, pointless ingenuity, as did Kenneth MacMillan's *Journey,* to Bartók's Music for Strings, Percussion and Celesta. Birgit Cullberg's *Miss Julie,* to music by Ture Rangstrom, is one of the narrative ballets whose movements have little interest beyond the story they tell; and in this instance the recital of some of the incidents of Strindberg's *Miss Julie* conveyed nothing of the real substance of this subtly intellectual play.

If Ballet Theater had wanted to get Robbins to revise *Fancy Free* it would presumably have found him, in September, at the Alvin Theater keeping his eye on his own production, *Ballets: U. S. A.* Two pieces on this program, *Afternoon of a Faun* and *The Concert,* had been done previously by the New York City Ballet; one, *N. Y. Export, Op. Jazz,* had been created for last summer's Festival of Two Worlds in Spoleto and was now receiving its first American performances (I was told that it was a reworking of material in *West Side Story,* which I had not seen); and *3X3* was a new curtain-raiser.

Afternoon of a Faun and *The Concert* are two of the pieces in which Robbins's impressive powers as a choreographer have served the perceptive mind and eye of a master of comedy. But at the same time that Robbins has produced his comedies he has created ballets embodying his serious thoughts about the world—*Facsimile* and *Age of Anxiety,* about lonely people; *The Guests,* about social snobbery; *The Cage,* about the lethal behaviour of insect-like females to males—of which the first two exhibited personal privacies that were embarrassing to look at, and the other two said their say in movements that achieved nothing beyond their uninteresting or unpleasant meaning. Now comes *N. Y. Export, Op. Jazz*, prefaced by the statement in the program that our teen-agers—feeling themselves "a minority group in this threatening and explosive world into which they have been born," and therefore feeling a strong emotional kinship with the minority groups, Negro and Latin-American, who have made the major and basic contribution to American popular dancing—"have so identified with the dynamics, kinetic impetus, the drives and 'coolness' of today's jazz steps that these dances have become an expression of our youth's outlook and their attitudes toward the contemporary world around them." But it is only in the final section of *N. Y. Export* that the teen-agers express their outlook and attitudes merely by dancing the dances that supposedly express their outlook and attitudes: in the earlier sections the expressing is done by "a formal, abstract ballet based on the kinds of movements, complexities of rhythms, expressions of relationships and qualities of atmospheres found in today's dances"—this being exemplified by the group of teen-agers with arms extended heavenwards in yearning, in the photograph on the program cover. For me a group of teen-agers with arms extended heavenward has no relation either to the realities of teen-agers' dancing or to any other realities in their lives; and though I found the mere dancing at the end exciting, I was left uninvolved by the earlier formal, abstract ballet based on this dancing.

As for *3 X 3*, it testified to Robbins's gift for the excessively arch.

Spring 1959 The New York City Ballet's winter season offered new ballets, a new principal dancer, and dancers in new roles. Two of the new ballets, William Christensen's *Octet* to the piece of that title by Stravinsky, and Birgit Cullberg's *Medea* to music of Bartók, I take to represent Balanchine's sheer desperation in his search for ballets by other choreographers; for the first was a slight classical piece in which one saw something like the

Balanchine movements put together without creative power; and the second, like Cullberg's *Miss Julie*, offered not a dance equivalent of the poetry of the original play of Euripides but a danced and mimed narration of the few incidents of a transformed and cheapened story of the play, which alternated between cliché and literally meaningful contrivance of the caliber of Medea's angry kicks at the prostrate Jason.

Balanchine's contributions were the new *Native Dancers*, to Rieti's Symphony No. 5, and the revival of the 1933 *Seven Deadly Sins*, to the text of Berthold Brecht (translated by W. H. Auden and Chester Kallman) and the music of Kurt Weill. *Native Dancers*, with its lighter-weight music, was a slighter piece of the kind of *Square Dance*: a dance toccata employing the virtuosity of Wilde and d'Amboise in a context supplied by a group of boys and girls, with new dance ingenuities from Balanchine's seemingly inexhaustible store, some of them involving horsey conceits related to the title (the boys were in jockey silks; the girls, in charming costumes by Peter Larkin, had their hair in ponytails; the setting by David Hayes was part of a racetrack). In *The Seven Deadly Sins* I find it necessary to distinguish the realization in production from what was produced: certain of the stage incidents, as contrived by Balanchine with the assistance of Rouben Ter-Arutunian's scenery, costumes and lighting, and as executed by Kent and her associates, worked effectively as theater; but what was staged so brilliantly began with the incongruity of an image of Berlin of the twenties projected onto Memphis, Los Angeles, Philadelphia and Boston; and to this initial incongruity were added the incongruities and perversities of the morality play about the dutiful daughter whose discharge of her moral obligation to her family was achieved by various immoralities which taught her the various moral lessons about pride, anger, lust and the rest. These were amusing at times in their cockeyed way; but for me the Brecht-Weill ideational world is one that yields no esthetic satisfactions.

The new dancer was Violette Verdy, who had appeared with the American Ballet Theater in September, and who operated in the New York

City Ballet style not only with exciting technical security and bravura but with the clarity and continuity of outline and the projected personal radiance and force that one sees in Kent's dancing, and that made Verdy literally stand out in the ensemble as Kent does. Interestingly, though Verdy's style was very strong and Kent's was exquisitely delicate I found that it was Kent who exercised the greater compulsion on my eye when the two appeared together in *Symphony in C* and *Divertimento*. And I found also that the two, with their radiated brightness of presence, made everyone else in those pieces seem drab.

In *The Four Temperaments* the *Melancholic Variation* had new and exciting effect from Moncion's powerful presence and the largeness and weight of his movements: clearly he was the predestined dancer for this episode. Villella, in Bolender's absence, danced in the first *Pas de Trois* of *Agon*, which Bolender makes amusing by looking as though the eccentric movements seem odd to him, but in which Villella's face was dead-serious as he exhibited the individual movements and their connections in the dance phrases with a clarity of definition they hadn't had in Bolender's performance, but also without a trace of their humorous effect in those performances. One wondered how Balanchine felt about this—whether he preferred the dance clear or amusing.

Villella's usual grin was in evidence in his triumphant performances in *Stars and Stripes*, *Western Symphony* and *Symphony in C*. And after his brilliance in these works it was astonishing to see him not achieve in *Candy Canes* in *The Nutcracker* the dazzling speed and brilliance of the regrettably departed Barnett.

Apollo suffered from an exaggerated and excessive muscularity in d'Amboise's performance; though much of what he did in this work —notably his soaring leaps around the muses— was excitingly effective. I might add that it seems to me logical that a ballet about a god and the muses should be danced in costume, and that the god, in particular, shouldn't be in the black tights that are the male dancer's uniform in the New York City Ballet, with a shirt that looks like two large handkerchiefs knotted together.

Summer 1959 A couple of years ago Danilova gave her impression of the Bolshoi Ballet, which she had seen in London: "Every member of the *corps de ballet* is a ballerina—the arms—everything! But the style of the dancing, the style of the productions, the scenery and costumes are from fifty years ago—like from a museum!" This was confirmed, in the *Giselle* that was the one work I saw performed by the Bolshoi at the Metropolitan, by the *corps* whose beautiful and precise execution of the dance of the Wilis elicited cheers from the audience; and on the other hand by the tastelessly lavish costumes of some of the noble ladies in the hunting party that Danilova may have had in mind as being "from fifty years ago—like from a museum."

Whatever may be said about continuing to use styles of the past in new works, it seems to me arguable that an old ballet like *Giselle* might legitimately be given a museum-style production which preserved its original form and style —as a nineteenth-century novel is published today, or a nineteenth-century painting is exhibited, in its original state. But in any case certain museum-like features of the Bolshoi *Giselle* were admirable. Thus, even before the curtain rose I found myself hearing for the first time an extensive musical prelude which was only one of a number of passages of music that I had never heard in other performances; and with some of these I saw dance episodes that I had never seen, including an extensive *pas de deux* of two villagers in the first act. On the other hand the detailed choreography of an old ballet is something that hasn't been preserved and can't be reproduced exactly; and the choreography of the Bolshoi *Giselle* as reconstructed by the Bolshoi's principal choreographer, Leonid Lavrovsky, differed constantly in dance detail from what we have seen in other performances—most vividly in the second-act lifts in which Albrecht raised Giselle in spectacular fashion to a position over his head. I recall seeing these lifts also in the film of Lavrovsky's *Romeo and Juliet*, and nowhere else; as far as I know, then, they are an invention of his—one which for me represents the present-day Russian style of the portentously gigantesque that was to be seen in much of *Romeo and Juliet*; and this contemporary detail was a false note in *Giselle*.

The lifts and the costumes were flaws; but they counted for little in the total beautiful and secure operation. At the heart of it—and always *of* it at the same time that she was a creature apart in force of presence and loveliness and eloquence of movement—was Galina Ulanova, whose performance placed her with the greats we have seen, including Markova in her first years with Ballet Theater. And as something achieved by a woman of forty-nine, and done with complete involvement of self, it shamed Markova who at a much earlier age began giving less and less of herself in smaller-and-smaller-scaled performances.

Fall 1959 Episodes, the New York City Ballet's final production in June, was in two parts. The first was Martha Graham's setting of two of the pieces of music by Webern that were used in the work—the early and traditional Passacaglia Op. 1, richly scored for a large orchestra, and the Six Pieces Op. 6, which exhibited the beginnings of the distinctive Webern style. The second was Balanchine's setting of the remaining pieces—the Symphony Op. 21, Five Pieces Op. 10, Concerto Op. 24 and Variations Op. 30 (in that order), which were in the fully developed Webern style of wisps of sound in fragments of phrases that made no coherent musical sense to my ears, and finally the marvelously contrived orchestration of the superb six-voiced Ricercare of Bach's *Musical Offering*. Miss Graham's part narrated a story of the life, loves and death of Mary Queen of Scots, with sumptuous costumes by Karinska, and on a stage which had handsome decorative forms by David Hays hung in the corners and a construction in the rear center

that was topped by what at first was a throne and later became a scaffold. Balanchine's part was an abstract ballet danced in practice costumes on a stage which retained Mr. Hays's decorative forms.

The modern-dance adherents, and specifically the admirers of Martha Graham, who were in the City Center at the performances of *Episodes*, have one thing in common with the members of the Bolshoi Ballet (who were reported to have been baffled and bored by Balanchine's *Serenade*, *Symphony in C* and *Agon*): they require that dance movement have story meaning. And they seem to require nothing more: it was enough, apparently, for them to see dancers in costumes which identified them as Mary Queen of Scots, Bothwell, Elizabeth Queen of England, make movements which denoted Bothwell's ambition to be King and his treating Mary "like a drab," or make the movements of a symbolic game of tennis between Mary and Elizabeth; it didn't matter to them, apparently, that the movements which embodied these meanings had nothing beyond that to excite the eye and the mind (as the dance metaphors in Balanchine's *Apollo* do): the mere literal spelling out of these meanings held the Grahamites spellbound; and at the end of this insignificant achievement their frenzied applause brought Miss Graham—smiling bravely through her look of agony—before the curtain again and again.

As against this poverty of dance imagination and invention behind the façade of costumes, stage decorations and props, Balanchine offered the profusion of what he contrived not only in ballet movement for his own dancers but in modern movement for the modern dancer Paul Taylor whom he used alone in his setting of the Variations Op. 30. In the settings of the Symphony Op. 21 and Concerto Op. 24 that preceded Op. 30 Balanchine carried further, with amazing inventiveness, the distortions and contortions of ballet movement he had presented in *Agon*, using more intensively, for example, the bending back of the foot that broke the usual line from thigh to toe. And between Op. 21 and Op. 24, the Five Pieces Op. 10—whose fragmentary substance I believe I once heard provoke an audience to laughter even by itself—was the musical basis for a *pas de deux* whose negating frustrations and grotesque distortions struck the City Center audience as funny now. The setting of Op. 30 continued all this distortion in its modern-style movement; then the concluding setting of the Bach Ricercare overwhelmed one with its return to ordered beauty in the music and in the ballet movement that was like a further and richer-textured development of Balanchine's *Concerto Barocco*—with groups of the *corps* providing a context of disciplined regularity for the solo couple that moved with the utmost freedom.

Bertram Ross exhibited impressive agility and control in the first part; and in the second part there were superb performances by Verdy and Watts in Op. 21, Adams and d'Amboise in Op. 10, Kent and Magallanes in Op. 24, Taylor in Op. 30, and Hayden and Moncion in the Bach Ricercare, with beautifully precise and sharp work by the *corps.* *(152–155)*

Postscript 1970 I later came to find both Webern's instrumentation of Bach's Ricercare and Balanchine's choreography for it excessively busy for the grave music.

1960   *Spring 1960* As I write, the New York City Ballet has presented two of the promised three additions to its repertory: *Night Shadow* [now *La Sonnambula*], which Balanchine created in 1946 for the Ballet Russe de Monte Carlo to a score fashioned by Rieti out of music by Bellini; and *Panamerica,* a new work that fills the entire evening with a number of pieces by Balanchine and other choreographers to scores by Latin-American composers. *Night Shadow* is concerned with a Poet who happens into an early-nineteenth-century party where he becomes involved first with a Coquette who presumably is the Host's mistress, then with a Somnambulist, who presumably is the Host's wife, and for this is killed by the Host. It is, then, a piece in which Balanchine's powers of choreographic invention serve his dramatic imagination and theater sense, producing the inanities of the guests' dancing, the banalities and grotesqueries of the *divertissements* for their entertainment, the impassioned *pas de deux* of the Poet and the Coquette, and then a supreme stroke of *fantaisie Balanchine*—the *pas de deux* of the Poet's encounter with the Somnambulist, in which, unable to make contact with her mind, he experiments with her moving body, spinning it, impelling it now in this direction now in that, grasping the candle in her hand and swinging her by it now this way now that. The Bellini music is chosen well for the varieties of movement, with some of his most beautiful melodies for the sleep-walking episode; and Esteban Francés provides a fine set and suitably violent-colored costumes for the guests. In 1946 Danilova, as the Somnambulist, took one's breath away with the intensity of her movement across the stage on points at her first entrance, and the powerful concentration of her quieter movement later in the episode; in the new performance Kent didn't have this power but took one's breath away with the loveliness of her limpidly flowing movement. Quiet power of presence and projection made Bruhn superbly effective as the Poet; the part of the Coquette calls for precisely the alluring femininity that Jillana radiated; and Villella's brief appearance in the Harlequin's dance was enough to amaze and delight one anew with his soaring and spinning, his sinuous grace even in slow turns. *(156)*

Panamerica—with effective scenery by David Hays and colorful costumes by Esteban Francés and Karinska—began with *Serenata Concertante,* a piece of music by Juan Orrega Salas (Chile) that rattled along pointlessly, with choreography by Gloria Contreras, whose straining invention contrived classical movements and formations different from Balanchine's that had nothing but their labored ingenuity. But later Contreras produced some engaging music-hall-style entertainment to the somewhat more attractive *Ocho por Radio* of Silvestre Revueltas (Mexico). Moncion's ingenuities, in his attempt at escape from the Balanchine idiom—to a piece of bad music, the *Choros No. 7* of Villa-Lobos—were at times a little more interesting. Taras, making no attempt to escape, used the Balanchine idiom effectively with *Variaciones Concertantes*, an agreeable piece by Alberto Ginastera (Argentina). And d'Amboise dodged around the difficulty by producing not a dance piece but a skillfully made Grand Guignol number to music whose quality I cannot recall, the *Sinfonia No. 2 of Hector Tosay (Uruguay)*. As for Balanchine, his ever freshly inventive imagination produced a superb *pas de deux* to *Preludios para Percusion* by Luis Escobar (Colombia), which provided no more than a minimum sound-track for the movements; an adagio in the wrestling style of the one for Adams and Mitchell in *Agon*, but this time for three dancers, which was the outstanding thing in the big work that Balanchine put together to some bad music by Carlos Chavez (Mexico), the *Sinfonia No. 5* for string orchestra; and an attractive big piece in popular style to the engaging *Danzas Sinfonicas* of Julian Orbon (Cuba). The performances that call for mention are those of Wilde and Bruhn, and later Wilde and Villella, in the Balanchine *pas de deux*; Adams, Moncion and Magallanes in the wrestling adagio of the second Balanchine piece; Verdy, Villella and Wilde in the Taras piece; Bruhn and Verdy in the d'Amboise piece.

Additional brilliance in the superb company was promised not only by the participation of Bruhn but by the return of Tallchief; and in the *Swan Lake* that opened the season Bruhn fulfilled expectation with his intensely expressive dramatic performance and with the leaps and turns accomplished with quiet elegance that make him the pre-eminent *danseur noble* of today. But Tallchief's very first movements brought a shock: the well-remembered Tallchief image—of lovely bodily deployment and configuration achieved seemingly without effort—was now gone (as on an occasion years ago the radiance that Tatiana Riabouchinska's dancing had spread over the stage was suddenly gone). One waited for it to reappear; but it did not in this *Swan Lake*, or in *Symphony in C* the following week, or in *The Nutcracker*; only in the special style of Eurydice's part in *Orpheus*, with its twists and angularities, did she operate impressively. Bruhn, in those clas-

sical ballets, continued as dazzlingly as he had begun; and in one performance of *Divertimento No. 15* it was exciting to see the difficult details of the Fifth Variation executed this time with a reserve of technical power that gave them unstraining assurance and elegance.

Among the dancers in new roles, Verdy contributed clearly and beautifully articulated and outlined movement to the Dewdrop part in *The Nutcracker*, the first movement of *Symphony in C*, the Hayden part in *Agon*, and was a brilliant Firebird; and Moncion, substituting for d'Amboise, operated in the Op. 10 of *Episodes* with an additional power that made one wonder why he hadn't been used in this piece from the beginning. In the revival of *Prodigal Son* Moncion was replaced by Villella, who in the opening scene—after sauntering onto the stage like a boy from Brooklyn—leaped and spun more effectively than Moncion, and was moving in the final scene of the return, but was less adequate than Moncion in his *pas de deux* with the Siren, and didn't even begin to achieve what Moncion used to achieve in the scene after the despoilment—the long line of movement, continuous in outline, flow and tension, from the moment that he began to sink to the ground to the moment when he dragged himself off the stage. And Conrad Ludlow, evidently intended for solo activity, exhibited extraordinary and touching warmth and sweetness as partner of Kent in *The Nutcracker* and of Tallchief in *Danzas Sinfonicas* of *Pan America*, but revealed in the *Nutcracker pas de deux* that army service had cost him much of his elevation in leaps. (*148, 132–133*)

Summer 1960 The theater sense that is served by Balanchine's powers of choreographic invention was to be seen most recently in *The Figure in the Carpet*, with which the New York City Ballet, in its spring engagement, completed its activity of the year. Sponsored by the Shah of Iran in honor of the Fourth International Congress of Iranian Art and Archeology, the work had two preliminary scenes, *The Sands of the Desert* and *The*

Weaving of the Carpet, which led to *The Building of the Palace,* the scene of a dazzling court spectacle in the form of a reception of foreign ambassadors by the Prince and Princess of Persia, with stunning scenery and costumes by Esteban Francés and richly varied invention by Balanchine to Handel's *Royal Fireworks* and *Water Music.* Handel's music has nothing to do with Iran, but it is superbly suited to Balanchine's invention for a court spectacle— ranging from the classical *pas de trois* of the Prince and Princesses of Lorraine, brilliantly executed by Villella with Susan Borree and Suki Schorer, through the noble intricate dance of the Spanish Duke and Duchess of Granada, elegantly executed by Judith Green and Moncion, the delicately amusing dance of the Chinese Duke and Duchess of L'an L'ing, delightfully executed by Patricia McBride and Magallanes, to the grandly involved *pas de deux* of the Prince and Princess of Persia, impressively executed by Hayden and d'Amboise. And in the introductory scenes the music has as little to do with desert sands and the weaving of a Persian carpet as some of the classical ballet movements that Balanchine devised for them—e.g. the enchanting solo of Verdy—but goes perfectly with those movements. *(157–158)*

The company's spring engagement opened with a new Balanchine *pas de deux,* to unfamiliar music by Tchaikovsky originally intended for *Swan Lake,* and with breathtakingly beautiful new details contrived for the exquisite style of Verdy. But the company cancelled its scheduled repetitions of *Theme and Variations,* the lovely classical ballet to Tchaikovsky's music of the same title that Balanchine made for Ballet Theater some years ago and introduced into the New York City Ballet's repertory at the end of this year's winter engagement, when it was danced with clarity and quiet brilliance by Verdy and Villella. *(164–169, 117–118)*

At the Metropolitan in April Ballet Theater presented two new works. One was Birgit Cullberg's *Lady from the Sea,* another of her narrative ballets which again offered not a dance equivalent of the total substance of the Ibsen play but a danced and mimed narration of its bare plot in movements that alternated between the obvious and the desperately contrived, with no interest or value beyond the story they told, and sometimes not even that. The other was *Dialogues: Serenade for Seven,* an abstract classical ballet by Herbert Ross, who gave the company one striking piece, *Caprichos,* years ago but has disappointed resultant expectations ever since, and did so again this time with his strained-for and pointless ingenuities.

Winter 1961 Reappearing here after three years, the Royal Ballet presented several new works. Two were evening-length ballets by the company's principal choreographer, Frederick Ashton—a new version of the old comedy classic, *La Fille mal Gardée,* and a new dramatic ballet, *Ondine*; two were shorter pieces by its younger choreographers: MacMillan's *Le Baiser de la Fée* and Cranko's *Antigone.*

Ashton's most distinguished achievements, for me, have been his comedies *Façade,* to the music of William Walton, and *A Wedding Bouquet,* to the music of Lord Berners and the words of Gertrude Stein. And in *La Fille mal Gardée* his comic gift gave us brilliant things like the clog dance of Mother Simone that might have been a number in *Façade,* the grotesque solo of the half-wit suitor Alain, the episode in which Colas made love to Lise while she danced a *pas de deux* with Alain—but these with a considerable amount of comedy which the audience found more amusing than I did. The work also offered resourcefully contrived classical solos and duets for Lise and Colas; but for me it was much too long and included material that I found boring. John Lanchberry adapted the original music of Hérold; Osbert Lancaster designed the scenery and costumes; and there were excellent performances by Nadia Nerina as Lise, David Blair as Colas, and Alexander Grant as Alain.

Ondine is one of the works of Ashton that have exhibited only the uninteresting ingenuities of the resourceful craftsman. For his adaptation of the story of the involvement of a water sprite with a mortal he devised movements that he was quoted as saying were intended to suggest "the ebb and flow of the sea" and to achieve "an unbroken continuity of dance, which would remove the distinction between aria and recitative," but that had no merit for me beyond the exquisiteness of their execution by Fonteyn. The work had an ugly contemporary score by Hans Werner Henze that was inappropriate to the character and atmosphere of the story; on the other hand it had appropriately spectacular scenery by Lila de Nobili; and it had fine performances by the other principals, Somes, Farron and Grant.

Inevitably, as I watched the detail of MacMillan's setting of Stravinsky's *Le Baiser de la Fée*, I recalled what Balanchine had produced at the same points, and noted that MacMillan achieved only a pleasantly inventive use of the ballet idiom where Balanchine had achieved wonderfully imaginative metaphors for the dramatic action. At the end of the village scene, for example, the MacMillan *pas de deux* of the Fairy and the Boy was one that could have occurred in any other ballet; whereas in the Balanchine version the *pas de deux* was the Fairy's violent taking possession of the Boy. So with what followed this episode: in the MacMillan version the Fairy conducted the Boy to his Bride in further supported *arabesques* and turns; whereas Balanchine at this point gave us one of his supreme examples of *fantaisie Balanchine*: the Fairy stood behind the limp body of the Boy, her right arm extended over his shoulder and pointing forward, and with her left hand gave him a push that impelled him a few steps; moving up behind him with her extended right arm still pointing forward, she gave him another push that impelled him another few steps; again she moved up behind him with her extended right arm pointing forward and gave him a push that impelled him off the stage; and as she followed him off with her extended right arm pointing forward the curtain fell. What remains to be added about the MacMillan piece is that the scenery of Kenneth Rowell was overpowering in design and color, and that the performances of Svetlana Beriosova as the Fairy, Donald

Macleary as the Boy, and Lynn Seymour as the Bride were excellent.

As for Cranko's *Antigone*, it told its story of violence largely in expressive movement derived from the modern dance that leaves me unaffected; it used a noisy score by Mikis Theodorakis and had an obtrusive setting by Rufino Tamayo; and it was performed well by Beriosova, Macleary, Blair, Gary Burne, Somes and Farron.

Spring 1961 After the soft style of the Royal Ballet it was exciting to see again the sharp clarity of the New York City Ballet; and after the disappointing new choreographies of the Royal Ballet's Ashton, MacMillan and Cranko, not only was it exciting to see the New York City Ballet's new works of Balanchine, but there was pleasure from the contributions of Bolender, Moncion and Taras to the work called *Jazz Concert*. This comprised settings of four pieces of music by European composers concerned with American ragtime and jazz: Stravinsky's *Ragtime* (not the 1919 *Piano-Rag Music* but the 1918 piece for a small instrumental group), which was set by Balanchine; Milhaud's *La Création du Monde* (1923), set by Bolender; Poulenc's *Les Biches* (1923), set by Moncion; and Stravinsky's *Ebony Concerto* for Woody Herman's Orchestra (1945), set by Taras. Milhaud incorporates facsimiles of what he heard into what might be called *Impressions of American Popular Music*; and Bolender used this as the serviceable sound-track for a work in which a brief prologue concerned with male and female from Adam and Eve down through the ages led to an account of the rise and fall of a girl named Peaches in the period that ended with the 1929 stock-market crash. This account, with its strokes of comedy and brilliant sequences of Broadway musical-show dancing of the period, testified to the talents of Bolender that would be profitably employed in a Broadway musical show; it also provided the occasion for the classically trained dancers of the company to reveal an engaging proficiency in musical-show dancing; and there were additional pleasures from Janet Reed's comic gift in the role of Peaches, Mitchell's sinuous strutting in the role of her Negro tempter, and Villella's leaps and spins in the role of her humble admirer.

Poulenc's score is pleasantly inconsequential; and Moncion operated with more engaging results in the lyrical Adagietto for Sara Leland and Andantino for Leland and Anthony Blum, than in his kidding of the social behavior and dances of the early twenties. Leland and Blum danced their pieces charmingly.

In sharp contrast with the bland Milhaud and Poulenc scores are the two in which Stravinsky subjects the ragtime and jazz idioms to manipulation by his powerful mind. With the more elaborate *Ebony Concerto* Taras used a Balanchinesque vocabulary skillfully and effectively—the effect being most striking in the opening Allegro, in which the movements of the group headed by McBride and Mitchell on the dark stage were seen in silhouette against a lighted backdrop. And for the sourly parodistic *Ragtime* Balanchine used only two dancers in his play with the style of Negro jazz dancing. The sharply outlined and articulated movements for Adams were (like the movements of the climactic *pas de deux* in *Agon*) something special in which she achieved the clarity of definition and the superlative in performance that she does not, for me, achieve in *Swan Lake, The Nutcracker* and *Apollo*. As such they were also further evidence of Balanchine's eye for a dancer's capabilities—the eye that led him to pick for Adams's partner a boy from the *corps*, Bill Carter, whose easy, large style complemented hers delightfully.

The series in *Jazz Concert* was continued in *Modern Jazz: Variants*, Balanchine's setting of a commissioned work by Gunther Schuller in which material in an atonal idiom of serious music was the context for material in the style of modern jazz. Schuller's atonal serious idiom was not a medium of expressive communication for me; and I was left cold by his modern-jazz-style writing for the orchestra and in the solos for the piano, bass, vibraharp and drums of the Modern Jazz Quartet. But for Balanchine the

work provided the sufficient sound-track for a series of superb pieces in which he combined movements of ballet and movements derived from Negro jazz dancing—intricate acrobatic and erotic duos for Adams and John Jones and for Hayden and Mitchell; a solo for Jones, with background movements of a group of girls, that worked up from a slow, sinuous beginning to larger, more animated movements and subsided into a slow, sinuous conclusion; a leisurely solo for Adams, with background movements of a line of boys, in which she did more of what she had done so effectively in *Ragtime*; a solo for Hayden whose faster acrobatic intricacies also were something special in which she achieved the superlative in performance that she does not, for me, achieve in *Swan Lake* and *The Nutcracker*.

Another new work of Balanchine, *Variations from Don Sebastian*, to some of Donizetti's simpler-minded music, was an elaborate and joyous virtuoso showpiece in which the solos and duos of the two principals, with their new intricacies and jokes, were interspersed among dances by the supporting group. The spectacular feats calling for enormous technique and strength were the kind of thing Hayden does brilliantly; but in a later performance Verdy gave them an additional transfiguring elegance and distinction; and in this performance Villella imparted his ease and fluidity to the leaps and spins that Watts had executed with evident effort. *(158)*

Unspectacular and quiet, on the other hand, were the movements Balanchine contrived to go with *Monumentum pro Gesualdo*, Stravinsky's beautifully wrought recomposition for orchestra of three of Gesualdo's madrigals. The piece called for nothing more than the clean execution it received from Adams, Ludlow and the supporting group.

And the remaining new work was Balanchine's setting of Brahms's *Liebeslieder Walzer* Opp. 52 and 65 for vocal quartet and piano four hands—music which one wouldn't expect Balanchine to be interested in, but which elicited from him one of his loveliest creations. The rising curtain revealed a candle-lit ballroom with four pairs of dancers in mid-nineteenth-century ball costume in the center and the musicians in similar costume at the left; and with the start of Op. 52 the dancers began a series of waltzes that enchanted one with their varied visual design and expressive character, and with such striking details as Magallanes hiding his face from Verdy with his hand at one point in their slow dance of dark estrangement. This series ended with the dancers leaving the stage through the French windows at the back and the curtain falling; and after an interval the curtain rose again to reveal—on a stage now lighted by a large chandelier—the girls in long ballet skirts and toe shoes for a series of waltzes made ethereal and brilliant by the extensions, the lifts, the spins of ballet. At the end of this series, when the last pair of dancers had left the stage, the musicians continued with the final slow waltz of Op. 65 as the ballroom resumed its original candle-lit appearance and the dancers—the girls in their original ball dresses—returned slowly to listen and, at the end of the piece, to applaud the musicians as the curtain fell. David Hays provided the handsome décor, Karinska the beautiful costumes; the music was performed well by the singers, Angelene Rasmussen, Mitzi Wilson, Frank Porretta and Herbert Beattie, and the pianists, Louise Sherman and Robert Irving. Adams (with Carter again), Hayden (with Watts), Jillana (with Ludlow) and Verdy (with Magallanes) all danced superbly; but Verdy's sharp clarity and accuracy, her way of completing the configuration of body with delicate flick of hand or toe, and the general elegance and distinction I mentioned earlier, made her performance stand out among the others; and a solo around Adams gave Carter another opportunity to exhibit a large easy grace. *(159–163)*

The season lost by the temporary absence of Kent; it gained by Verdy's appearances in new roles—her lovely Sugar Plum Fairy in *The Nutcracker*, her distinguished second movement of *Symphony in C*, and, just before the end of the season, her long-delayed Odette in *Swan Lake*, which overwhelmed one with the quietly vivid beauty and distinction of what was familiar

and what was newly devised by Balanchine for her personal style. *(144–145)*

Summer 1961 The new work of the New York City Ballet's brief spring season was Balanchine's *Electronics*, to a composition by Remy Gassmann utilizing the sounds produced by the Studio Trautonium, the electronic musical instrument invented by Oskar Sala. What was striking about these electronically produced sounds was their new timbres, varying from eerie to thunderous; and what Gassmann produced with them was, to my ear, not a work of any musical interest but a sound-track suitable for the science-fiction fantasy that David Hays's glittering crystalline scenery and the tight-fitting white costumes with glittering gold and silver hair created the appearance of. I put it this way because the movements of the choreography were not those of a new synthetic dance vocabulary devised, according to John Martin in *The Times*, as an analogy to the synthetic musical vocabulary, and capable of being taken as the movements of beings in a science-fiction world. Instead they were more of what one had seen in other recent works of Balanchine; and one could say that facing the same fact that had faced him in *Episodes*, he had dealt with it in the same way. That fact was the configuration of the human body, which, in *Episodes,* he could not destroy and reduce to the *disjecta membra* analogous to the fragmentation of Webern's music, but could only subject to grotesque distortions. And it was this grotesquerie that one saw again in Verdy's solo to Gassmann's electronic sounds; also one saw adagios like the one of Adams and Mitchell in *Agon*, in which this time Adams and d'Amboise (or Ludlow) went through even more complicated erotic entanglements whose difficulty became obtrusive; and on the other hand one saw Villella do leaps, turns and *entrechats* that he would have done in a ballet to music of Tchaikovsky. Though all these were of course contrived with Balanchine's authoritative expertness and ingenuity, they did not, for me, add up to one of the especially treasurable Balanchine achievements; and I would say the whole idea was one of his mistakes.

In addition Balanchine revived four episodes of *Ivesiana*, the 1954 work to pieces of music by Charles Ives. The first of these, *Central Park in the Dark*, beginning and ending slowly in a modern idiom that made no coherent musical sense to me, and breaking into ragtime for a few moments, provided the sound-track for the slow entrance and swaying movements of the *corps*, the powerful metaphors of an episode of sexual violence, executed by McBride and Moncion, and the slow withdrawal of the *corps*. *The Unanswered Question*—strings continuing with quiet chords, while at intervals a trumpet repeated the same phrase, and at other intervals flutes broke into agitated exclamations—performed a similar function for a striking episode in which Kent entered standing on the shoulders of four boys who caught her when she fell, passed her around their bodies and moved her in other ways out of the reach of Deni Lamont, who dragged himself after her. My impression is that in 1954 the boy on the ground never succeeded in touching her; but this time she was delivered once, rolled up in a ball, into his arms for a moment and withdrawn before being raised to the standing position in which she was carried out, with Lamont dragging himself after her. The ragtime of *In the Inn* was the basis for an episode, brilliantly danced by Adams and Mitchell, in which the style of Negro jazz dancing was subjected to distortions that seemed to me to have been made even more amusingly eccentric and grotesque, and more erotic, than in 1954. And with *In the Night*, reminiscent of *Central Park in the Dark*, the dancers entered from both sides slowly on their knees, and continued to move across the stage in this strange way until the curtain fell.

Villella was given the Moncion part in Robbins's *Afternoon of a Faun*, with McBride in the part danced originally by LeClercq and later by Kent; and with them the piece now became one about two sweet young innocents, which didn't say what it had said when one had seen two evidently knowing youngsters begin a movement of emotional involvement that ended each time in their turning to see how they looked in the mirror. I was left wishing I could see the piece with Moncion and Kent again; and I had a similar wish about Balanchine's *Prodigal Son*: Villella's appearance of a young innocent and his agility are assets in the earlier scenes of this work; but he doesn't have in the later scenes the power of presence and projection, and in the scene after the despoilment in particular the feeling for continuity of tension and flow of movement, that Moncion brought to them.

As for Ballet Theater, the rising of the curtain for Balanchine's *Theme and Variations* brought the first shock of the garish new costumes; then came the successive shocks of the performance, as the technical and stylistic inadequacy of Toni Lander revealed itself in an operation which was made grotesque and ludicrous by the airs and gestures that pretended to the grandness and grace and charm she lacked; as Royes Fernandez executed his virtuoso solos without virtuoso brilliance; and as the *corps* went through its formations without the exactness and clarity they called for. One writhed at the thought of how this travesty of Balanchine's lovely and distinguished work must have impressed the Russians and West Europeans who saw it last summer. On the other hand Dania Krupska's new *Points on Jazz*, to engaging music by Dave Brubeck, offered an excellent performance by Scott Douglas, Elizabeth Carroll, Sally Wilson and the *corps*; but it was wasted on the arty banalities spiced with sensational acrobatics that had Igor Moiseyev sitting up and forward in his seat with alert interest. Mr. Moiseyev was content to sit back in his seat during *Grand Pas*, Frederic Franklin's restaging of the last scene of the 1946 Balanchine reconstruction of *Raymonda* (which Balanchine made into his *Pas de Dix*), though this piece brought the only excitingly great moments I can report—those in which Bruhn performed his feats of virtuosity with brilliance and elegance. Tallchief's assured competence was the more impressive for what one had just seen Lander do; but her movements didn't have the lovely fluidity they used to have.

Winter 1962 The Leningrad Kirov Ballet that appeared here last fall is the present embodiment of the company of the Maryinsky Theater of Tsarist St. Petersburg—the company which Petipa trained, for which he and Ivanov created *Swan Lake* and *The Sleeping Beauty* in the 1890's, and which has continued to perform these two ballets ever since. Moreover, it was the Maryinsky's school that produced Nijinsky, Pavlova, Karsavina, Fokine, and later Danilova, Doubrovska and Balanchine, who danced in the Maryinsky Theater before they joined Diaghilev's company in Western Europe and came to this country. It is, then, not only the present Kirov company that derives from the old Maryinsky, but, through Balanchine and Doubrovska, the New York City Ballet, and in some degree, through Karsavina and the dancers who settled in London and Paris to teach, London's Royal Ballet and other Western European companies.

But continuity doesn't preclude change; derivation from the same source doesn't preclude dissimilarity. There are, for one thing, the gradual but inevitable changes that occur in a company's dancing and its ballets in the course of time, which may be small. Thus Danilova after seeing the Kirov company could say that after forty years it was still the old Maryinsky—not, I am sure, because there were no changes in what it did, but because they were slight (except for the male dancer lifting the ballerina over his head, which appears to be standard practice in Soviet Russian ballet, and which I doubt that Danilova saw at the Maryinsky Theater forty years ago). On the other hand there are the changes produced by personal intervention, which may be large: the Kirov still executes much the same movements, and does so with the same quiet elegance, as Danilova remembers; but the New York City Ballet executes movements, and does so with an energy and sharp clarity, whose striking dissimilarity from the Kirov vocabulary and style of execution represents the impress on the traditional ballet movement and execution of the mind and imagination of Balanchine.

Concerning the Kirov *Swan Lake* that I saw first there is, then, this to say: it offered the Petipa-Ivanov choreography revised by Konstantin Sergeyev (to include a new character, a Jester, and to provide a new happy ending), which looked as though it was close to the original and which was very different from the Balanchine choreography of the second act performed by the New York City Ballet; it offered the movements of the old choreography executed in a style very different from that of the execution of the Balanchine movements; and I must add that it offered the old movements executed with a precision that the less adequately rehearsed New York City *corps* doesn't exhibit. But as against the excitingly beautiful and imaginative Balanchine movements, those of the Kirov version, even performed with elegance and precision, were insipid and boring. And in the principal part Kaleria Fedicheva didn't exhibit the exquisite fluidity, elegance and distinction of the New York City's best dancers, Verdy and Kent. Altogether the Kirov *Swan Lake* I saw was mediocre and uninteresting.

Not so, however, *The Sleeping Beauty*. Here there was no recollection of Balanchine's work to keep one from enjoying the Petipa choreography revised by Konstantin Sergeyev—only one's recollection of the Nicolai Sergeyev reconstruction offered by the Royal Ballet, which was similar in style and executed with a similar mild elegance. Nor did the recollection of Fonteyn's unique performance as Aurora lessen one's pleasure from the loveliness of Alla Sizova's operation. Yuri Soloviev was a more brilliant Prince than Somes; Inna Zubkovskaya a radiant Lilac Fairy; Sergei Vikulov and Natalia Makarova an excellent Blue Bird and Princess Florine. And the scenery, though not as beautifully imagined as Oliver Messel's for the Royal Ballet, was impressive. The Kirov *Sleeping Beauty*, then, was a memorable experience.

So was the *Giselle*, which offered technically

accomplished dancing and expressive acting by Irina Kolpakova in a superb performance of the title role, better dancing than acting by Vladilen Semenov as Albrecht, a brilliant first-act peasant *pas de deux* by Ninel Kurgapkina and Soloviev, and beautiful work by Inna Korneyeva and the *corps* as Myrtha and her group of Wilis in the second act.

A mixed program included two charming Petipa pieces—a short one, *Bayaderka*, performed well by Fedicheva and Vikulov, and a *pas de deux*, *The Corsair*, performed with enchanting style and dazzling virtuosity by Sizova and Soloviev. And it ended well with a Cossack number, *Taras Bulba*, put together by Boris Fenster. But the other pieces of present-day Russian choreographic invention—Vassily Vainonen's to music from Tchaikovsky's *Nutcracker*, and worst of all, Leonid Yakobson's *The Hunter and the Bird* and *The Gossips*—made it clear that one should see the Russians only in the old classics.

Ballet Theater's new works included William Dollar's *Divertimento-Rossini*, a pleasant Balanchine-style classical piece to Rossini music arranged by Britten; Birgit Cullberg's *Moon Reindeer*, which, to a noisy score of Knudaage Riisager, told its long story in movement that exhibited enormous effort and ingenuity in the achievement of the unattractive; and a work of more consequence, Harold Lander's *Etudes*. This used a score which Riisager made out of the Czerny Etudes that exercise the hand in various types of piano technique; and it offered a series of sequences which exercised the dancers in the movements of classical ballet—sequences which led from the simplest warming-up movements at the bar in a gradual crescendo of intricacy, speed and brilliance to a dazzling conclusion. It was a masterful use of the medium and was superbly executed by the soloists—notably Lander and Fernandez—and the *corps*.

Mastery is evident in Robbins's operation, but with other things that make the operation unenjoyable for me. W. J. Turner once observed that he didn't like the Brahms of the symphonic works who sets out to be a great creator, and preferred the Brahms of the sequences of variations who is a mere musician. Similarly I don't like the Robbins who is a Serious Thinker About the Condition of Man and the World and produces the portentous tosh of *Events*, a new piece he presented his company in last fall. Nor do I like the Robbins who must break new paths and produces *Moves*, a "ballet in silence about relationships"—not that it doesn't include occasional striking details but that they would be even more effective with music, and that some of the movements make me squirm with their implied "relationships," as I squirmed at the exhibition of personal privacies in *Facsimile* and *Age of Anxiety* years ago. What I don't like, that is, is some of the things that come through in Robbins's work, including the sticky sentimentality and excessive cuteness. His company is an engaging one which does efficiently all the things it shouldn't have to do; but Veronika Mlakar and Jay Norman or John Jones don't perform *Afternoon of a Faun* adequately for someone who has seen it done by LeClercq or Kent and Moncion.

Spring 1962 The first week of the New York City Ballet's season brought a new work of Balanchine, *Valses et Variations* [now *Raymonda Variations*]—another of the display pieces in which his exploitation of virtuosity has achieved delightful art. It was a companion piece to *Pas de Dix*, using music from an earlier act of the ballet *Raymonda* as against *Pas de Dix's* music from the last act, and using music and dancers in a Balanchine version of the kind of piece that might have used them in the Petipa period—a version, that is, employing Balanchine's ever new developments and elaborations of the movements he learned at the Maryinsky's school, and the syntax he has developed for their combinations in sequences and textures. Thus the piece could have served as a demonstration to the Leningrad Kirov company of what Balanchine had done with the Maryinsky style; and the movements devised for the particular capacities of the dancers demonstrated what *they* could do with it: in addition to the numbers which exhibited the virtuosity of Wilde and d'Amboise, there were solos for five of the girls—Suki Schorer, Victoria Simon, Gloria Govrin, Carol Sumner and Patricia Neary—which showed what accomplished dancers they were.

With this new work the company presented part of its repertory, with important changes of cast resulting from the absence of Adams and Hayden. *Agon*, for example, had Kent in the part in which Adams achieves one of her most impressive performances, and which it was fascinating to see transformed by the exquisite fluidity Kent brought to it—the fluidity that also was enchanting in *Scotch Symphony* and *Serenade*. Govrin operated effectively in Adams's part in *Liebeslieder Walzer*, but was painfully unequal to the taxing demands of the Siren in *Prodigal Son*. And McBride, though technically impeccable, lacked power of presence and projection in the Hayden part in *Liebeslieder Walzer*, the part of the Sleepwalker in *La Sonnambula*, in which she substituted for Kent, and in *Serenade*. In addition one performance of *Afternoon of a Faun* had Moncion again giving the piece the effectiveness he used to give it with his powerful presence. And a performance of *Apollo* had a realization of the title role by Ludlow—in movement whose beautiful plasticity became impressively grand in style—that was the finest since Eglevsky's in 1945, and that not only was free of the angularity and stiffness of d'Amboise's performance but included a few details that d'Amboise omits. *(136–137)*

The last weeks of the season brought the other of Balanchine's new works an evening-length ballet version of *A Midsummer Night's Dream*, wonderfully imagined by Balanchine and brilliantly realized in his choreography, the scenery and lighting of David Hays, and the costumes of Karinska. The succession of scenes in the first act dealt with several of the dramatic themes of the play—the quarrel of Oberon and Titania, the confusion of the lovers, Titania's infatuation with Bottom—for which Balanchine used not only parts of Mendelssohn's music for the play but other Mendelssohn pieces which, it turned out, worked

perfectly with the dance movements that were for the most part superbly contrived for each dramatic purpose. I say for the most part because in one instance what was exciting to look at seemed to me dramatically wrong: Villella's Oberon was impressively regal, but the dance to the music of the Scherzo, in effect, had Oberon executing the brilliant leaps and turns of Villella instead of Villella performing the movements of a king (as Hayden, in her dances as Titania, performed the movements of a queen). But with this one exception what Balanchine contrived was not only fascinating to the eye but dramatically right. And this act concerned with the play's dramatic themes was followed by a second act devoted to the festivities on the occasion of the triple wedding of Hippolyta and Theseus and the two pairs of lovers at Theseus' court—principally a little ballet for two soloists and a small supporting group. The occasion seemed to me to call for something more imposing than the little ingenuities Balanchine devised for the inconsequential fast movements of the early Mendelssohn symphony he used for the ballet; and he achieved it in his beautiful invention for the more impressive middle movement. The ballet was followed by a stately dance by the three couples and the Courtiers—after which there was a return to Titania and Oberon in the forest, with Puck, as in the play, having the last word. This last word was Mitchell's, whose Puck was one of numerous excellent performances—Hayden's as Titania, Villella's as Oberon, Verdy's and Ludlow's in the second-act ballet, Jillana's, McBride's, Magallanes's and Bill Carter's as the lovers, Roland Vazquez's as Bottom, Schorer's as the principal Butterfly. *(170)*

Winter 1963 My previous experiences of the 1963 Bolshoi Ballet included the filmed *Giselle* and *Romeo and Juliet* and a *Giselle* at the Metropolitan Opera House in 1959. The *Giselles* revealed the strength of the company—its performances of the classics in which one saw the secure and beautiful operation of a large group of dancers who were not only highly accomplished but adequately rehearsed; the *Romeo*, with its story-telling in Soviet gigantesque style, revealed the company's weakness—its lack of new ballets of the quality of the old. And the same strength and weakness were evident in the program of three small pieces that I saw last September (by accident I missed seeing the big classics and the big new work, *Sparta-cus*). On the one hand the fourth act of Petipa's *Bayaderka* was made enjoyable for a spectator of today by the performance of the company's first dancers, Maya Plisetskaya and Nicolai Fadeyechev, three accomplished lesser female soloists, and the precise *corps*. On the other hand the more recent fourth act of Nina Anisi-mova's *Gayane* offered only a succession of brilliant numbers in Caucasian style. And Asaf Messerer's new piece, *Ballet School*—which like Harold Lander's *Etudes* offered a series of sequences exercising the dancers in movements ranging from children's practice at the bar to spectacular feats of star soloists—merely pre-sented one dancer or group of dancers after another performing one sequence of move-ments after another. The dancers included the most brilliant members of the company, whose movements were exciting to see; but the se-quences were not, as they had been in *Etudes*, made into an integrated progression with the varying textures and the developing structure that produced the cumulative effect of a ballet.

Summer 1963 I said in a recent chronicle that Stravinsky's *Le Baiser de la Fée* is not what Winthrop Sargeant hears—a Stravinsky orches-tration of music that is an imitation of the style of Tchaikovsky; that it is instead, from first to last, an operation of the Stravinsky mind, which not only elaborates and transforms the Tchaikovsky fragments it uses, but fits these transformed elements into contexts of writing of its own imagining. I speak of this now be-cause Balanchine's *Bugaku*, the first of the New York City Ballet's new works last spring, is a similar operation of the Balanchine mind, which—out of what it has seen in Japanese paintings and in the performances of the Gagaku

company—has created its own Japanese-style movements of female and male dancers that flow into and out of Balanchine-style ballet movements. Like any other procedure, this one justifies itself or not by the way it works in the object presented to eye or ear; and in *Bugaku* it works as impressively as in *Le Baiser de la Fée*. Indeed the impressiveness is, in the end, that of an extraordinary *tour de force*: except for a single moment of animation that interrupts the climactic adagio of the boy and girl, the music of Toshiro Mayuzumi whines, drones and blares its way in slow tempo for a half-hour; and it is an extraordinary *tour de force* to have cre-ated movements—the slow assuming of exquis-ite Japanese-style configurations by the girl and her companions, the vigorous Japanese-style movements of the boy and his com-panions, the adagio of the five couples, leading to the adagio of the boy and girl alone—which, as they succeed each other in that half-hour of slow tempo, hold the eye without a break in their fascination and tension.

In this they are helped by the way they are executed. As always, Balanchine's imagination has operated in terms related to the particular capacities and styles of his dancers. With Kent it is the capacity for exquisite delicacy in bodily configuration and movement—to say nothing of the mere physical strength behind this, which in *Bugaku* makes possible the secure slow-motion execution of the delicate configura-tions and movements with unbroken continuity. With Villella it is the virtuoso powers exercised with an elegance and grace that are personal as well as physical, and with a force of mere presence that becomes tremendous in the cli-mactic adagio—another in the style of those of *Agon* and *Episodes*, in which the boy doesn't merely support the freely moving girl in her spins and *arabesques*, but instead closely holds and controls and manipulates her body in extra-ordinary configurations and involvements with his own. (Mimi Paul, in one of the perform-ances, achieved a sufficient approximation of Kent's delicacy; but the Mitchell personality and style didn't work well in the boy's part: one image that remains in my memory is that of Mitchell stepping with a fussiness that was almost dainty, as against the simplicity and strength of Villella's movements.) *(171–175)*

The title of Balanchine's other new work, *Movements*, is that of the recent Stravinsky piece to which it is danced. The music of the six brief sections presents what my ears hear as successions of fragments of sound—tonally unrelated, and without coherent expressive meaning—like those of the Webern music Balanchine used in *Episodes*; and his settings of them are new and powerful elaborations of the distorted, angular and jerky style he used with that music. Six girls provide contexts for the entanglements in which d'Amboise manipulates the body of Suzanne Farrell, a girl taken from the *corps* this season, who in a succession of solo parts—in *Concerto Barocco, Liebeslieder Walzer*, John Taras's *Arcade*, and finally *Movements*—exhibited increasingly impressive style and technical power. *(126, 130, 161–2, 175)*

Taras's *Arcade*, to Stravinsky's Concerto for Piano and Wind Instruments, is a skillful use of the Balanchine idiom which gives Farrell and Mitchell material for brilliant performances.

As important as Balanchine's new contributions to the repertory was the restoration of two of his greatest works of the past, *Concerto Barocco* and *The Four Temperaments*. "Before," he said a few weeks before the season, "I could not give *Concerto Barocco* because I never could be sure of having the eight girls: always two would be missing and I had no replacements. Now we have *three* groups of eight girls! We have the best company in the world!" And in the two performances of *Concerto Barocco* I saw, the dancing of the eight girls behind Hayden and Farrell glowed with a brilliance that no earlier group had exhibited—the new brilliance of the company this year that justified Balanchine's high opinion of it. *The Four Temperaments* also was done superbly, except for the *Phlegmatic Variation* in which Mitchell's performance was not an adequate replacement for Bolender's. *(126–130, 124–5)*

And there were new dancers in old parts. Verdy was the first Eurydice, in *Orpheus*, to exhibit the joy she could be expected to feel at her liberation. Jillana achieved a convincing grand style in *Swan Lake*; McBride, on the other hand, worked too hard at it. Jillana's Siren in *Prodigal Son* was less successful—one damaging detail being the snarl on her face during the *pas de deux* of seduction, which would have been bad even if it hadn't resembled the snarl that was one of the high points of the burlesque seduction in Bolender's *Souvenirs*. Mimi Paul—taken from the *corps* last year for an astonishing solo performance in the second movement of *Symphony in C*—repeated it with even more authority in its exquisite and grand style. And Lamont contributed an extraordinarily imagined and brilliantly executed Harlequin to a performance of *La Sonnambula*. *(120)*

Despite the general brilliance of the operation, then, there were performances with leading parts danced ineffectively. D'Amboise has the virtuosity that enables him to dispose of a display piece like the Tchaikovsky *Pas de Deux* with an ease that makes the performance a pleasure to see; but his attempt at god-like grandeur in *Apollo* produces only a pompousness damaging to the piece. On the other hand, Ludlow's inadequacy for the technical feats of *Pas de Deux* is as painful to witness as it must be for him to exhibit; but his few performances in *Apollo* a couple of seasons ago were the most beautiful and satisfying since Eglevsky's in 1945. Matching of right dancer to right part would assign d'Amboise to *Pas de Deux* and Ludlow to *Apollo*; but what one saw was *Pas de Deux* with Ludlow and *Apollo* with D'Amboise. And though Ludlow was replaced by Villella in a few later performances of *Pas de Deux*, he didn't replace d'Amboise in any of the later performances of *Apollo*.

Fall 1963 After curtain calls for Lynn Seymour and the other soloists of the Royal Ballet who had danced engagingly in a *divertissement* from Bournonville's *Napoli*, the curtain rose again for a *pas de deux* from his *Flower Festival at Genzano*. For a few moments the stage was empty; then a couple appeared at the back: Rudolf Nureyev escorting Merle Park to the center of the stage, where he released her and bowed deeply with a curving overhead sweep of the arm. It was something I had seen done many times—something that every dancer does well enough, a mere preliminary that may receive only half one's attention even when done by a good dancer; and it was almost over when I was suddenly aware that the mere flow of changing bodily configuration was extraordinary, and that with the aura of presence and style it was one of the most extraordinary things I had ever seen. And it sufficed to reveal what sets Nureyev apart from the other great male dancers known to most of us. Whether Karsavina did or did not say he was even greater than Nijinsky, anyone can see that Nureyev, on the stage, exercises—through his movements, through his mere presence when he is motionless—the kind of extraordinary compulsion we have been told Nijinsky exercised. It operates in even the quietest, the least of his movements; and it operated in those with which, in the opening adagio of the *pas de deux*, he created a heightening context for what Park did (very much as Franz Rupp's excitingly alive piano-playing creates a heightening context for the singing he is accompanying). In these movements he held one's fascinated attention legitimately, with the extraordinary way he did what the piece required him to do—not illegitimately, with anything done specifically to get attention. And the same was true of the breathtaking execution of the feats of virtuosity in his solo and in the coda.

So, a night later, with *Giselle*. For the *New Yorker's* Winthrop Sargeant, Nureyev came to life in this ballet only in his seemingly effortless execution of Albrecht's spectacular solo near the end: until then he had given the impression of being "merely a slim, decorative, graceful, and somewhat sulky young man." The solo was indeed an impressive achievement; and so, in its different way, was Sargeant's not seeing what there had been to see up to that point: Nureyev's dramatic performance, which from Albrecht's first impetuous rush onto the stage held the eye with the power of presence and expressivity that was sustained through every detail; the extraordinary things he made of Albrecht's movements in the dances with Giselle and the Villagers in the first act; and above all what he made of the

adagio with Giselle in the second act, with movements extraordinary not only in themselves but in the way they worked with Fonteyn's to heighten their beauty and effect.

Winter 1964 For its brief fall season the New York City Ballet announced no new works, but only revivals of Balanchine's *Square Dance* and *Bourrée Fantasque*. One hoped that this time Balanchine would present the charming and brilliant ensembles of *Square Dance* with the engaging music of Vivaldi and Corelli and without the square-dance-caller's calling of what the dancers did. But he is stubborn about his mistakes; and so this time again the movements of great elegance were accompanied by the appalling jingling words ("Now watch her feet go wickety-wack") that—blared out by the loud-speakers—so obtruded themselves on ears and mind as to make it almost impossible to hear the music and see the movements. The piece had Wilde again in the principal role that demands all her extraordinary strength and endurance for the sequences of movements in which she is made to look her best.

The performance of *Bourrée Fantasque* I saw had Hayden again in the romantic middle movement; but the brilliant opening movement—with its amusing details for the solo couple and fascinatingly complex sequences for the *corps*—provided young Mimi Paul with a new role which she carried off very well; and Mitchell also did well in a role suited to his style. As for the boisterous finale, McBride made her exciting lifts a little too violent with the concluding kicks that I don't remember being done originally.

Paul also danced the Verdy role in *Episodes*, and surprised one with not only the clarity and force but the dramatic point and wit of her execution of the eccentric movements. And her strong and vividly expressive Calliope in the final *Apollo* deserved the attention that none of the muses got from d'Amboise, whose idea of a god-like attitude in that situation was to sit staring up at the Second Balcony like a grim wooden Indian. In addition, Suzanne Farrell, perhaps the most impressive of the young soloists recently emerged from the *corps*, took over the first role in *Concerto Barocco*, bringing to it her secure fluidity, with especially beautiful results in the unending invention that holds one spellbound in the great middle movement. Patricia Neary did well in the second solo role of *Concerto Barocco* and in the Adams role in *Episodes*; and her long legs made her an effective Polyhymnia in *Apollo*. *(128–9)*

An event of major importance was Villella's performances as the Prince in *Swan Lake*, since they were the first by a regular member of the company that brought to this role the illusion-creating physical appearance, presence, dramatic expressiveness and elegance it has called for in vain all these years. I saw his performance not with Verdy's Odette, but with McBride's, which was more relaxed than in her first try last year, and quite lovely in its flow of movement, but slight and lacking in force, like all her dancing. *(144–145)*

Completely unexpected, therefore, was the power of McBride's dancing in the role of the girl who turns on her lover and destroys him, in Taras's new ballet, *Fantasy*, to Schubert's Fantasy Op. 103 for piano four-hands. This was another skillful Taras use of the Balanchine idiom, with a dramatic idea that worked well with the melancholy opening and closing sections of the Schubert piece, but not with the cheerful animated middle section. The other new ballet, d'Amboise's *The Chase*, was so insignificant as to call for no comment except sympathy with Kent for the waste of her talent, and with those members of the audience who had paid their money for the originally scheduled *Apollo* and were given *The Chase* instead.

Spring 1964 With both Kent and Verdy absent the first two weeks of the New York City Ballet's winter season, the rising younger dancers made impressive appearances in additional first-line roles. The opening *Divertimento No. 15*, for example, had—with only Wilde of earlier casts—Mimi Paul, Schorer, Sumner and Simon, all operating beautifully, but Paul standing out among them in the impassioned elegance of her style—notably in the *arabesques* and lifts of the Adagio in which she was supported by Bruhn. And outstanding too was the unstraining elegance of Bruhn's variation. A night later Paul's performance in the second movement of *Symphony in C* was made even more effective than it had been by an additional fluidity of the arms that now initiated, now completed the lovely movements of the rest of her body. And in the first movement McBride exhibited, in addition to her accuracy and clarity, a new exquisite fluidity of arms enlivened by a new energy. *(149)*

Then there was Farrell's performance in the first of Balanchine's new works, *Meditation*, to a Tchaikovsky piece for violin and orchestra. This was a *pas de deux* astonishingly different from all of Balanchine's other separate *pas de deux* in that it had an expressive content—the boy's intense grief, from which the girl drew him with her love—and that it conveyed this content not only through the beautiful dance metaphors of Balanchine's usual practice, but also directly and explicitly through expressive movements, facial expressions and desperate embraces such as I don't recall his using before. Farrell exhibited again the secure fluidity that had made her movements excitingly beautiful in an impersonal work like *Concerto Barocco*, and with this an unexpected and deeply moving projection of the personal emotion of the new piece. And another surprise was to see d'Amboise completely convincing and moving in a serious role. In large part this was caused by an important change in his physical appearance: instead of the hair neatly parted on the side that gave us in *Swan Lake* or *Apollo* the face of a clean-cut lad from Dedham, Mass., there was now a wig that changed the face astonishingly to that of a boy—any boy anywhere—sunk in grief. He should use it in those other roles.

I thought I had an explanation of the enriching changes in Paul's dancing when Verdy returned and I saw her in *The Nutcracker*, *Episodes* and *Swan Lake*: clearly Paul had been looking at Verdy too—at her special elegance of style, and in this the particular elegant fluidity of her arms. There was an overwhelming demonstration of this at the very beginning of *Swan Lake*, just before Odette comes face to face with Prince Siegfried (danced beautifully on this occasion by Villella): the flow of her arms above her head and around her body was the most beautiful I had ever seen. I thought I saw additional new details throughout the work —some with new dramatic point, some with new dance effect; and every dazzling movement had her extraordinary exactness and perfection of execution.

Balanchine's other new *pas de deux, Tarantella,* to music of Gottschalk, was a delightful *perpetuum mobile* of blended Italian-style and ballet movements for an engagingly brilliant Villella and vivacious McBride. But a far more important new achievement of Villella was his first performance in *Apollo.* It has been difficult to understand Balanchine's not being bothered by d'Amboise's stiffness and pompousness in this work; his not preferring the beautifully sensitive performance of Ludlow two years ago; and—when he was not satisfied with Ludlow— his not having Villella perform in it. The delay gave Villella time for a lot of thinking about the role, which showed itself in details like the new-born Apollo's unsteadiness on his feet, his attentive watching of the muses in their solos; but more important was the characteristic relaxed grace of his operation and the beauty this gave to his movements. One of the impressive moments of d'Amboise's performance is his grandly soaring leaps around the lined-up muses in the *pas d'action,* which I had thought no one could equal; and I was unprepared, therefore, to see Villella not only do the leaps themselves with similar impressiveness but come down after each in a configuration of his body that was more beautiful than d'Amboise's. Of the dancers who appeared with Villella in the work for the first time, Schorer offered a performance of Calliope's solo that was completely achieved in its clarity and continuity; but Sumner hadn't yet mastered the movements of Polyhymnia's solo, and McBride didn't get beyond the mere conscientious execution of the movements of Terpsichore's. And I should mention here that in the performances of *Apollo* with d'Amboise Paul's Calliope was another of

her distinguished achievements, but Hayden didn't present an image one could accept as *Terpsichore's. (176, 137–138)*

Fall 1964 A report on the New York City Ballet's spring season must begin with the New York State Theater, in which the company gave its performances and probably will continue to give them beyond the two years of its present commitment. Whereas the newspaper reviews had reported the defective sound in Philharmonic Hall after the very first concert there and had continued to report it thereafter, the reviews of the New York City Ballet season were enthusiastic about the new theater and continued so in the face of dissent and protest from the public. And under the title *The Essence of a Theater, Newsweek* published one of those news-magazine-style pieces in which what is reported omnisciently as fact includes opinion —often, as in this instance, favorable opinion which accepts publicized intention as valid and as realized in what was achieved. The "essence" of the title turned out to be one defined by a statement of the theater's architect, Philip Johnson: "The essence of a theater is elegance, just as the essence of a church is spirituality"; and the piece reported in this connection that the "seats are deep red plush, the fronts of the rings [balconies] are gold leaf; the lights . . . are cut and faceted like giant diamonds"; that "the theme of elegance reaches a peak in the 50-foot-high, 200-foot-long promenade" of which "the travertine floor is inlaid with strips of red marble, the ceiling is gold leaf, the railings of the promenade balconies are travertine and bronze filigree, etc. etc." And as the piece accepted Mr. Johnson's view of all this as "the essence of a theater," so, when it considered the real essence of the new theater—namely, how it served the purposes and needs of performers and spectators—it again accepted his view that "a horseshoe . . . shape is best fitted for the stage and the people looking at it—with its curved corners, it brings you in close to the performers," and that with the five horseshoe-shaped balconies which brought 2,178 of the

2,729 seats within 100 feet of the stage he had achieved "the first modern *Volkstheater*, a theater of the masses . . . a non-aristocratic, large house," and thus had fulfilled the intention expressed in his quoted statement to Balanchine, "George, I designed it for you": a theater suitable for ballet to be performed in and to be seen in.

The quoted statement of Balanchine, "Just what I always wanted," may well have expressed his satisfaction with the new theater as a place in which to rehearse and perform his ballets; though even here one wonders whether he liked everything—in particular the diminishing effect on some of the ballets of the enormously increased height of the proscenium. And one wonders whether the statement represented satisfaction also with the new theater as a place in which to see his ballets: after a week or so I no longer saw him occupying his own seat in the first row center of the First Ring. For myself I can report that on the one occasion when I sat in the first row center of the First Ring I was still too far from the stage to be able to see the dancers' faces distinctly; and from the third, fourth, fifth and sixth rows in which I sat the other times the dancers were tiny figures —made to seem even smaller by the high proscenium frame of the stage space—of whom not only the subtleties of personal style were lost, but even the large movements were diminished to the point of ineffectiveness, and what at closer range would have been the thrilling trajectory of a soaring leap was reduced to miniature in size and impact. I felt myself to be not in contact with the dancers; and an actor who sat with me at one performance commented: "No emanations."

This was the "epic intimacy" referred to in the *Newsweek* piece as I experienced it in the center of the First Ring. And someone who had paid $4.95 for a seat on the side of this balcony reported that the horseshoe shape which brought him close to the dancers prevented his seeing them on part of that side of the stage, precisely as it did in the Metropolitan Opera House, whose notorious "blind" seats one would have thought would have kept anyone from repeating the error of its horseshoe shape

today. Moreover, the difficulty of seeing increased with each successively higher balcony, as I learned from someone accustomed to seeing the company's performances from the Second Balcony of City Center, who reported the frustrating experience of seeing them from the similarly priced but much more distant Fourth Ring of the New York State Theater. What, then, in Mr. Johnson's words was a theater for the seeing of ballet by the masses, in fact was one in which the performances could be seen satisfactorily by the occupants of the several hundred seats in the Orchestra from, say, row H (center) to row P, but not by the occupants of the rest of the 1044 Orchestra seats that were too close or too much on the side or too distant, and not by the occupants of the 1685 seats in the five balconies. His real concern had been with a theater to look *at*, not to see *in*; and that was what he had produced.

Reporting, then, on what I saw with less than full adequacy, Balanchine's new work for the New York City Ballet, *Clarinade*, got its title from the music, Morton Gould's *Derivations* for clarinet and jazz band, an even worse Gould piece than the one Robbins used for *Interplay*; and what Balanchine devised for it, though not one of his great works, impressed me as better in its genre than the analogous Robbins invention in *Interplay*, with the blues movement bringing the amazing new ingenuities that each new supported adagio elicits from Balanchine. This movement was danced beautifully by Farrell and Blum; and Govrin and Mitchell were excellent in the fast movements.

The season's other novelty was the company's first performance of Tudor's *Dim Luster*, originally produced some twenty years ago by Ballet Theater. Somewhere around that time Carl Van Vechten remarked to me: "The trouble with Balanchine as a choreographer is that he isn't going anywhere. Tudor is going somewhere." And a few years later, after Ballet Society's production of Balanchine's *The Four Temperaments*, Van Vechten said he had liked only the *Phlegmatic Variation*. Last May Van Vechten was present for the New York City Ballet's first performance of *Dim Luster*, which was preceded by a performance of *The Four*

Temperaments; and I wondered whether this time—watching in the Balanchine piece the succession of astoundingly original and powerful details in the three Themes—he had again failed to see the gigantic step they constituted in the going somewhere by Balanchine that still had not stopped. And after *Dim Luster* I wondered whether Van Vechten had seen this time that in the choreography of this piece Tudor had not gone an inch beyond the three movements of *Lilac Garden* that were his total dance vocabulary; and that his going in the new piece was merely to a new story line presenting the characters in new names (the Gentleman with Her, the Lady with Him), new costumes and a new set, but particularizing the old emotional frustration and nostalgia in the terms of the same vocabulary of gesture and mime. I am not objecting to the addition of a Tudor ballet to the company's repertory, but to the addition of a poor one: the company should have revived *Lilac Garden*, in which Tudor's use of his style was freshly motivated, not a work in which it was the repetition of mannerisms. In fact I think the company has reached the point where it ought to enrich its repertory with the outstanding works of other choreographers besides Tudor: not only the Lew Christensen-Virgil Thomson *Filling Station* again, but the Loring-Copland *Billy the Kid*, the de Mille-Copland *Rodeo*, the de Mille-Respighi *Three Virgins and a Devil*. And I go so far as to suggest the historic Fokine-Stravinsky *Petrushka* (with Lazovsky), and even the historic Fokine-Chopin *Les Sylphides*.

In addition to waltzing gracefully to Strauss's *Burleske* in *Dim Luster*, Villella and McBride made impressively effective appearances in *Raymonda Variations* and the Tchaikovsky *Pas de Deux*—except that in the second piece she seemed to me not yet to have achieved transcendent mastery of her solo. In *Apollo* too her solo still exhibited conscientious effort instead of relaxed ease; but her work in the rest of the ballet was lovely. Schorer repeated her beautifully achieved Calliope; Carol Sumner this time executed Polyhymnia's solo with assured mastery; and Villella's Apollo again had its touching warmth and expressiveness at the

beginning, its ennobling grace and beauty later (it continued its one inaccuracy: Apollo's failure, in the *pas d'action*, to join the three muses in swinging their arms forward and backward. Villella had done this correctly at his first performance, but not thereafter).

In the continued absence not only of Verdy and Kent but of Hayden, the younger dancers appeared in additional first-line roles. Most impressive in her suppleness and clarity was Farrell as Titania in *A Midsummer Night's Dream*, Terpsichore in the *Apollo* with d'Amboise, and in the *Pas de Deux* of *Agon*. Govrin exhibited her strong clarity in the final Ricercare of *Episodes*, and was effective in her solo, but a little big for her partners to lift easily, in the second *Pas de Trois* of *Agon*; and Blum was excellent in the first *Pas de Trois*. Neary did well in the first movement of *Symphony in C*; and a new soloist, Marnee Morris, proved fully adequate to the demands of the last movement. And after performances last fall and winter that were at times painful to watch, I was unprepared to see Tallchief, in *Serenade*, operating again with her former security and ease and lovely fluidity. *(170, 151)*

Winter 1965 The New York ballet season 1965 was opened this year by the Leningrad Kirov Ballet, which exhibited much the same strengths and weaknesses as when it first appeared here in 1961—though the weaknesses this time were for me more obtrusive and important. The strengths were the excellence of the dancers— the *corps*, the lesser soloists and some of the principals—and the precision and finish of their thoroughly rehearsed operation, enough to make the long slow entrance of the corps in a series of *arabesques* at the beginning of Petipa's *Bayaderka* one of the most impressive and exciting things the company offers. One weakness appeared later in this piece, in the dancing of one of the principals, Kaleria Fedicheva, an efficient athlete completely without the elegant fluidity and style, the personal radiance, that ennoble the dancing of Alla Sizova and Irina Kolpakova: possessing only these two real ballerinas, the company has to use a mere athlete in ballerina roles, as it did again later in the same gala program when it presented Petipa's *Corsair pas de deux* with Fedicheva instead of Sizova who had danced it the night before. But even more important was the weakness revealed by two of the other pieces on the program, Konstantin Sergeyev's ballet, *A Distant Planet*, and Vassily Vainonen's choreography for a few passages from Tchaikovsky's *The Nutcracker*: the excellent dancers are presented in feeble ballets.

Nor are these only the new ballets. In 1961 I reported concerning the Kirov *Swan Lake*, with its Petipa-Ivanov choreography revised by Sergeyev, that to someone who had been seeing the excitingly beautiful and imaginative movements of the Balanchine version of Act 2 the movements of the Kirov version were insipid and boring. And this time I must make the same report about the movements of Sergeyev's revision of another Petipa ballet, *Raymonda*—as against the enchanting movements of Balanchine's choreography for some of the music of the Glazunov score, *Raymonda Variations*, which exhibit *his* developments and elaborations of the Petipa vocabulary and syntax. It was presumably similar movements that made Balanchine's version of the entire ballet for the Monte Carlo Ballet Russe in 1946 an exciting experience for me in spite of the absurd story, the sleazy scenery, the inadequacy of most of the principals. And it had also the great performance of Danilova in the title role; whereas the Kirov performance I saw had Fedicheva, who contributed nothing that relieved the tedium of the occasion.

This time even the Konstantin Sergeyev revision of Petipa's *The Sleeping Beauty* presented by the Kirov Ballet seemed to me inferior to the version of Nicolai Sergeyev performed by England's Royal Ballet, whose effectiveness is heightened, moreover, by the distinguished and imaginative scenic context provided by Oliver Messel, as against Simon Virsaladze's mediocre and drab sets for the Kirov production. But the performance I saw was irradiated by the loveliness and elegance of Sizova's dancing in the title role—this in addition to the superb

dancing of Yuri Soloviev and the fine work of the others; and so it was, for me, the one memorable experience of the Kirov engagement.

As it happened, the New York City Ballet's opening program of its fall season began with *Raymonda Variations*, whose choreographic invention as executed by the dancers trained in the Balanchine style was an even greater pleasure to see after the Kirov presentations. André Prokovsky, in the role danced originally by d'Amboise and later by Villella, got applause with the evident exertion of physical powers that achieved the difficult things he did—as against d'Amboise's or Villella's exertion of greater powers to produce the appearance of the difficult things being done with no effort. Prokovsky thus provided additional contradiction of the idea Balanchine holds to in the face of the many demonstrations to the contrary —that there are no differences between dancers, and stars represent only publicity. The difference between even as competent a dancer as Prokovsky, and d'Amboise or Villella, is clear to any eye; and while Balanchine may nevertheless have to use Prokovsky in a role that calls for d'Amboise or Villella, there should be recognition of the lessened effectiveness of the role when he is so used.

A further demonstration of this kind was provided in the next work on the opening program, Balanchine's *The Four Temperaments*. As astounding today in the flow of its original invention as it was the first time in 1947, it is performed for the most part as impressively today as in 1947 by the new dancers Balanchine has had to use—notably by Mimi Paul in the Third Theme. There have been excellent performances also by Schorer in this part, by Rapp in the *Melancholic Variation*, by Neary in the *Choleric Variation*; and this time there was Govrin in the *Sanguinic Variation*, in which one expected to see her suitable strong clarity, only to be surprised by her relaxed, spacious performance, which gave the movements an entirely new and attractive character. But in place of Bolender's unforgettable opening solo in the *Phlegmatic Variation* there have been the unsuitable quick and sharp movements of

Mitchell's flashy style, which this time were even quicker and sharper and more damaging to the character of the piece. And I might add that even worse, a few nights later, was Mitchell's performance in *Bugaku*, in which his exaggerated crouching and lunging, his ostentatiously over-elaborate preparation in Japanese-wrestler-style of every movement of body, arm and hand in the *pas de deux*, produced a caricature of the role in place of the powerful realization of it that Villella achieves with his quiet elegance and sustained tension.

Govrin's *Sanguinic Variation* in *Four Temperaments* was the first of several appearances by the younger dancers in new roles. *Symphony in C*, the second night, had Farrell dancing the second movement with her beautiful fluidity, as against the exquisitely inflected detail and the grand style of Paul's performance. In a *Donizetti Variations* with Villella, Sara Leland danced with impressive precision and clarity and humor, but not with the bravura required to bring down the house; however, the precision and clarity produced a satisfying Polyhymnia in an *Apollo* with Villella. And McBride and Blum brought a youthful freshness to *Allegro Brillante* that made it newly attractive. *(120)*

The season's first new work was Balanchine's revision of his Act 2 of *Swan Lake,* in which he eliminated what he had retained of the Petipa choreography, including the *pas de quatre*, and added new numbers of his own: an exquisite waltz for a group of Swans, another for Odette and four Swans, a brilliant one for Prince Siegfried. And though one wouldn't think so from the grumbling in the press — which seemed to consider it outrageous for Balanchine to make his own setting of music of his choice from the Tchaikovsky score — the result is a most beautiful work. Rouben Ter-Arutunian's somber new setting is good; his costumes for the Hunters unattractive; but at last — thanks, perhaps, to the Ford Foundation millions — d'Amboise's costume includes a wig which lessens the incongruity of his American appearance in the role of Siegfried. He should be made to wear one in all such roles, including Apollo; and if necessary an additional grant should be requested from the Ford Foundation for the purpose.

In place of the new ballet of Tudor, which was not ready, the company presented Taras's *Piège de Lumière*, which he created in 1952 for the company of the Marquis de Cuevas, and which is what one thinks of as being a ballet for the Paris public, with its story about escaped convicts in a jungle who set a trap of light for the big, brilliantly colored butterflies of the region that provide the occasion for spectacular costumes and choreographic ingenuities. These produce one theatrically effective scene — of the long progression of butterflies dancing across the stage toward the dazzling light, with an imaginative solo by the Iphias, danced well in one performance by Blum and in another by Prokovsky. The rest, which had Tallchief as the Queen of the Morphides and Mitchell as one of the Convicts, I found uninteresting. The costumes are by André Levasseur; the less impressive scenery by Felix Labisse.

D'Amboise's last two ballets left me unprepared for his *Irish Fantasy,* in which his indebtedness to Balanchine is evident but he uses what he has learned from Balanchine interestingly and with effective details of his own contriving — for example in the supported adagio. The performance I saw had d'Amboise himself in the dazzling feats of virtuosity that were not much more difficult than those brilliantly executed by Blum and Frank Ohman; and Farrell was delightful in the Allegros and exquisite in the Adagio. The music is by Saint-Saëns; the lace fore-curtain ingeniously designed to become a canopy over the stage is by David Hays; the charming costumes are by Karinska.

The final new work was Balanchine's *Ballet Imperial*, which he created, with *Concerto Barocco*, in 1941 for the Latin-American tour of the American Ballet, and which was last performed in New York in the later '40s by the Monte Carlo Ballet Russe. One was grateful for the opportunity to hear again Tchaikovsky's rarely played Piano Concerto No. 2, which is so superior to the ubiquitous No. 1, and to see again the invention which the music elicited from Balanchine. The principal roles were danced brilliantly by Farrell, d'Amboise and Neary; but their unmistakably American looks were disturbing in their imperial Russian roles, especially in the mimed dramatic episode of the second movement. The enormous draperies painted on Rouben Ter-Arutunian's scenery were too heavily obtrusive; but Karinska's costumes were beautiful. One hopes Frederic Franklin, the former *maître de ballet* of the Monte Carlo Company, who staged *Ballet Imperial* for the New York City Ballet, will be asked to stage two other Balanchine masterpieces that were in the Monte Carlo repertory, *Danses Concertantes* and *Le Baiser de la Fée*.

In what seemed to be a more thoroughly rehearsed *Prodigal Son*, Villella's performance had newly and well thought-out details which were less important than the increased continuity of his movements in the scene after the despoiling; but Shaun O'Brien, as the Father, damaged the end again by advancing toward the audience and then turning sharply to face the Son like a stern drill sergeant.*

Spring 1965 Wondering about the New York City Ballet's "new" production of *The Nutcracker*, I found it difficult to believe that Balanchine could think up a new Christmas party for the first act in place of the beautifully imagined old one; and it turned out that he had left the entire first act unchanged, and in the second act had changed only the opening scene with the Angels and the dances for *Hot Chocolate* and *Coffee*. What was entirely new was the scenery of Rouben Ter-Arutunian; and I didn't like the lacy Christmas-card-like frame around

---

*After I had sent in this report I saw Mimi Paul's Odette in *Swan Lake*, in which the image created by the contour of her body and the fluidity of its movements was impressively beautiful in the early scenes, and became excitingly so in the later solo with the four Swans, when she had relaxed sufficiently to operate with freedom and authority in movement completely, perfectly and breath-takingly achieved in its grand style. One flaw must be mentioned: her fluid bodily movement ends in a sharp bend of the wrist and a raising of the index finger which—in the rapidly repeated fluttering of the arms—became disturbingly obtrusive. I also saw an *Apollo* with d'Amboise, whose continuing thought and work on his misconceived realization of the title role showed itself in a further increase of its stiff, angular and over-muscular pompousness to the point where I felt I couldn't bear ever to see the role so monstrously distorted again.

the proscenium, thought the huge masses of snow that threatened to engulf the dancing Snowflakes in Act 1 were bad, and was appalled by the setting for Act 2, which—instead of the subtly imagined scene that Tchaikovsky's wonderful orchestral prelude prepared one for—offered a piling up of sundaes and the like in the pictorial style of an ice-cream ad. But Karinska's genius for color and shape in costume outdid itself in some of her new costumes—the Spanish ones for *Hot Chocolate* above all.

The *Times* and *Herald Tribune* critics are right in contending that the New York City Ballet should announce dancers as well as ballets in advance, but wrong in their reason. The company's policy of not announcing dancers is objectionable, they say, because its result is that someone attending a performance in the expectation of seeing a ballerina like Melissa Hayden sees some inexperienced young dancer or other instead. But I find this irresponsible slinging around of words objectionable. Hayden is a very efficient dancer, but—lacking the exquisiteness of changing bodily configuration, the poetic aura that one can see Fonteyn's dancing has—Hayden is not what one can see Fonteyn is, a ballerina. And for anyone who judges not by names and words but by what he sees, the "inexperienced young dancers" Mimi Paul and Suzanne Farrell whom the company has been offering occasionally in place of Hayden are not only amazingly strong in technique but equally amazing in the qualities of exquisite style and poetry that make them more fascinating to watch than Hayden. But I agree that it should be possible for anyone who prefers Hayden to Paul or Farrell to see Hayden. And in general it seems to me that when a ballet is performed on different nights with different dancers the company should make it possible for a person to see it with the dancer he prefers—*Raymonda Variations* with d'Amboise rather than Prokovsky, *Apollo* with Villella rather than d'Amboise, *Swan Lake* with Verdy rather than Wilde, or, if he prefers, the other way round.

Summer 1965 The first of the new works of the New York City Ballet's winter season was

Balanchine's *Pas de Deux and Divertissement,* which framed part of the earlier *Sylvia pas de deux* with new dances by a group of girls headed by a soloist, converting it into another of the elaborate show pieces like *Raymonda Variations* that Balanchine has done occasionally in recent years. The new material was charming and made effective use of Schorer's delightful style of sharply precise small-scale movement. And Karinska's costumes for the girls—with their bright red bodices and delicately colored skirts and underskirts—added another to her many extraordinary achievements. The principal roles were danced effectively at the première by Hayden and Prokovsky, with later performances offering the excitingly beautiful dancing of Farrell or Kent.

The second new work, Taras's *Shadow'd Ground,* presented a series of episodes evoked by the epitaphs in a graveyard. The music, Copland's *Dance Panels,* seemed to me not to justify its title; the movements devised to go with it I found weak and uninteresting; and the scenic production distracted the eye with four large panels on which were projected a succession of colored photographs.

In the final new work, Balanchine's *Harlequinade*—derived from the ballet *Les Millions d'Arlequin* that he saw as a child, and using its music by Drigo—his powers of dance invention operated in the service of his superb sense for the theater, and in this instance for comedy. The number for the drunken police patrol, and what was presented to the eye—in costume, make-up and movement—as the character of Léandre, were only two high points in the entertaining progression of dance and pantomime contrived, as always, in terms of the particular capacities and styles of the dancers—not only of Villella and McBride, the Harlequin and Columbine, but of Lamont and Schorer, the Pierrot and Pierrette—in the frame of Rouben Ter-Arutunian's amusing scenery.

As important as the new works was the return of Balanchine's *Liebeslieder Walzer.* Seen after an interval of two years, its inexhaustible flow of constantly varied invention for one piece of music after another in the one basic rhythm and style—now with the touching implications of a romantic episode, now with powerful dramatic implications—had an increased impressiveness that placed the work, for me, with his major achievements. When it was first done, Verdy's was the outstanding performance; and this time her coaching was evident in the images of her clarity, elegance and distinction that one saw in Sara Leland's performance of the same role. On the other hand Farrell made no attempt to reproduce Adams's cool, aloof performance; instead, with her own inflections of arms and hands she created an entirely new character—youthfully warm, impulsive, touching—in excitingly beautiful dancing that was as outstanding in these performances as Verdy's had been in the first ones. Farrell's partner, Kent Stowell, didn't achieve in his solos the superb style in large movement that Carter had exhibited; but James DeBolt was an effective replacement for Watts. The others—McBride, Jillana, Magallanes and Ludlow—repeated their excellent contributions to the early performances. *(161–162)*

In addition a performance of *Scotch Symphony* had Farrell, in the second movement, again creating a different character—youthfully impulsive, capricious, even playful, and utterly captivating—from the grandly romantic ones created by her predecessors. A performance of *Serenade* had Mimi Paul operating with her strength and authority in her beautifully fluid style. And several other young dancers— Sumner, Simon, Neary and Schorer—demonstrated their technical and stylistic adequacy for the difficult roles they took on in *Divertimento No. 15.*

With the exciting experiences provided by these young dancers there were the ones offered by Kent, whose return to the company enabled one to confirm one's recollection of the exquisite flow of her movements in *Serenade* and the second movement of *Symphony in C,* her additional projective force in *La Sonnambula,* the quiet power of her slowly and securely executed delicate movements in *Bugaku* (and her return to this piece brought Villella back to it, to confirm my recollection of the superb effect of his quiet and contained exercise of strength, as against the destructive effect of Mitchell's fussing and hamming). But one thing, it turned out, I had not remembered as I should have: the overwhelming beauty and dramatic expressiveness of Kent's performance in *Swan Lake*. (171–175, 143)

Fall 1965 Critical writing, as I have pointed out, includes the making of imaginary points about imagined artistic happenings; and this was true of some of the newspaper reviews of the American Ballet Theater's 25th-birthday season at the New York State Theater. These described not what was actually presented to the eye by the actual company, but instead what *would* and *should* have been—and in the reviewer's imagination therefore *was*—presented by the company they wanted, and therefore believed and proclaimed, the American Ballet Theater to be: a company with a personnel and a repertory that made it America's greatest, the American counterpart of the Russian Bolshoi and Kirov and the English Royal Ballets. In these reviews the company had in Lupe Serrano and Toni Lander ballerinas comparable with Markova and Alonso years ago; in Fernandez and Scott Douglas, male virtuosos comparable with Youskevitch and Lazovsky. But not on the stage of the New York State Theater, where the actual Serrano one saw was a technically proficient dancer who appeared to produce the fluid movements of the *Nutcracker pas de deux* with arms and legs of steel; where the actual Toni Lander's movements, her manner, and her facial expressions in the *Grand Pas—Glazunov* made one think one was seeing Beatrice Lillie in a spoof of the ballerina operation; and where the actual Fernandez and Douglas were anything but impressive as their partners. What the actual *Giselle* with Serrano was, as against the one in the reviews, I didn't get to see; but I can report that Balanchine's *Theme and Variations* danced by Serrano with Fernandez, in their ugly new costumes, was not what it had been when danced with elegant brilliance by Alonso and Youskevitch, in their original beautiful costumes. However, though the actual company has no great dancers, it has several good ones—notably Ruth Ann Koesun, whose exquisitely modulated Waltz with guest-dancer John Gilpin was the high point of her lovely dancing in a good performance of *Les Sylphides;* and Sallie Wilson, who also danced beautifully in this piece. It still has Kriza, with lessened agility as a dancer, but with undiminished powers of presence and dramatic projection in his comic role in deMille's *Frail Quarry* (originally *Tally-Ho*), his grimly amusing one in Herbert Ross's *Caprichos*. With Koesun and Wilson in *Caprichos,* with Wilson and guest-dancer Carmen de Lavallade in *Frail Quarry*, the actual performances of these pieces were good, as was the performance of Robbins's *Fancy Free*.

So with the repertory that in the reviews was "matchless" in size and variety. In actuality the long Ballet Theater list includes the many worthless pieces—dropped after a season or two—that have been commissioned year after year with the lack of artistic judgment and discrimination that was exhibited again in what was presented this time. The revivals included—among the fine pieces like *Billy the Kid, Fancy Free, Caprichos, Lilac Garden*— de Mille's entertaining *Frail Quarry*, but also her *Fall River Legend*, one of her serious pieces of Americana, this one concerned with the Lizzie Borden case in hour-long boring detail. And the new works too included on the one hand as impressive an achievement as Robbins's *Les Noces*, which I will say more about in a moment, but also two more American pieces by de Mille whose American subjects— a country calendar of the seasons in *The Wind in the Mountains*, an aspect of the racial problem in the South in *The Four Marys*—didn't increase the moderate interest of the movements which de Mille's resourceful use of her personal vocabulary and style devised for them. The new works also included Glen Tetley's *Sargasso*, a "milestone" in the columns of the *Herald Tribune*, but on the stage of the New York State Theater a laughable monstrosity of modern-dance-style "expressive" contortion and distortion; and Bentley Stone's *L'Inconnue*, which even in the *Herald Tribune* was a mere experimental workshop product that didn't warrant presentation in a professional theater to the general public. And the historic Bournonville *La Sylphide* as reconstructed by Harald Lander was—as against the historic *Giselle*— not very interesting to the eye of today; though

I must add that it gave Toni Lander a role in which she operated more impressively than in *Grand Pas—Glazunov*.

It was not merely in this context that the performances of Robbins's *Les Noces* were the exciting occasions of the Ballet Theater season: the work was one of the notable achievements of the powers which this most outstandingly gifted of American choreographers has exercised in ballet with only occasional success. The successes have been those of a master of comedy—whether the robust comedy of *Fancy Free* or the delicately, wryly humorous perception of *Afternoon of a Faun*; the failures have been those of the master of comedy who felt that to be a serious artist he had to deal with serious subjects in a serious manner, and who produced ballets embodying his thought on the human condition—ballets like *Facsimile* and *Age of Anxiety*, about lonely people, and exhibiting personal privacies that were embarrassing to look at. But in *Age of Anxiety* the four lonely people got involved now and then with a lot of other people in episodes which provided occasions for Robbins to exercise his power in the orchestrating of large groups. And in *Les Noces* —where Robbins operated under the conditions and limitations imposed not only by Stravinsky's score but by a scenario and text concerned with a Russian peasant couple in the ritualized public situations of their marriage—his dealing with these situations was the varied and exciting detail of the *perpetuum mobile* of imaginative large-group orchestration that he fitted to the unending reiterations of the music—all against the background of on-stage instrumentalists and singers and the huge icon figures of Oliver Smith's backdrop. Wonderfully imagined and moving, after all this, was the end: the last poignant percussive sounds of the music, and the boy and girl standing in embrace alone on a small platform. *(176–177)*

Much of the advance publicity about the Royal Ballet's season at the Metropolitan Opera House was concerned with one of its new works, the evening-length *Romeo and Juliet* of the company's principal choreographer, Kenneth MacMillan—his setting of the Prokofiev score used in the ballet presented by the Bolshoi company a few years ago. The MacMillan work got forty-three curtain calls at its London première; it was warmly praised by the perceptive English critic Clive Barnes; and at the Metropolitan it was applauded by an audience which apparently was content to see richly costumed dancers on a sumptuously set stage make movements that told the familiar story. But for someone who asked in addition for movements that exhibited imaginative invention in the manipulation of dancers' bodies, this *Romeo* was an evening-long bore. The crucial instances of this were the episodes of Romeo and Juliet alone; and here I will not speak of the ever new and fascinating ways that Balanchine keeps discovering for a pair of dancers to move in relation to each other, but will instead recall the breath-takingly beautiful movements Tudor devised in his individual style for the bedroom *pas de deux* of his *Romeo and Juliet* years ago. MacMillan could produce nothing of this kind, nothing even adequate, for this supreme moment—nothing but the few clichés of his vocabulary and occasional laborious ingenuity that revealed the poverty of invention concealed at other times by story-telling and hubbub.

But most of the publicity was about Nureyev; and its magnitude and character—in particular some of the unpleasant personal details in the news-magazine cover stories in brashly omniscient news-magazine style—caused some people to feel they should express disapproval of the offensive ballyhoo or of the offensively egotistic behavior of its subject by not going to see Nureyev, and other people to suspect that the ballyhoo was about someone not really extraordinary and worth seeing. Both were wrong: the ballyhoo happened, in this instance, to be about someone really extraordinary and worth seeing; and what he did on the stage was something to go and see regardless of what he himself did elsewhere or what anyone else said about it in news-magazine publicity stories. If Fonteyn didn't let the appalling things Nureyev was reported to say to her deprive her of the fascination and stimulation of dancing with him, a spectator shouldn't let them deprive him of the experience of, say, the bravura dancing, overwhelming in its brilliance, power and projective force, that Nureyev did in the *Laurentia pas de six*.

I will add that he is someone to go and see regardless of the things he sometimes does on the stage. At one point in Odette's supported adagio in Act 2 of *Swan Lake* he did a couple of leaps which could have been interpolations of his own and, as such, egotistic intrusions; but as such they were a momentary flaw in what was for the rest a progression of intensely beautiful and poetic movement that wonderfully framed and heightened the effect of Fonteyn's marvelous dancing; and as such they were something to treat as one treated Glenn Gould's perverse thumping out of meaningless bass figurations in his great performance of Mozart's Concerto K.491: something to regret as one noticed it and then to put out of mind for the great things that followed. *(178)*

But some things he did on the stage that were criticized didn't seem to me to deserve the criticism. In an article in the *Herald Tribune* Michael Harrington contended that the "star treatment" of Nureyev had resulted in fixing "the attention of millions upon the worst in the ballet tradition: that a prettified banality should serve as the backdrop for an individual genius" —this specifically in the first act of *Swan Lake*, in which for almost an hour Nureyev "strolls, bows, receives flowers, sits, broods, mimes, and in general pays scrupulous respect to all the dear, dead traditions, those holy dodo birds of ballet." All this was for the Tsars, as against Balanchine's *Serenade*, *The Four Temperaments* and *Agon*, in which he "[integrated] the angularities and dissonances of modern dance—and, more importantly, of modern life—into the ballet vocabulary" and "gave the chaotic, traumatic, breakneck experiences of these times an aesthetic form." I doubt that Balanchine would accept these as the facts about his ballets; and Mr. Harrington is equally remote from fact in his idea of the Royal Ballet's putting on *Swan Lake* to display egotistic posturing by Nureyev, and indeed in his idea of Nureyev's operation in the first act as mere egotistic posturing. *Swan Lake*, *The Sleeping*

Beauty and *Giselle* have been in the Royal Ballet's repertory for many years, as three great classics of ballet which it is as legitimate for the Royal or the Bolshoi or the Kirov to present today as it is for a theater company to present plays by Shakespeare, Congreve and Chekhov. And this year the company presented a new staging of *Swan Lake* by Robert Helpmann, with revisions and additions to make the work more plausible and effective for audiences of today than the company's earlier reconstruction of the original ballet as it was performed in St. Petersburg early in this century. Thus, in the original first act the action stopped when the dances in celebration of the Prince's birthday began, and he sat watching them as an interested but motionless spectator until they ended, when dramatic action resumed and he resumed his miming in it. But in the newly staged first act the action continued and was integrated with the dancing: now and then the Prince, as he watched the dancers, was impelled to join them for a few minutes; at other times he sat visibly abstracted and brooding, his thoughts elsewhere; and his troubled state of mind was conveyed further—when his guests left—in a new meditative solo. The new details in the Prince's role were executed by Donald MacLeary and Christopher Gable when they performed it; and on these occasions they were noticed by the audience, as Helpmann intended them to be. And the only difference on the one occasion when Nureyev executed them was their more powerful communicative effect.

With the New York City Ballet giving us only the great ballets of today, we must be grateful to the Royal Ballet for its presentations of the great classics of the past, and additionally grateful for the presentation that includes Nureyev, whose style wouldn't work in Balanchine's *The Four Temperaments* or *Agon* but does work with superbly enhancing effect in *Swan Lake* or *Giselle*.* It is these classics, and

*This is the answer to the statement Balanchine is reported to have made, that Nureyev is old-fashioned and not for today. Nureyev dances in the style he learned in Russia—the style other Russian dancers learned—the style one sees in Russian productions of the old classics—and a style that works in the Royal Ballet's productions of them.

others of this century like *Les Sylphides*, the original Diaghilev *Firebird* and *Petrushka*, that are the interesting and valuable part of the Royal Ballet's repertory for us, not the ballets of present-day English choreographers—not MacMillan's *Romeo*, or his even worse *The Invitation*, or Ashton's boring *Daphnis* and *Chloë*, or his *Marguerite and Armand*. The performances of those classics with Fonteyn in previous visits, and now with Fonteyn and Nureyev, have been some of the most distinguished, moving and unforgettable artistic operations we have seen here; but even without Fonteyn, and without Nureyev, they are, and probably will continue to be, almost the only Royal Ballet offerings worth going to see.

More justified was the advance publicity about the new work of the New York City Ballet's spring season—not just a new ballet of Balanchine, but one of evening length, *Don Quixote*, to a specially commissioned score by Nicolas Nabokov, with scenery and costumes by Esteban Francés. (And some of this publicity was concerned, properly, with Balanchine's one appearance in the title role at a benefit preview before the première.) Balanchine was served well by Francés, most notably with the magnificently somber set and Courtiers' costumes for the second act in the ducal palace. But personal loyalty to a friend—an admirable quality, but not in artistic matters—resulted in Balanchine's being handicapped by one of the feeblest, most boring and, after a couple of hours, most irritating pretenses at music-making in my experience. However Balanchine had overcome similar handicaps before, and he triumphed over the Nabokov score this time.

Don Quixote and Sancho Panza would seem to lend themselves to being realized on the stage in dance; and one must suppose that such a realization by Balanchine would have been fascinating—in addition to making the work a ballet throughout. But he chose to make them mime roles, and the work a mingling of mime, spectacle and dancing. In the mime and spectacle one observed the play of Balanchine's mind, his theater sense, his fantasy, his humor—most powerful in the second act, which

began with a ceremonial dance of the Courtiers that chilled audiences into complete silence at its conclusion, and, after a series of *divertissements*, reached a climax in the Courtiers' baiting of Don Quixote. And the dancing offered additional examples of the fascinating new invention that keeps coming from that inexhaustible mind—notably the solos of Paul and Blum in Act 3, and one number in a genre I don't remember having seen before in Balanchine's work: the enchanting *Pas de Deux Mauresque* in folk-dance style of Schorer and John Prinz, among the *divertissements* of Act 2. (Balanchine previously had taken girls out of the *corps* for solos revealing the capacities he had perceived; now he had done this with a boy.) These were in addition to the marvelously beautiful and varied invention for Farrell in her appearances in different guises in the course of the work. *(179–183)*

To the mime scenes Farrell brought the moving expressive projection she had first exhibited in *Meditation*. With this, and with her breath-takingly beautiful dancing, her operation left one overwhelmed. Of the other dancing, Paul's stood out vividly in its distinction of style, with impressive contributions by Schorer, McBride, Morris, Neary and Blum; of the other miming, Rapp's of the old knight in his world of illusion was effective and touching, and Lamont's of Sancho offered the few telling strokes of a superb comic. (Balanchine's one appearance in the title role was made, unfortunately, in a performance which wasn't entirely ready and at times distracted his attention from his role; also, it was made, it seemed to me, in a state of great fatigue. But even with the lessened force of presence and projection it was something I am grateful for having seen.)

Don Quixote came after a month of repertory and was followed by performances of *A Midsummer Night's Dream*; and interesting in that connection were some of Balanchine's remarks in a *Life* article, in which he enunciated an attitude on ballet curiously different from his attitudes on other arts. We may today, it appeared, look at Michelangelo, and presumably listen to Mozart; but in ballet "we have got to enjoy the now"—the ballets made with the dancers of today, which exist only with these dancers, and which therefore are the only ones that do exist for us—not the ballets made with the dancers of 100 years ago that existed only with those dancers. "It is like a butterfly. I always say butterflies of yesterday don't exist"—which is Balanchine's answer when one begs for revivals of his *Cotillon*, *Le Baiser de la Fée*, *Jeu de Cartes*, *Danses Concertantes*. Actually the New York City Ballet's repertory consists mostly of Balanchine butterflies of various yesterdays, ranging from the recent *Bugaku*, *Liebeslieder Walzer*, *Episodes* and *Agon* to the *Prodigal Son* and *Apollo* of almost 40 years ago, performed by other dancers than those he made them with; and one may therefore ask why not also *Cotillon*, *Le Baiser de la Fée*, *Jeu de Cartes* and *Danses Concertantes*. But when Balanchine says *he* is interested only in what he is making with the dancers he has now, he may be confirming someone's suggestion that he is interested only in the making of a ballet and loses interest once it is made. This suggestion was offered as a possible explanation of what I found difficult to understand: Balanchine's permitting defects in the performances of his ballets to continue uncorrected—defects ranging from the zigzagging lines instead of the absolutely straight ones needed for the proper effect of his choreographic designs in *Swan Lake* or *Ballet Imperial*, to Shaun O'Brien's entrance in the manner of a severe drill sergeant rather than a forgiving father at the end of *The Prodigal Son*, or Mitchell's hammed-up performance in *Bugaku*, or d'Amboise's stiff pompousness in *Apollo*.

Last spring's season offered McBride's effective performance in *Ballet Imperial*, Schorer's in the first movement of *Symphony in C*, and the excellent Helena of Paul and Hippolyta of Neary in *A Midsummer Night's Dream*. And the long-awaited return of Verdy enriched performances of *Liebeslieder Walzer* and *Episodes* with her unique and exciting combination of exactness, enchanting elegance and style, dazzling brilliance, and dramatic power.

Wondering what the dancer's eye was aware of in Verdy's dancing, in addition to the elegance and style that enchanted the non-dancer's eye, I asked members of the company.* One of them, recalling Verdy's first movement of *Symphony in C*, said: "It was so elegant, with such quality; and the phrasing—the way she fell off those points! It's beautiful to see someone fall when she *wants* to fall and *controls* the fall; and it's one of the hardest things to do. It's hard enough just to find the balance; and some dancers just hit it and go on. But Verdy gets the value out of *reaching* the point, and *phrasing* it: of getting up to it, and hitting it, and then going off it. And that's finished dancing."

It was such details that the dancers spoke of— "these small, delicate things," as one of them put it. Thus, at the beginning of the Tchaikovsky *Pas de Deux*, "she steps back, back, back— and rests; then she begins the first phrase— pirouettes—and looks down; and just the tilt of the head is so sweet and right." Or, later in that piece, "she goes upstage and her partner pulls her: she goes just far enough—then turns and is back to him." Again, in that piece, "the skirt of her costume flows and floats in the same way she does; and it's an extraordinary thing that she can make her body act like this soft material." And in the *passés* she does at one point, there is the way she uses her eyes: "It's a very small thing to think of when you're making a performance; but it's a big thing from the audience's point of view. Very few realize it and understand it; but Verdy does. When she does this *passé, passé*, hold, it's not only the foot and the leg and the body and the arms, but the eyes too, with everything reaching the same point in time perfectly. And in the *passé* it's not just the foot and leg moving up from the stage to the knee: she brings them up as though they bounced right from the music. Another example of this feeling for music comes near the end of the piece, where she does some turns, then stops, but doesn't really stop: she hits that final pose with the music, but as the music continues and diminishes her arms and fingertips are still going with it, then the air just beyond her fingertips: her movement goes through her body, her arms, her fingertips, and pushes the air a bit, before it ends." *(164–169)*

*Actually only Villella.

These last details come from someone for whom "the most distinctive thing about Verdy is the musical quality she has. It's an extraordinary, complete musical understanding, almost like Balanchine's in the way she can make you *see* the music. She did that with the first movement of *Episodes*. I didn't understand the score; but when I watched her I could understand the music and could see what Balanchine was after. Certain lunges didn't make sense—choreographic sense—to me when I saw someone else at rehearsal just lunge and turn, lunge and turn. Then I saw Verdy do them, and I said, 'Of course.' When she lunged and turned I saw a motivation for the lunge and turn—both in visual terms and in relation to the music." *(152)*

This musical understanding, one dancer thought, had a great deal to do with "the amazing way Verdy understands a new role and develops it immediately, as soon as it is started. I have to learn the steps and the counts and digest them, and bring something to the role after that; but she brings something to it while she's learning the steps: you can see her doing it. I remember when a dancer was showing her the steps of a role: when Verdy repeated them they weren't just the steps any more, the way she suddenly brought them alive and made things happen and explode."

The musical understanding works with what she has as a dancer. "She has natural gifts for dancing," someone said. "Her feet are good, with a wonderful turn-out, which is so difficult to acquire. Her legs are good; her body is in good proportion, with the size and length of the legs right for the rest of the body; her head is the right size; the contour of the arm is nice. All these things make for the over-all picture. In addition she knows her way, so to speak, around the stage—which is important. And she looks beautiful on the stage: she can make herself look absolutely lovely—and chic, really chic—on the stage. Whereas off-stage she's just not interested: she has her heart and her soul and her life in this thing called ballet—this theater business. In Russia, when we had a performance at eleven in the morning, she would be in the theater at eight, preparing, and doing her make-up for an hour and a half.

"Also, she is a thinking dancer; and because she works with her mind as well as her body, she works well by herself. It's important to take your classes—to feed on that steady diet of technique; but you also have to be able to work alone; and this is something Verdy does very well. She knows her body, and what she has to give it; and the only trouble is that she may get so involved in her work that she will go too far and knock herself out. She does a bar for an hour and a half, where ordinarily a bar is 35 minutes. Then she does floor work; then she goes back to the bar with toe shoes. She has all this fantastic discipline, this fantastic dedication to the essentials that have to be worked at day in and day out. It's easy to get by on a slim diet of work, and many dancers do; but the really great dancers are the ones who work on absolutely everything, and who work with their minds as well as their bodies, like Verdy. Erik Bruhn is an incredible dancer; but he didn't just happen to get that way. The same with Verdy: she's not a great dancer because she just happened to become one, but because she faced and accepted the challenge, the demands of the endless thing that goes on day after day, with all the small details that are so hard to keep up and keep going. Just the carriage of the hand: it has to be worked on; and Verdy has the will to work on it. And everything else: the holding of the head, the ease here, the strength there, the stretch here, the pull there—everything."

What this endless work produces was described by a dancer to whom I spoke admiringly of Verdy's *Swan Lake*. "It's terrible when you are excited by someone who is dancing beautifully, and then you see a hand or a look of the head that is wrong. You want to see a complete performance: that's beauty! that's art! And a complete performance that isn't calculated—that is spontaneous, that just happens. Verdy gives you that. And she gives it to you in *Stars and Stripes* as well as *Swan Lake*. Some dancers are good only in certain things: they are lyric dancers, or dramatic dancers, or romantic dancers, or *demi-caractère* dancers. But Verdy is such a rounded dancer that I can see her doing any role. The remarkable thing, in fact, is that this French dancer, coming here to another style and another repertoire, has pointed up Balanchine's intentions in certain roles more than any of his other dancers. She's brought out things in roles that no one ever saw—that were always there, and that I'm sure Balanchine wanted to begin with, but that other dancers just didn't bring out. She made a great impression on the company because everything she did she made her own—she made a real performance of. She did it right from the start with the first thing she danced, the first movement of *Symphony in C*: it was *never* danced so well. She did it with *Firebird*: that was absolutely superb! She put it on and wore it: when she came out on stage she was that bird! And she did it with roles that were dull, that nobody wanted to dance, and that she made fantastic. The first movement of *Western Symphony*, for example: it's not very distinctive, but she completely understood it and took the western thing with her French flair, so that she got all the humor out of it that was intended and made it a scream. The same with *Stars and Stripes:* instead of just a bunch of girls running around with her leading them, she made it into a real parade, baton-twirling situation, and interesting thing, with her darting in and out and livening up the atmosphere." *(144–145, 132–133)*

There was more; but these are the most important things I was told about Verdy.

1966   *Spring 1966* The reviews of the Royal Danish Ballet—about the great company in exciting performances of a remarkably varied and interesting repertory—again reported what the reviewers wanted to see and imagined they saw, instead of what actually was presented to their eyes. The company is an excellent one, well-trained and well-rehearsed, and exhibiting an attractive sweetness, but also a lack of the sharpness and force we are accustomed to in the dancing of the New York City Ballet—this blandness being relieved only by the powerful personal styles of a few of the soloists—Bruhn, Kronstam, Niels Kehlet. But it appeared this season in a repertory which ranged from mildly interesting to extremely boring. Mildly interest-

ing were the few Bournonville ballets that have been in the company's repertory since their early-19th-century premières—*La Sylphide*, Act 3 of *Napoli*, and, new this time, Act 1 of *Konservatoriet*. But whereas ten years ago the modern works included Fokine's *Les Sylphides* and *Petrushka* and Balanchine's *La Sonnambula*, this time there were none of these or of the other Balanchine pieces in the company's repertory, but only Ashton's boring evening-length *Romeo and Juliet*, Culberg's interminable *Miss Julie* and *Moon Reindeer*, a lesser Robbins product, *Fanfare*, Petit's trashy *Carmen*, and a new piece, Flemming Flindt's *The Private Lesson*, whose movements offered nothing of interest beyond their detailing of the story of a psychopathic dancing teacher who is driven to kill his pupil. Of the classics of the ballet repertory there was only *Coppélia*, of which the Danish version this time seemed to me less effective than the Russian one performed by the Monte Carlo Ballet Russe years ago; moreover, the Danish dancers' execution of the simpler movements was unexciting, and the lift which a great dancer might have given to the performance with the personal radiance and magnetic compulsion of her Swanilda was something Ruth Anderson did not give to the performance I saw. Unexcitingly executed too were the exhibition dances in Act 3 of *Napoli*, except for Kehlet's brilliant moments, until the crescendo of the final tarantella. But the company's quiet style was suitable for the exercises of the ballet class in Act 1 of *Konservatoriet*, which got a charming performance, with particularly lovely dancing by a girl named Lise la Cour. *(196)*

Of the New York City Ballet's Christmas performances of Balanchine's *The Nutcracker* I saw one with Farrell's exquisitely phrased dancing of the Sugar Plum Fairy, and with John Prinz giving *Candy Canes* an elegant style which was more attractive than the recent unsuccessful attempts at the extraordinary speed and brilliance of Barnett's original performance. The new scenery didn't improve with further acquaintance.

Summer 1966 To the works from its older

repertory—including the classics *Giselle* and *Les Sylphides*, fine modern pieces like *Theme and Variations*, *Billy the Kid*, *Fancy Free* and *Caprichos*, and lethal bores like *Fall River Legend* and *Miss Julie*—Ballet Theater added an early major work of Tudor, his dramatic ballet *Pillar of Fire*, which is for the many who find more to interest them than I do in the Tudor style and what it embodies. Of last year's new works the company repeated not only Robbins's stunning *Les Noces* and de Mille's pleasantly inconsequential *The Four Marys* and *The Wind in the Mountains*, but Tetley's monstrosity, *Sargasso*. And with these it offered several new works, of which I saw Tetley's *Ricercare*, somewhat less extreme in its unattractiveness than *Sargasso*, and Bolender's *Kontraste*, a filling out of time with little inanities, except for one substantial episode reminiscent of the extraordinary *Unanswered Question* of Balanchine's *Ivesiana*.

But an event of real importance was the fine new staging of Act 2 of *Swan Lake* by David Blair of the Royal Ballet—the first installment of what will be a production of that company's reconstruction of the entire Petipa-Ivanov original. As against the Balanchine version, which makes of the act an entity in and for itself, the one presented by Ballet Theater opened with action related to the preceding act: the Prince dismissed his Huntsmen in order to meditate alone in the disquietude he had exhibited at his birthday fête in the first act; and one heard here all of Tchaikovsky's music for the scene, not just the few passages torn out of context that Balanchine uses. And whereas Balanchine makes the Prince's first encounter with Odette an animated *pas de deux* in which he wins her, in the Ballet Theater version it was a mime scene in which she acquainted him with her predicament. This was followed by the traditional choreography derived from the Petipa-Ivanov original, its effect heightened by the excellent scenery designed by Oliver Smith, costumes designed by Freddy Wittop, and lighting by Jean Rosenthal. But no amount of such heightening could make the steely movements of Serrano appear to be those of Odette, Queen of the Swans. And this was one of the painful realities of Ballet Theater's present condition that couldn't be con-

jured away by wishful fantasies in the press: the company had the dancers for Robbins's *Les Noces*; it had Koesun and Wilson who were capable of the poetic lyricism of *Les Sylphides*; it had Eleanor D'Antuono and Bruce Marks who could manage a respectable performance of *Theme and Variations*; but it didn't have dancers with great style in addition to brilliant technique for *Giselle* and *Swan Lake*, which it presented nevertheless, ineffectively, with the inadequate dancers it did have.

I have seen only two of the New York City Ballet's new works. Merce Cunningham's *Summerspace* is a reworking of a piece he made for his own company; and with its attractive *pointilliste* scenery and costumes of Robert Rauschenberg and what might be described as the *pointilliste* sounds of Morton Feldman's music, it offers *pointilliste* movement—a succession of brief unrelated sequences, each concerned with a little pattern of movement in the way a Chopin Prelude is concerned with a piano figuration, but not building up a structure even on the miniature scale of the Chopin Prelude, and not contributing to any larger structure. Some of the sequences are striking and impressive; but some are gimmicky and cute.

Balanchine's *Variations* is a sequence of three settings of Stravinsky's *Aldous Huxley Variations*—the first using a group of girls, the second a group of boys, the third Farrell alone. The Stravinsky piece is incomprehensible and ugly to my ears; but the Balanchine movements fitted to it are fascinating to the eye. They are in line with the long solo Balanchine devised for Paul Taylor to Webern music in *Episodes*, which was in effect an étude that exploited Taylor's capacities: *Variations* offers three such études which exploit the capacities of the two groups and the solo dancer in the fascinating invention that continues to come in an unending stream from Balanchine's mind. *(196)*

Fall 1966 It was difficult to imagine in advance what had induced Balanchine—who admires the music of Mozart, Bizet, Chabrier and Stravinsky—to make a ballet out of something as different and bad as Brahms's Piano Quartet Op. 25, and with its badness magnified by Schönberg's excessively and tastelessly busy instrumentation. And while he had, as recently as last year's *Don Quixote*, shown himself able to produce superb dance invention for bad music, the opening Allegro of the Brahms, danced by Hayden and Prokovsky, looked like a mere filling out of time with a mechanical use of the Balanchine vocabulary. The filling out of time continued, though with somewhat more attractive movements for McBride and Ludlow in the Intermezzo, and a few exquisite details for Kent in the Andante; and here one saw a first manifestation of real inventive power in the brief but stunning solo for Villella: the large movements in *andante* tempo with which he filled the stage space in a progression of enormous tension and grandeur. And in the final *Rondo alla zingarese* the delightful invention in folk-dance style that Farrell danced enchantingly with d'Amboise suggested that it may have been this finale which attracted Balanchine to the Brahms work. The tasselled draperies designed by Peter Harvey contributed only their obtrusiveness; and Karinska's costumes were agreeable to the eye, except for the one that made Hayden look dumpy and heavy.

The New York City Ballet's final new work, Taras's *Jeux*, used the Debussy score that Diaghilev commissioned for the 1912 ballet of Nijinsky. Listening to it by itself, one hears a succession of mere mannerisms of the matured Debussy orchestral style, with no ideas like those of *La Mer*, *Ibéria* and *Rondes de Printemps*; but it turned out that this operation of mere style worked powerfully as sound-track for a stage action. In fact it suggested a more powerful stage work than the one Taras provided in his realization of the Nijinsky scenario about a young man who, searching for a lost tennis ball, encounters two emotionally involved young girls, interposes himself between them, wins one, then the other, then both, only to run off in the end in pursuit of another tennis ball. The piece began well, with the music preparing one for Raoul Pène DuBois's fine set of a clear-

ing near a lake, and Villella's leap as he crossed the stage in pursuit of the first tennis ball. But then came the two young girls: one, Allegra Kent, made to look a little absurd by her costume of filmy trouserettes, the other, Melissa Hayden, hardly a young girl, and costumed to look like a grotesquely oversized Baby Snooks. This made their involvement in the movement devised by Taras somewhat repellent; and for their subsequent involvements with the man Taras provided the necessary supported turns, *arabesques* and lifts, which he failed to make fresh, imaginative and distinguished.

In addition to the new works there was a new scene for the rustics in the first act of *A Midsummer Night's Dream*, in which they began a rehearsal of their play which was disrupted by Puck, who placed on Bottom the ass's head that caused the others to flee in terror. The scene was an improvement in an already superb act; whereas worse than nothing was done for the second act that badly needs improvement. In this act the opening dance of the Courtiers is another of the rare instances of Balanchine's seeming to fill out time mechanically; and the first movement of the little *divertissement* is one of the rare instances of his being defeated by poor music. However with the lovely opening section of the second movement of Mendelssohn's little symphony there is the exquisite *pas de deux* of the two soloists, and with the somber middle section the impressive dance of the six boys; but even this dance of the boys was omitted last spring. The performance had distinguished contributions by Villella and Farrell in the first act, and by Kent in her second-act *divertissement* with d'Amboise.

Balanchine also introduced an effective new happening into the first act of *Don Quixote*. While the newly armed knight paced back and forth, Sancho Panza brandished a sword in trial movements whose gigantic shadows appeared on the backdrop, causing the knight, when he excitedly became aware of them, to make futile lunges at them with his spear. Then the gigantic shadows of his own lunges appeared on the backdrop, and he now began to lunge at these. I use the word "happening" because seeing *Don Quixote* again confirmed my impression that the work is an assemblage of Balanchine happenings, using incidents in the Cervantes book for what are expressions of Balanchine's mind, personality and gifts for dance and theater. These happenings include a number of pieces of marvelous dance invention: Farrell's first solo in Act 1; the opening dance of the Courtiers and the *divertissements* in Act 2—above all the *Pas de Deux Mauresque* for Schorer and Prinz; the supported adagio for Farrell, the solos for Paul, Morris, Blum and Farrell in Act 3. And these are interspersed among pieces of theater invention—some funny, some touching, all wonderfully imagined—of which only the religious procession in the last scene gets to be ineffective and irritatingly boring because of the atrocious Nabokov music that drones on interminably. Except for this the succession of happenings provides an absorbing and exciting artistic experience, especially as they are realized by the dancers I have mentioned and by Rapp and Lamont in their mime roles of Don Quixote and Sancho Panza.

For the rest, one deplored the dropping of four of the greatest Balanchine works—*Concerto Barocco, Symphony in C, The Four Temperaments* and *Episodes*—too high a price to pay for the new *Brahms-Schönberg Quartet, Jeux* and *Summerspace* (a more reasonable and acceptable price would have been *Con Amore, Piège de Lumière, Ebony Concerto, Irish Fantasy* or *Dim Luster*). But even without these four, Balanchine's *Apollo, Prodigal Son, Serenade, Ballet Imperial, La Sonnambula, Divertimento No. 15, Swan Lake, Agon, Liebeslieder Walzer, Bugaku, Raymonda Variations, Donizetti Variations,* Tchaikovsky *Pas de Deux, Meditation, Tarantella, Harlequinade* and a half-dozen others provided, every night, the exciting experiences that the visiting Royal and Bolshoi and Kirov provide only with occasional performances of classics like *Swan Lake, The Sleeping Beauty* and *Giselle*—the ones with particularly distinguished dancers. It is true that Balanchine's *Swan Lake* with Hayden is not what it is with Kent or Verdy or Paul, and that his *Apollo* with d'Amboise is not what it is with Ludlow or Villella; and the company did present *Swan Lake* with Hayden as well as Kent and Paul, and

Apollo only with d'Amboise. But the works come through excitingly even with the poorer dancers.

Farrell added *Swan Lake* to her repertory; and her second performance, which I saw, was something completely and securely achieved and breath-takingly beautiful in her individual style. Paul danced the Jillana role in *Liebeslieder Walzer,* giving it her characteristic elegance and distinction; and with the enchanting contributions of Verdy and Farrell and the lovely dancing of McBride, the realizations of this marvelous piece were two of the season's great events. And a last-minute substitution gave a lucky audience Verdy's extraordinary performance in *The Firebird.*

The company's great male dancer, Villella—great by virtue of what he has beyond mere dazzling technique—exhibited, in his first years, elegance not just in the sense of grace, but in the sense in which mathematicians use the term about a demonstration, meaning the economy and simplicity resulting from the elimination of everything superfluous. He affected one powerfully even when he stood motionless at the side of the stage watching his partner's movement in the center, or when he moved toward her very simply and with the minimum gesture of arm and hand. In those days he brought to mind the similar elegance of Youskevitch; but whereas Youskevitch retained his economy and simplicity to the very end, Villella has in the last two years exhibited an increasing and disturbing tendency toward superflous elaboration and complication. It began, as I recall it, with an ardently weaving body as he approached his partner, a more elaborate movement of the arm ending in an excessive curling of wrist, hand and fingers. And he now no longer stands still: in *Donizetti Variations* last spring, while his partner danced alone, he kept moving about the stage with his arms going like semaphores. This was not the scene-stealing of an Eglevsky: Villella is a wholly generous partner and serious artist; and what he did was, I am sure, the result of an attempt to make his performance better. And that, I am equally sure, is the explanation of his present heavy italicizing, in *Bugaku,* of the movements that had more impressive dignity and nobility as he did them with unemphatic simplicity and strength the first years.

An additional reason for regretting the absence of *Concerto Barocco* from the season's repertory was the publication in the programs of several passages from Edwin Denby's 1948 collection of his dance criticism, *Looking at the Dance*, including one about the slow movement of *Barocco* in which Denby described the detail of two of its greatest moments. The passage would have enabled people in the audiences to see what otherwise they might not have seen; and in this way they would also have learned what a real critic is and does: that he is the professional spectator with powers of perception which the non-professional doesn't have; and that he begins by perceiving what his reader may not have noticed, then describes it in a way that enables the reader to perceive it—the result being in effect that the reader operates with the critic's perceptions, sees through his eyes, hears with his ears. Accurate perception—the ability to see or hear what is placed before him—is not the only equipment of the critic: intellectual and moral discipline enter into the operation too. But it is the first, basic and essential equipment, without which the operation cannot begin; and the primary reason for the bad criticism that fills newspapers and magazines is that accurate perception—the ability merely to see or hear what is set before the critic—is exceedingly rare.

Some magazine articles of the English dance critic Clive Barnes a few years ago revealed him as one who could see—not as well as Denby saw, but well enough to create the expectation last fall that he would be the dance critic *The New York Times* and its readers have needed all these years. But his performances in *The Times* revealed his lack of the discipline I referred to a moment ago. The critic must be able not only to see but to hold his pen strictly to what he has seen; but Barnes, in addition to doing his reporting job, has been concerned with being bright, funny and lovable; and the objection to this is that when a critic's eye is partly on the effect he wants to make, it is by that much less on the thing he is ostensibly writing about.

Thus, bubbling along and throwing out little *obiter dicta* to amuse, to please, to shock, Barnes peppered his reviews with nonsense. He wrote, for example, that "Miss Hayden dances like a prima ballerina should," and credited her, in a review I have misplaced, with the loveliest arms in ballet. Or he admired Verdy's glittering performance in *Firebird* for its "soft radiance." Or he described in Farrell's dancing in *Don Quixote* its "sweet perfection and terribly touching immaturity." Or he urged Ballet Theater to scrap its distinguished Eugene Berman production of *Giselle* and reinstate the pre-1948 Lucinda Ballard production (which he can hardly have seen). And in addition to such statements in his reviews of particular ballets and performances there were the ones in his general think-pieces. I recall in one such article a statement to the effect that Balanchine and the New York City Ballet badly needed competition—which made no discernible sense in relation to the company's repertory and performances: what were the shoddy works Balanchine had been content to get by with in the absence of the competition that would have compelled him to create masterpieces?

And so, in his *New Republic* review of Denby's new collection of his critical writing since 1948,* Barnes referred, incredibly, to John Martin as "a dance critic who might be regarded as Denby's peer." And he wrote about the collection: "It is even better than his first"—which was the gracious thing to say, but not true. "Indeed it is probably . . . the best book of dance criticism ever written"—which it is not. The best book of dance criticism ever written was the first collection, *Looking at the Dance*, which took its place next to the collections of the best music and theater criticism ever written—those of Bernard Shaw and Stark Young. The new collection includes some writing as fine as that of *Looking at the Dance*—notably a description of Markova operating with lessened powers in 1952 that creates images of her movements as vivid as those created by the writing about Markova in the earlier book. But

Dancers, Buildings and People in the Streets, by Edwin Denby. Horizon Press.

the regular reviewing of performances that Denby did, first in *Modern Music* and then in the *Herald Tribune* during the war years, yielded a far greater amount of such vivid descriptive writing about ballets and dancers for inclusion in *Looking at the Dance* than the infrequent writing he has done since 1949 provided for the new collection. And the new book includes a great deal—involved in style, or obscure, or excessively technical—that does *not* enable one to see the things it is describing. But its best certainly is something not to miss; and in publishing it Horizon Press has done the public a valuable service—an even more valuable one if the publication of this book should lead to the reissuing of *Looking at the Dance.*

Postscript 1970 Before the appearance of the preceding article in mid-October 1966 Mr. Barnes—in a Sunday article defending the New York City Ballet's newly introduced subscription system, which I had attacked in the Summer *Hudson Review*—wrote that "when Mr. Haggin is not riding hobby-horses about Toscanini, Balanchine or his fellow music critics [this from the man in whose writing Frederick Ashton is a King Charles's head] he can talk a lot of sense." But then he read my evaluation of his *Times* operation in the preceding article; and he read also in one of Robert Garis's superb articles on ballet in *Partisan Review* the comment that "since this gifted English critic began to write, and to write far too much, for the *New York Times*, much has been odd in his performances." And his reply to Garis and me was a Sunday article in November titled *Difficulties Facing the Aspiring Critic*, which opened with this Barnesian statement: "Even to write about dance badly can be, as I know from personal experience, an extraordinarily difficult thing." And to write about it well, it turned out, required the professionalism that was lacking in most of the writing on the subject. "Only two New York papers [*The Herald Tribune* was still in existence at that time] find it necessary to employ a professional [dance] critic." In the weeklies, monthlies or literary quarterlies, in which "one would hope to find criticism," one found either silence or

(and this is really worse) a drama critic, or music critic, or even some kind of cultural voyeur, occasionally waving his prejudices like tomahawks, and often trying to assess complete dance seasons on the basis of only a scattered handful of performances. At times it seems that their technical knowledge is minimal and their dance background underprivileged.

As against the music critic and the cultural voyeur the professionals were

people who have worked at dance criticism. They will have seen at least 1,000 and probably nearer 2,000 performances (for dance criticism, in the absence of written or mechanical records, is exclusively a pragmatic craft) . . . What differentiates [the professional] from his non-professional rival [sic] is simply that he has an enormously wide performance log in all branches of the art. The opinion of a man who is seeing "Swan Lake" for the first time might be interesting, but it will never be informed. Music critics are often perceptive but they rarely have the time, or for that matter the inclination, to acquire the right to *public*, as opposed to private, opinions.

But if dance criticism was a pragmatic craft, for which one qualified merely with the experience acquired by seeing a sufficient number of performances, then I certainly qualified in this way, and so did Garis. It was not, as he claimed, from our writing that Mr. Barnes got his idea of our underprivileged dance background; it was, characteristically, from his imagination, and in my case from his effrontery. Effrontery, since he knew from my *Brooklyn Eagle* statement—included in a collection of my criticism, *Music Observed*, which I had been told he had read—that I had begun to see Balanchine's ballets, and presumably those of other choreographers, as early as the last Diaghilev season; and he knew from other articles in the collection that I had continued to see Balanchine's and other choreographers' ballets to the present, and my writing on *Swan Lake* was not that of a man who had seen it for the first time. As for Garis, he had begun later than I, with Markova's and Danilova's performances in the early '40s; and as an occasional visitor to New York he had seen less than I, a New York critic who had attended several performances a week; but in twenty years he had seen enough to be able to write those articles in *Partisan Review*. This was evident in the articles; but the more important thing they revealed was that he was someone who saw what he looked at *now*—which brings us to the heart of the matter. Garis, that is, writing in 1968 about the new Balanchine ballet, *Metastaseis and Pithoprakta*, described the striking sequence near the end in which Mitchell began the motions of supporting Farrell in a *pas de deux* but actually didn't touch her; whereas in Mr. Barnes's several pieces of writing on the work this striking sequence went unmentioned. And this was one of the instances in which Garis, though he may have attended fewer than the 2,000 performances Mr. Barnes required, had the first essential of the critic's equipment: the eye that sees what it looks at—which Mr. Barnes with his 2,000 performances did not have. Moreover, as the statement about the Verdy-Magallanes duet in *Liebeslieder Walzer* that I discuss on page 105 demonstrated, even what the Barnes eye did see it often saw incorrectly. And what became evident in time was that his writing was largely an irresponsible chatter not about the actual happenings on the stage but about the inventions of his imagination.

One other thing. Mr. Barnes, in the spring of 1968, devoted a Sunday article to Lincoln Kirstein and a paperback reprint of three Kirstein pamphlets issued by Dance Horizons; and a year later he dealt in another Sunday article with John Martin and Dance Horizons' paperback reprints of Martin's books. On the second occasion he observed that "as a writer and, I suppose, as a critic, [Martin] has been overshadowed by . . . Edwin Denby, who happens to be the finest English-speaking dance critic of all time"—only to add characteristically "which, incidentally, is altogether less of a distinction than it sounds." More important, neither on this occasion nor on any other did Mr. Barnes reveal the fact that Denby's *Looking at the Dance*, long out of print, had been reissued by Horizon Press. I will hazard this guess at the reason for Mr. Barnes's silence about *Looking at the Dance:* the new edition had an introduction in

which I said Denby had not only an eye that could see but a discipline that resulted in his reader's seeing the dancer's performance, not a performance by Denby; and though as a guest speaker in Denby's book I didn't embarrass him by naming names, Mr. Barnes knew who I thought lacked this discipline. In any case his professed admiration for Denby begins to look very much like John Martin's for Balanchine; and with it Denby needs no enemies.

Winter 1967 What one has experienced in art conditions one's further experience; and the difficulty some of us have with much of the Royal Ballet or the Bolshoi or Ballet Theater is that we are looking at it with eyes which have seen Balanchine's ballets, and after these find nothing to interest them in MacMillan's *Romeo and Juliet*, Ashton's *Daphnis and Chloë*, Culberg's *Miss Julie* and *Moon Reindeer*, de Mille's *Fall River Legend* and more recent pieces of Americana, Glen Tetley's *Sargasso* and *Ricercare*. This was my difficulty in September with the Joffrey Ballet's first season as the new resident company of the New York City Center—my difficulty even with pieces like Robert Joffrey's own *Pas de Déesses* and *Gamelan*, Gerald Arpino's *Viva Vivaldi* and Gloria Contreras's *Moncayao I*, which were put together with skill and pleasant to look at, but which offered the little ingenuities of minor talent, as against the fascinating and exciting achievements of great creative power in Balanchine's works. And the difficulty was much greater with most of the other pieces—Arpino's *Incubus* and *Nightwings*, Contreras's *Vitalitas*, Loring's *These Three*—whose movements embodying dramatic ideas or generalized emotional turbulence ranged from uninteresting to awful. From this Joffrey-Arpino-Contreras repertory I got the impression of a semi-professional operation; and contrast of the professional was provided only by Balanchine's *Donizetti Variations* and Ruthanna Boris's *Cakewalk*. The supporting dancers did well in the Balanchine piece; but Susan Magno, who substituted for Stephania Lee, lacked the clarity and style which her solo part required, and Robert Blankshine, who replaced Luis Fuentes, lacked the physical stamina for his taxing part. *Cakewalk*, years ago, in the context of Balanchine's works, had been merely entertaining; but now, seeing it after *Vitalitas* and *Incubus*, I appreciated the solidly professional competence that had produced it. Moreover, it was a piece which the talented company seemed to enjoy doing most, and did best; and it gave me the most enjoyable moments of my evenings in City Center.

It seems clear that the Joffrey Ballet's major problem is that of all the other companies except the New York City Ballet: repertory, and more specifically ballets which can interest and impress people who have seen Balanchine's work. It seems clear also that the Joffrey Ballet is not getting such ballets from Joffrey, Arpino and Contreras—any more than the other companies are getting them from their more celebrated choreographers. But if, as it seems, Balanchine is friendly and co-operative, the solution of the problem is for the Joffrey Ballet to add further ballets of his to its repertory. Not, however, those that are in the current repertory of the New York City Ballet, in which the Joffrey Ballet shouldn't attempt to compete with that company. Rather, it should combine benefit to itself with a valuable service to the public by putting back on view certain great Balanchine works of the past that he is not interested in reviving himself. Clive Barnes suggested one— the *Divertimento* to Haieff's music, which certainly is worth having again; but I think of *Le Baiser de la Fée* and *Danses Concertantes*, which Frederic Franklin could restage, if necessary with the help of some of the dancers of the earlier productions; of *Card Game*, which Bolender and Reed should be able to reconstruct; even of *Cotillon*, which Lazovsky, Lichine, Riabouchinska and Toumanova might be able to reconstruct.

I would extend my suggestion beyond the Joffrey Ballet. The campaign, aided by foundation money, to promote the teaching of ballet throughout the country makes no sense unless there are companies that will employ the dancers when they have finished their studies; the companies have no chance of establishing themselves unless they can offer ballets which the people in their communities find worth paying to see; and these ballets are not likely to be provided by local choreographers. The solution is a universal repertory like that of music, which would make available to any company anywhere not only the classics of the distant past like *Swan Lake*, *The Sleeping Beauty*, *The Nutcracker* and *Giselle*, but the great contemporary ballets of Balanchine, modern classics like Fokine's *Les Sylphides*, *Firebird* and *Petrushka*, Massine's *Le Tricorne*, Ashton's *Façade* and *A Wedding Bouquet*, Tudor's *Lilac Garden*, and American classics like Christensen's *Filling Station*, Loring's *Billy the Kid*, de Mille's *Three Virgins and a Devil*, *Rodeo* and *The Frail Quarry*, Robbins's *Fancy Free* and *Afternoon of a Faun*.

Summer 1967 The one program of the National Ballet I saw, during its brief season at New York's City Center, offered Balanchine's *Serenade;* two pieces, *Danse Brillante* and *Homage*, effectively contrived in the Balanchine style by the company's director, Frederic Franklin; and Job Sanders's *Bachianas*, which was more modern dance than ballet, and uninteresting. The performances were good ones by a company with a well-trained *corps* and better female soloists than male—one girl, Andrea Vodehnal, being especially good. But in *Serenade* it was evident that the dancers were less strong than those of the New York City Ballet; and it seems to me, therefore, that instead of having his company perform the same Balanchine pieces as the New York City Ballet, which it cannot do as well, Franklin should revive for it the great works of the past that Balanchine is no longer interested in, such as *Danses Concertantes* and *Le Baiser de la Fée*.

Villella was reported to have said his ballet *Narkissos* represented no more than a desire to try his hand at choreography. And the result, produced by the New York City Ballet last fall, revealed some skill in contriving effective movements for his solos and his dances with

McBride and Michael Steele, but no ability to do as much for the *corps*, or to relate the passages for soloists and *corps* in the continuous, coherent progression of a ballet.

D'Amboise's *Prologue*, concerned with the characters of Shakespeare's *Othello* before the beginning of his play—with its dances characterizing the noble Othello, the exquisite Desdemona and the sinister Iago, excellently performed by Moncion, Paul and Prinz; its dances of the minor characters; its Elizabethan music; its rich costumes and set by Peter Larkin—added up to a Royal Ballet or Ballet Theater type of piece, somewhat better than theirs. And Taras's *La Guirlande de Campra*, taking its title from the undistinguished variations by contemporary French composers on a theme of the eighteenth-century composer Campra, offered competently made but undistinguished dances whose only interest was that of their execution by Verdy, Paul and some of the other dancers.

Balanchine's contributions began with *Ragtime*, a new setting of the 1918 Stravinsky piece. Clive Barnes objected in *The Times* that Balanchine had ignored the difference between what jazz meant to him in 1966 and what it had meant to Stravinsky in 1918; but to my eye and ear the difference was one between something living and something drained of life; and I enjoyed the living thing Balanchine produced around Stravinsky's desiccated skeleton. I also enjoyed Farrell's and Mitchell's dancing in it.

Next there were the new happenings Balanchine introduced in the Village Scene of *Don Quixote*: the knight's encounter with a group of vicious-looking beggars, ending absurdly in his dignified dancing with one of them; a gypsy dance beautifully performed by Farrell; a juggler's dance brilliantly performed by Paul Mejia.

And in April there was first *Trois Valses Romantiques* to Chabrier's music of that title, which Balanchine put together in place of a new Taras work that was postponed. It was pleasant but not of great consequence (for me there was the awareness that the setting of the third waltz was miles removed from the wonderful invention for this music in *Cotillon* years ago). And it left one unprepared for the marvelous three ballets of *Jewels*, which offered the operation of

Balanchine's amazingly undiminished powers in the terms of his personal dance vocabulary in all the variety it has acquired by now, but also in the terms of the individual styles of his dancers, and all these basically conditioned by the different styles of the music. Thus the first ballet, *Emeralds*, to music of Fauré, offered pieces devised for Verdy to enchant the eye with her aristocratic elegance in pose and movement—in the deployment of her body in supported turns and lifts, the inflection of her arms and hands (those lovely arms that Clive Barnes thinks are Hayden's). And it offered a solo for Paul to delight one with her special pointed-up elegant fluidity; an excitingly original *pas de deux* in which—powerfully held and guided by Moncion, in a manner reminiscent of the *pas de deux* of *Agon* and *Episodes*—Paul stepped about on her points. The third ballet, *Diamonds*, to parts of Tchaikovsky's Symphony No. 3, offered a long impassioned *pas de deux* for Farrell and d'Amboise, which exhibited her large, open, grand and breath-takingly beautiful movements; a fast scherzo for three girls in which Farrell and d'Amboise made brilliant solo appearances (and in which Balanchine inserted a little joke: a few peasant-dance-style arm movements of the girls, occasioned by a folksong-like phrase of the trombone); a finale for large ensemble, with further solo episodes for Farrell and d'Amboise, and a dazzling coda which attained grandeur with the majestic orchestral pronouncement that preceded the final stretto. Between these two ballets in pure classical style, *Rubies*, the most strikingly original and fascinating and exciting of the three, fitted to the perversely rhythmed fast movements of Stravinsky's Capriccio a perpetual motion—exhibiting among other things the exuberant and spectacular virtuosity of Villella—in the witty and amusing style, with borrowings from American show dancing, that Balanchine first devised thirty years ago for another Stravinsky neo-classical score, *Jeu de Cartes*. That style now had additions from the recent ballets to modern scores: the amusingly perverse inflections of body in the movements in which Villella, McBride, Neary and the *corps* disported themselves; the amusing episode in the first movement in which four boys, each grasping a hand or a foot of Neary, moved it now here, now there, as in the Concerto Op. 24 of *Episodes*; the dead-pan perversities of Neary and the *corps* that ended the movement. There were perverse twists and bends also in the *pas de deux* of the middle movement, in which Villella, again, held and guided McBride in the powerful manner reminiscent of *Agon* and *Episodes*.

I have had to try to give some idea of this latest Balanchine masterpiece; but I have done so only too aware of the correctness of a friend's exclamation after *Rubies:* "Indescribable!" *(184-195)*

As for dancers I saw in new roles, Farrell's charmingly idiosyncratic inflection of arms and hands didn't work well, to my eye, in *Bugaku*, where it made personal what should be ritualized. But her Sleepwalker in *La Sonnambula*, in which her arms were fixed in one position, was more effective. Verdy and Paul made distinguished contributions, in their different styles, to a *Serenade* I saw. Paul also was a lovely Sugar Plum Fairy in *The Nutcracker*, and was convincing in an *Afternoon of a Faun* in which it was a pleasure to see Moncion's powerful performance again. Kay Mazzo's pert face made her less believable in this piece; but she was superbly effective in the Concerto Op. 24 of *Episodes*. Prinz didn't have the physical power with which to make the effect in *Tarantella* that Villella does; but his elegance and clarity in a *pas de trois* in *Emeralds* were a pleasure to see; and in *Illuminations* his impressive performance included dance details I couldn't recall seeing years ago. *(147, 155)*

Fall 1967 It would have been wonderful to see on the stage the great things American Ballet Theater and the Royal Ballet did last spring in Clive Barnes's reviews in *The Times*. Ballet Theater's new *Swan Lake* was one. This was the complete four-act ballet, with the original Petipa and Ivanov choreography that Nicholas Sergeyev, a former *régisseur* at the Maryinsky Theater, reconstituted in 1934 for what was then the Vic-Wells Ballet, later be-

came the Sadler's Wells, and now is the Royal Ballet, which has itself replaced the Sergeyev with the revised version of Robert Helpmann. The Sergeyev original was reproduced for Ballet Theater—with a few revisions and additions—by the Royal Ballet's David Blair; and in Mr. Barnes's review this production now offered "the best version of the ballet anywhere to be found," and gave the company an additional role and purpose—of "bringing the best out of the past into American ballet." It was the best by virtue of Blair's staging, which gave it "its individual flair and special quality," and Oliver Smith's scenery and Freddy Wittop's costumes, which made it "a most properly sumptuous production." True, while it was the best staged in the world, it was not the best danced: the company hadn't performed it the 72 years the Kirov Ballet had had *Swan Lake* in its repertory, or even the 33 years the Royal Ballet had been dancing it; therefore it was "as much a promise as an achievement." But "the promise is bright." For though "the depths of the role [Odette-Odile] eluded her," Toni Lander "danced exceptionally well" in a portrayal that "was always stylish and clean"; Bruce Marks's "natural nobility [made] a strong impression as a slightly haughty and headstrong Prince," and "his dancing combined elegance with bravura"; and "the company as a whole has not looked in such good condition for many seasons."

I would have liked to see all this instead of what was done on the stage of the New York State Theater. The Sergeyev *Swan Lake* was what I saw the Sadler's Wells Ballet do here in 1949; but I didn't recognize it in what Ballet Theater did now. For one thing, the Sadler's Wells production did have sumptuous scenery in a style resembling that of the 19th-century Russian original; whereas the backdrop of Ballet Theater's Act 1 had what looked like an Osbert Lancaster spoof of Ludwig of Bavaria's Neuschwanstein; and the great hall of the palace in Act 3 looked like a big public room in a Broadway hotel. And in the Sadler's Wells performance the choreography was executed by the incandescent Margot Fonteyn and an impressive partner, by accomplished lesser soloists, and by the excellently trained and precise *corps*; whereas in the Ballet Theater performance Lander achieved what looked like a Beatrice Lillie spoof of the role, in which every swan-like quiver of arm and hand—and in fact every movement of whatever part of the body—was comic in effect; Marks danced well, but had no princely force of presence to go with his prince's costume; in the first-act *pas de trois* the fast turns were done at half-speed, and even then were too much for one of the girls, who had to be turned by the boy to the end of the turn she couldn't complete; and there was as little brilliance in the operation of the *corps*. In all, a dismal performance, with which *not* to introduce this great classic of the past to the American public. As I said last year when Ballet Theater presented Act 2 as the first instalment of this new *Swan Lake*: the company no longer has dancers of the magnitude of technique and style required to give this work its effect; and that means it isn't equipped for the great new role Mr. Barnes assigned to it.

Again, in the first scene of *Harbinger*, the new ballet by Eliot Feld, I saw a fresh dance vocabulary used unpredictably and effectively in the fast tempo of the second movement of Prokofiev's Piano Concerto No. 5; but the attempt to achieve such individual and effective invention in the slow tempo of the second scene was unsuccessful; and I remember only partial success in the remaining scenes. Even with these weaker scenes it was an impressive first work of a talented man; but it wasn't the *Harbinger* that was done in Mr. Barnes's review. In classic ballet, he said, this century had produced a few true originals—the last, perhaps, being Kenneth MacMillan, who in 1955 suddenly "exploded upon an unexpectant world. The explosion is all important. Choreographers are seldom born—they explode. One exploded last night. His name is Eliot Feld." And the audience, which seemingly always knows, had instantly known his *Harbinger* "for what it was—a new phase in American dance." The dancers too "knew what was happening— and danced accordingly. They went through the sweeps and flurls of Mr. Feld's fascinatingly original choreography as if it were a brave new world. I think it may well prove to be just that." The dancers also danced very well in the piece I saw; but I wish I had seen the one they danced in Mr. Barnes's review.

I wish too I had seen all the fascinating ballets of MacMillan that Mr. Barnes has written about instead of the boring ones presented in the theater. The great original in classic ballet of this century, George Balanchine, once said he had begun to do choreography "because I wanted to move people around"; and if one defines the choreographer's gift in terms of his statement, it is the ability to move dancers around in ways that are fascinating and exciting to see. This is the gift Balanchine clearly has, but MacMillan has never exhibited in the ballets I have seen. It was therefore an agreeable surprise to get, in the new *Concerto* presented by Ballet Theater, a manifestation of such skill in the moderately interesting movements MacMillan devised to go with the lively first movement of Shostakovich's Piano Concerto No. 2. But with the slow movement there were again only the usual strained-for ingenuities without visual interest; and in the finale the ingenuity achieved only bits of cuteness. And so I must again regret not having seen the *Concerto* Mr. Barnes wrote about, in which, throughout, there was the dancers' "playing an attractive and tender game with the music," and MacMillan's utilizing "space with unobtrusive craftsmanship and a constant eye-engaging contrast between diagonals and parallels of movement." But I can report that the dancers danced well in the piece I saw.

Ballet Theater's revivals included Tudor's *Undertow* and *Dark Elegies*; and feeling sure I would see not the masterpieces in Mr. Barnes's review but only the works I had seen twenty years ago and had stayed away from thereafter, I stayed away again. But Copland's score induced me to see de Mille's *Rodeo*—the one Mr. Barnes characterized correctly as "show-biz treacle," not the other one he described as de Mille's "best ballet, engagingly simple, winningly unpretentious." It was danced adequately, if not as well as I could remember: at the point in the second scene where the Champion Roper swings himself sideways into the air, alternately to the right and left, I recalled Frederic Franklin's extraordinary feat of giving the movements the appearance of effortless casualness, as against the impressively effortful accomplishment of something obviously very difficult that brought Edward Verso a storm of applause. As for other older works, the company that had looked painfully incompetent in *Swan Lake* gave a brilliant performance of Lander's *Etudes* with d'Antuono, Douglas and Young in the leading roles, and a fine one of Fokine's *Les Sylphides*, with Koesun outstanding in the Prelude and the *pas de deux*. But though the corps danced well in Balanchine's *Theme and Variations*, and Ted Kivitt executed his solos impressively, d'Antuono didn't have the elegance and style her role requires.

That leaves what—though I speak of them last, as something outside of the company's own operation—were the most distinguished artistic happenings of Ballet Theater's season: the guest appearances of Erik Bruhn. He brought with him young Carla Fracci of La Scala, with whom he danced first in a *Romeo and Juliet pas de deux* he had devised to music from the Prokofiev score, which served its purpose of exhibiting Bruhn mostly in impassioned rushes, but also in a few leaps and spins, breath-taking merely as physical movements, and ennobled by his unique elegance; and Fracci in supported turns and lifts in which—in part, perhaps, because of her tight hairdo and unbecoming gown—she didn't operate with comparable impressiveness. But *Giselle* provided her with the conditions and opportunities for a performance that was technically brilliant, plastically beautiful and expressively moving. As for Bruhn, his Albrecht overwhelmed one again with the brilliance and beauty of movement achieved with elegance of style that was overwhelming in the performances with Markova years ago; and whereas then it was the abundant power of youth that inevitably caused him to overshadow a Markova operating, however marvelously, with lessened reserves of strength, now it was the authority acquired in the years since then that caused him to overshadow young Fracci. *(197)*

Probably I was seeing the Ballet Theater *Giselle* for the first time since the performances of Markova and Bruhn; and I found the Berman scenery—even badly lighted—as distinguished as I had remembered it to be. Mr. Barnes, who finds Oliver Smith's crudely unimaginative Act 3 of *Swan Lake* "properly sumptuous," last year urged Ballet Theater to throw out the Berman *Giselle* and reinstate the pre-1948 Lucinda Ballard version, and this year rejoiced over the announcement of a new production next season that would replace the "pitiable" Berman scenery and costumes. In addition he used the occasion to say he *had*, in 1946, seen the Ballard *Giselle*, which I had said he could hardly have seen; but what is important is the perception and taste Mr. Barnes exhibited about what he saw; and if he didn't, as I thought, merely assume the Ballard *Giselle* must have been better than the Berman, but judged it to be better after seeing both, it means he looked at the Ballard with as little perception and taste as at the Berman.

As for the Royal Ballet, one of the things I would have liked to see was the MacMillan *Song of the Earth* about which Mr. Barnes wrote that MacMillan, "in what must surely be regarded as his best work to date, has been incredibly successful in catching the special mood of Mahler's farewell to earthly pleasures." For the piece I saw was an interminable succession of the usual MacMillan strained-for ingenuities without any visual interest in themselves and any relevance to the expressive connotations of Mahler's *Das Lied von der Erde*. And I would also have liked to see the *Shadowplay* of Tudor that justified for Mr. Barnes the ballet's triumph in London: the "strange and engrossing work" with "the look and feel of a major work," whose choreography concerned with "the realms of experience and the attainment of grace" was "beautifully apt and untroubledly imaginative." For the piece I saw was a by no means engrossing realization of the ballet's idea in terms suggested by the Kipling *Jungle Book* that had inspired the Koechlin music—with the boy's progress to grace a passing through experiences with monkey-like

Arboreals, a formidable male-seducer-like Terrestrial, a seductress-like Celestial.

The Ashton *Monotones* I saw seemed, for once, to be much the same as the piece done in Mr. Barnes's review: two *pas de trois,* as slight as the *Trois Gnossiennes* and *Trois Gymnopédies* of Satie to which they were danced, but more interesting to the eye than *Daphnis and Chloë* and Ashton's other recent large-scale works. And what turned out to be another exception to those boring works—one that was made engaging by the humorous touches of the mind that produced Ashton's early comic masterpieces, *Façade* and *A Wedding Bouquet*—was his *Midsummer Night's Dream* ballet, *The Dream,* which I hadn't seen during the company's previous visit. It made points—for example, with the solo of Bottom—which Balanchine in his version does not make, but did not make some which Balanchine does, notably with the solos and *pas de deux* of the lovers; and it achieved nothing like the moments of imaginative power and grandeur which make Balanchine's version the work of major stature that Ashton's is not. One other important difference must be noted: Ashton's cutting some of Mendelssohn's music into snippets that he repeated at intervals as *Leitmotiven,* as against Balanchine's skillful fitting of the profusion of choreographed action into the successive pieces of music in their entirety. And so it must again have been a different Ashton *Dream* than I saw that led Mr. Barnes—when comparing it with Balanchine's version—to see them demonstrating in "two of the greatest choreographers of our time" similarities not only in "their understanding of the choreographic idiom, their genius in giving almost every choreographic phrase an individual trademark," but in "their musicality."

I seem to have seen the same *Brandenburg Nos. 2 & 4* of John Cranko as the one Mr. Barnes characterized as a disaster. And the *Paradise Lost* of Roland Petit that struck him as thin and trivial probably was the one that struck me as *kitsch.* Mr. Barnes thought it showed Petit to be a master of the theater, but less of a master of choreography; but I found it to be *kitsch* contrived with a choreographer's

gift for visually arresting movement. Every bizarre or distorted movement of the Man, every acrobatic involvement of the Man and the Woman—unlike the elaborate ingenuities of MacMillan and Cranko—was something striking to the eye, which employed the capacities of Nureyev and Fonteyn with impressive effect.

These extraordinary capacities were better employed in *Swan Lake*—the new Helpmann revision, which may be less good than the original presented by Ballet Theater, but was made to look better by being danced better. Actually the anonymously choreographed meditative solo of the Prince added at the end of Act 1 is something beautifully imagined; and as executed by Nureyev with his tremendous contained power it provides one of the production's great moments. It did so again this time; but it was overshadowed by the great moments Fonteyn created with the bodily configurations in motion and pose whose beauty and perfection were achieved with an elegance—in the sense not only of grace but of economy—that caused "its effect upon the mind," as W. J. Turner said of a Mozart piece, to be "out of all proportion to its impingement on the senses." Nor was it only these two great dancers but the other soloists and the *corps* who were equal to what the work asked of them.

Fonteyn was not seen this time in what for me was her greatest performance—her Princess Aurora in *The Sleeping Beauty.* Of those who took over the role, I saw Antoinette Sibley, who had been outstanding among the dancers of the first-act *pas de quatre* in *Swan Lake* two years earlier, and who now achieved a secure and beautiful performance of Aurora. She was also a lovely Titania in *The Dream,* in which the company's most impressive young male dancer, Anthony Dowell, was Oberon. Another excellent young dancer, Donald MacLeary, was the Prince Florimund in *The Sleeping Beauty;* and Michael Coleman's exciting elevation made him a brilliant Blue Bird in his *pas de deux* with the charming Jennifer Penney.

I have left to the last the other great event for me—besides the Fonteyn-Nureyev performance of *Swan Lake*—in the Royal Ballet's season: the Bronislava Nijinska *Les Noces*, first produced by Diaghilev in 1923, performed here by the Ballet Russe de Monte Carlo in 1937 or 38, and now revived for the Royal Ballet by Nijinska herself, with scenery and costumes after the original designs of Natalie Gontcharova. I had wondered whether it would seem different after thirty years; but it proved to be as singular, powerful and moving now as in 1937. Nijinska produced nothing comparable in the ballets I saw after that; indeed it was hard to believe these diffuse and feeble works had come from the mind that had achieved *Les Noces*. And seeing it now made it clear that Robbins hadn't produced its equal either. A basic difference was that Nijinska elaborated her ritualistic *perpetuum mobile* out of recognizably Russian peasant movements, whereas he used his own vocabulary—the one he had used in the large-group orchestrations of *Age of Anxiety* and *West Side Story,* among others—with only occasional suggestions of Russian movements. This gave her piece authenticity and purity, as against the aura of Broadway around his version. And as the authenticity and purity were heightened by the context of nothing but the austere Gontcharova scenery, so the Broadway aura was heightened by the context of the modern grand pianos and percussion instruments with their performers in modern evening clothes, the chorus and the conductor at the back of the stage—this in accordance with Stravinsky's own original wish, but, it was now clear, a mistake.

Of the New York City Ballet's performances of Balanchine's *A Midsummer Night's Dream,* I saw one with a few new features—Lamont's Puck, which was very good, and a new wig of golden curls for Villella's Oberon, which was quite bad.

The film of the ballet that was shown once for the benefit of the New York City Ballet Fund was interesting in having provided Balanchine with the space in which to realize the scheme of Act 2 that he had been unable to realize in the theater. The act took place in an outdoor courtyard from which stairs ascended toward the back; and after their festive opening dance Theseus and his court withdrew to the sides and back, from where they watched the *divertissement* of the dancers. Also, the camera had made possible a few magical effects in Act 1 that are impossible on the stage. But to the degree that the dances were changed in deference to the conventions of the film, they suffered losses. Oberon's dance with the Fairies to Mendelssohn's Scherzo, for example, chopped into sequences that were seen now from one angle and now from another, lost the effect it has seen as a single progression in a fixed framed space in front of the spectator. Nor did it seem to me that the ballet gained anything with the enormous close-up views of faces that the camera made possible. Placing a camera in front of the stage and just photographing a stage performance wouldn't have produced a work of film art; but it would have produced a facsimile of the ballet valuable for people today and a hundred years from today unable to see it on the stage.

Spring 1968 One of the rare moments of truth in Clive Barnes's silly chatter about ballet in *The Times* was a statement about the Harkness Ballet after one of the performances of its first New York season at the Broadway Theater— that "it remains perhaps a company of splendid dancers in search of a splendid ballet." At the two performances I attended I did see splendid dancers—Elizabeth Carroll, Helgi Tomasson, Lawrence Rhodes, among others—but did not see them in even one splendid ballet. The one piece I found moderately enjoyable was *Zealous Variations* by the company's director, Brian Macdonald—a Balanchine-like dance ballet to music of Schubert; but Macdonald's invention in *Tchaikovsky* was much feebler; and the *Firebird* he devised for the entire 1910 Stravinsky score was appallingly bad. So were, in their different ways, de Mille's *Golden Age,* Butler's *Sebastian* and Alvin Ailey's *Feast of Ashes.*

Mrs. Rebekah Harkness seems to have had the idea, when she founded the company, that one needed only to assemble "choreographers, composers, designers and dancers" and provide a place for them to "participate in coordinated programs to create new works for the ballet stage," for works to result that would be as deserving of the public's attention as Balanchine's. One could have told her at the start that this result would be achieved only if her choreographers had powers of the magnitude of Balanchine's; and similarly, concerning her idea that her company would be giving young choreographers the opportunity for development that alone could produce additional Balanchines, one could have told her that the opportunity would produce this result only if it was given to people with initial gifts to develop like those Balanchine had started with. One could also have pointed out that there was no situation requiring this intervention of hers: not only were there established choreographers, a few gifted, most not, producing ballets for the existing companies, but they were being joined by young newcomers; and there was no reason to think we were losing the achievements of genius, old or young, for lack of the opportunities Mrs. Harkness was setting out to provide. One could have told her all this, and have predicted that her course of action would produce the dismal results that were exhibited at the Broadway Theater this year. But she doesn't seem to be someone whom this would have dissuaded from doing what she had decided to do.

New works by both established choreographers and young newcomers were presented in the two-week season at New York City Center that American Ballet Theater devoted to contemporary works. Tudor's *Echoing of Trumpets* was concerned with the suffering inflicted by brutal conquering soldiers on the women of a village devastated by war; and whereas for Clive Barnes the work presented "agony poetically realized" and was "Tudor at its greatest," for me its movements of brutal violence were nothing more than just that, and made the work one of Tudor's worst. In MacMillan's *Danses Concertantes*, a dance piece using the Stravinsky score, bits of cuteness were scattered throughout the uninteresting choreography produced by the mere ability to put movements together that made MacMillan a choreographer analogous to the composer with the mere ability to put sounds together. But far worse was his invention for the dramatic ballet *Las Hermanas*, with its clichés—for the tyrannical Spanish mother, the sex-starved oldest daughter, the sexually formidable seducer—that were laughable caricatures of themselves, its lurid sexual encounters, its incoherence that became farcical.

Young Eliot Feld, whose first ballet last year, *Harbinger*, was a dance piece with a lively first movement that was very good, this year offered one, *At Midnight*, with serious meaning—a meaning not derived from the Rückert songs of Mahler that it used. In the opening episode, to the song *At Midnight*, a half-naked man was manipulated by a group of other men in what could well have been the "[delineation of] the agony of man" that Clive Barnes took it to be; with the lovely song *Ich atmet' einen Lindenduft* came a *pas de deux*, apparently of two lovers; with the great song *Ich bin der Welt abhanden gekommen* a male dancer mooned about the stage in modern-dance-style movements which Barnes took to be those of the "alienated 20th century hero, the Outsider"; and with the repeated *Ich atmet' einen Lindenduft* the young couple reappeared, while not only the male dancer but a female dancer mooned about in those modern-dance movements, to show the "solitary poet . . . threading his way, comprehending an uncomprehending life, and constantly missing fulfillment with poetic grandeur." The *pas de deux* to the second song I found charming; the rest didn't work for me.

The Catherine Wheel, the first work for Ballet Theater of another of its young dancers, Michael Smuin, was for the most part a series of *pas de deux* strung on a dramatic idea taken from Schnitzler's *Reigen*; and for the most part the invention had freshness and was enjoyable to watch.

Last year it was the great performances of the great new production of *Swan Lake* which Barnes imagined he saw that gave Ballet Theater the role and purpose of "bringing the best out of the past into American ballet"; this year it was the fascinating new repertory and excellent dancers of the two-week season that established Ballet Theater, "for ten years or more the meek Number Two to New York City Ballet," as "now in its own right and in its own way a simply marvelous company." My eyes saw only the excellent dancers—among them Veronika Mlakar, Susan Casey, Christine Sarry, Eliot Feld, Edward Verso, Michael Smuin, William Glassman.

As for the New York City Ballet this season, I can report only on the first of Balanchine's new works, *Glinkiana*—four delightful fun pieces to music of Glinka, their humor added to by Esteban Francés, the only first-rate stage designer among those Balanchine works with nowadays. His single set framed four small backdrops which provided the four scenes for Balanchine's pieces: a French lower-class place of entertainment, for a piece, to Glinka's Polka, which poked fun at the kind of dance one would see there, and in which Verdy gave a marvelous take-off of the dancer who would perform it; a romantic scene, for a setting of Valse-Fantaisie in which Paul took one's breath away with her exquisitely pointed-up dancing, and a new young soloist, John Clifford, dazzled one with his quick and sharp but contained ebullience; a Spanish scene, for a piece, to *Jota Aragonesa*, which poked fun at the Spanish style, and in which Hayden's operation in that style was very funny; and finally another romantic scene, but this one with a statue of a rearing white horse that provided a comic counterpoint for the romantic *pas de deux*, to Divertimento Brillante on themes of Bellini, that McBride and Villella danced dead-pan. *(197)*

Summer 1968 What Balanchine says he did at the beginning—"I had learned to dance, to move; I loved music; and suddenly I wanted to move people to music, to arrange dances"—he has done ever since: he has simply moved people to music. On numerous occasions he has moved them to good music; and he has produced fascinating and exciting ballets to poor music or to what can scarcely be called music at all. The latest example of this is his *Metastaseis*

and Pithoprakta to the sounds put together by Iannis Xenakis, an extreme example of the writing in which my ears hear neither musical communication nor even mutual coherence. In *Metastaseis* Balanchine uses a large group of dancers in white tights who, when the curtain rises, are lying prostrate in a heap, but begin to stir, and soon are running about in a *perpetuum mobile* of ballet and acrobatic movements, until they collapse in a heap again. It is the kind of thing one has seen in the modern-style choreographies of others; and, as on earlier occasions, Balanchine seems to be demonstrating that what they do uninterestingly he can do interestingly. But it is in *Pithoprakta* that he gives us yet another example of his capacity for unending innovation in his own idiom. The piece begins with the spotlight picking out on the dark stage one group that begins to dance, then another, then one that includes Mitchell, naked to the waist, then another that includes Farrell in a costume suggesting a stripper. Later the small groups combine into a single large one; and after involvements with this large group the two principals have solos. Farrell's is like her long *perpetuum mobile* in *Variations*, with modifications that make it more sexy; Mitchell's astounds one with its shivery, disjointed, convulsive movements, and the character they create, which are unlike anything Balanchine has done before. And excitingly new too is what happens at the high point of the piece: Mitchell's shivering into position behind Farrell to begin the motions of supporting her in the movements of an adagio in which he actually doesn't touch and support her at all, until eventually he does grasp her hand in real support that continues to the point at which he releases her and shuffles and shivers his way slowly off the stage, while she sinks to her knees weaving her arms sinuously around her face as the curtain falls. *(200)*

After this operation of genius, the operation of mere competence in fitting movements to sounds: Taras's *Haydn Concerto*, to music that is a product not of Haydn's genius but of *his* mere competence. Such interest and attractiveness as the proceedings have is supplied by the dancers—Mazzo and Prinz in the Allegros, McBride partnered by Earle Sieveling in the

Adagio—whose contribution is limited by the blandness of what they are given to dance, and who operate under the additional handicap of the backdrop designed by Raoul Pène DuBois, a representation of a strongly patterned and colored inlaid table top or floor that is more compelling of attention than what is happening on the stage (with not a word of objection from Clive Barnes, who is so exacting about scenery, but apparently objects only to what is good, like the Berman *Giselle*).

The rest of this report is about dancers. A young member of the Royal Danish Ballet, Peter Martins, made a few guest appearances with the company, first in *The Nutcracker*. Golden-haired and handsome, he was not, in the performance I saw, the logical Cavalier for the dark, exotic and withdrawn Sugar Plum Fairy of Paul; but he partnered her skillfully in a style—of arms and hands—I found a little over-ornate, and danced his brief solo passage with unstraining brilliance. And his physical beauty was one of the strengths of a later performance in *Apollo* which, except for a few details, was superb. It exhibited numerous differences from what we have been seeing here—some of them merely differences in the style of dancing that Martins learned in Copenhagen; some of them actual changes in details of the choreography; and it was a few of these changed details that troubled me. Thus, in the *pas d'action*, instead of Apollo lifting Calliope and Polyhymnia and carrying them from the front of the stage to a point further back, he followed them as they walked to that point (it is hard to believe Martins lacked the necessary strength, but at the point in the coda where Calliope and Polyhymnia grasp Apollo's arms to be swung up in the air, he didn't swing them up very far). And at the end of Polyhymnia's solo, where Apollo rises for the striking movement in which his left hand grasps the thumb of his right, whose other fingers are extended, Martins lessened the effect of all this by remaining seated as he made the hand movement. On the other hand, he restored one effective detail: at the very end, where Apollo is pulling the muses toward the point where they will begin to walk toward Parnassus, Martins accompanied each pull with the flinging back of his free arm that used to be done by Eglevsky and Youskevitch, and that Balanchine evidently taught the first Danish dancer of the role in 1956 but didn't teach d'Amboise and Villella. Martins's guest appearances were reported to be a preliminary to his joining the company next year, which should add greatly to the brilliance of its operation. *(139–140)*

Meanwhile the company's own gifted young male soloists have been contributing to this brilliance in their new roles: Mejia in the finale of *Brahms-Schönberg Quartet*, the first episode of *Glinkiana*, the third movement of *Symphony in C*, the first *Pas de Trois* of *Agon*; Clifford in the second episode of *Glinkiana* and *Candy Canes* in *The Nutcracker*.

As for older dancers, Moncion, who years ago achieved a powerful *Melancholic Variation* in *The Four Temperaments*, this year looked as though he hadn't had enough rehearsal for mere security in the role (in any case I repeat my suggestion that he be given the *Phlegmatic Variation* to do). But much thought and thorough preparation were evident in the performance of the title role in *Don Quixote* that maintained, in its rich dramatic detail, a continuity of movement and tension and projective force from first moment to last. In this it presented an interesting contrast to Balanchine's own performance in the evening of the same day—one with wonderful moments when Balanchine was in action, but with discontinuities when he had nothing to do: whereas Moncion, at such times, stayed in character, involved even as he watched the others, Balanchine became an uninvolved spectator. Moreover, Balanchine, in action, sometimes improvised; and these improvised moments, though fascinating, broke the continuity that Moncion maintained unbroken in his succession of rehearsed details.

Of the female dancers, Marnee Morris exhibited her powers at a new high point of development in a number of new roles. Though in *Rubies* she wasn't as amusing as Neary in the eccentric movements Balanchine had devised expressly for Neary's physical appearance and dancing style, she made the movements amusing enough; and her secure and beautifully inflected fluidity achieved exciting performances in *Serenade*, the first movement of *Symphony in C, Divertimento No. 15* and the *Sanguinic Variation* of *The Four Temperaments*. In *Divertimento No. 15* tiny Schorer amazed one with the effect she gave to the variation in the Andante originally designed for long-legged LeClercq. And even more amazing was the new work that Verdy made of *Allegro Brillante* with the enchanting subtleties of her distinctive style.

One way in which it is distinctive is that it is so evidently a highly cultivated style. Art is something wrought; and every movement Verdy makes is beautifully, perfectly wrought. Nor does the long, patient work end there: it goes on to join each such movement to the next in a continuous flow that has the appearance of complete spontaneity. It was this continuous exquisitely inflected movement that Verdy produced in the long phrases of the second act of *Giselle*, in her two performances with the Boston Ballet (in Boston); and it would have made them great performances even without the additional distinguished contribution by Villella: the long flow of quiet, grief-laden movement of his entrance, its continuity wonderfully maintained in the dropping of his cloak and the turning of his head as he paused, the gathering up of his cloak as he went on; the power and grandeur of his leaps in his climactic solo. In addition there was the beautiful operation in their dancing together; the affecting acting in the final scene in which Giselle lifts the prostrate Albrecht and comforts him and then leaves him. It was a performance that should have been seen in an imaginative stage context, such as the wonderful one of Eugene Berman that Clive Barnes has been campaigning against; but its greatness and power triumphed over the actual nondescript and crudely lighted second-act set that Mr. Barnes pronounced effective. And nothing else could be faulted in the context provided by the Boston Ballet, which included the strong Myrtha of Anamarie Sarazin; the Hilarion of Warren Lynch, which was the best-acted I have ever seen; the lively first-act peasant *pas de deux* of Carol Ravich and Leo Guerard; and the good work of the *corps. (198–199)*

Mr. Barnes, let me add, used the occasion of a Bruhn-Fracci performance of *Giselle* in Houston to explain at last what he found wrong with the Berman set—that it was "a blue and personal vision of romanticism quite unsuitable for the naturalistic background demanded by 'Giselle.'" And this demonstrated what I had contended—that Mr. Barnes prefers chattering irresponsibly about what he imagines in his head to writing responsibly about what exists on the stage before him. For the supernatural second act of *Giselle* demands not a naturalistic background but precisely the romantic one of Berman about which I wrote, when Ballet Theater introduced it: "Not since Berman's décor and costumes for *Danses Concertantes* has there been anything so pictorially sumptuous and distinguished, and so dramatically active in its relation to everything that happens on the stage as...the grandly somber fore-curtain; the powerful décor of the 'tomb of Giselle amid the lonely cypresses'...; the costumes of the Wilis, with a film of black over the white, and green showing now and then underneath."

The Pennsylvania Ballet, which appeared for a week at New York's City Center, serves its Philadelphia public well in providing it with the opportunity to see Balanchine's *Concerto Barocco, Scotch Symphony* and *Pas de Dix* and Tudor's *Lilac Garden;* but it does that public a disservice in presenting among the works of other choreographers—such as Moncion's *Pastorale* and Robert Rodham's *Trio*, which are skillfully made and pleasant to look at—those of Butler, whose long series of talentless products attains a climax of sheer monstrosity in *Villon* and *Ceremony*. As for New York, the performances of the Balanchine and Tudor works by the company's moderately proficient dancers are nothing for the public that knows the works from the performances of the New York City Ballet and Ballet Theater; and while the City Center audience that yelled its approval of the Butler pieces would agree with the *Newsweek* writer who thought the company's New York visit was justified sufficiently by the world première of *Ceremony*, I disagree.

The Netherlands Dance Theater, which I was able to see only once at the City Center, has

94

dancers who are accomplished in the techniques of both classical ballet and modern dance; and it has choreographers who used them effectively in the three works I saw. Hans van Manen's *Dualis* began with ingeniously contrived movements in ballet idiom by a large group, then continued with modern-dance movements by a couple, which I found less interesting, as I did the later involvements of large group and couple. Job Sanders's *Impressions*—to Gunther Schuller's Seven Studies on Themes of Paul Klee, and taking Klee's paintings as points of departure—achieved humor, some of it obvious and corny, some subtle and fascinating. And very amusing was Benjamin Harkavy's *Pas de Deux* to music of Adolphe Adam—his idea of a virtuoso *pas de deux* of Adam's period, performed dead-pan by two excellent dancers, Marian Sarstadt and Gerard Lemaitre. The program ended with Tetley's *The Anatomy Lesson;* but having seen his *Sargasso* and *Ricercare,* I left this one unseen.

Fall 1968 Looking at Balanchine's work for the first time forty years ago, not with eyes made perceptive by the professional training of a dancer, but with those of a mere non-professional observer, I found what I looked at—*Apollo,* no less—bafflingly strange and obscure. But continuing to look in the years that followed, I found what I saw not only clear but extraordinarily, overwhelmingly beautiful and fascinating. And there was a point where it seemed to me that Balanchine's powers in the mere manipulating of his medium, the additional powers of imagination that he revealed in this manipulation, the inexhaustible fertility of his invention, its unending development and originality, his related powers in music and theater—all these made him a creative artist of the same magnitude as Picasso, and the only one of that magnitude not only in his own art but in any other.

This was in 1947, after he had produced several pure dance ballets—*Concerto Barocco, Ballet Imperial, Danses Concertantes, The Four Temperaments, Symphony in C.* And for people accustomed to ballets embodying a dramatic action, who complained that they found Balanchine's dance ballets meaningless, I made the point that classical ballet movements, like the sounds of music, could be used as a purely plastic medium in assemblages in which they were meaningless, but also in assemblages in which they communicated what Aldous Huxley had called "the eloquence of pure form"; and that Balanchine's dance ballets had provided some of my most exciting experiences of this eloquence. In their succession, I said, they were like the succession of Mozart's piano concertos, in which the same language and style were used to fill out the same formal scheme, but the objects produced were constantly new and fascinating, delighting one with the ever fresh play of mind and wit in the endlessly inventive manipulation of the medium.

What Balanchine has produced in the twenty years since then has done more than confirm that view of him as a creative artist: the new works have given me new perceptions of the nature of his operation and its magnitude. And it is seeing *Jewels* several times again last year—each time with new awareness of its marvels—that has intensified these perceptions and impels me to speak of them. For example the *pas de deux* in *Emeralds,* in which Paul enters, held and escorted by Moncion with grave ceremony, and makes delicate step after step on pointed toe to the *moderato* beats of the still Fauré music—at one point in the progression stepping away from Moncion's arching body and extended arm and hand, then back to them; at another point interrupting her stepping for a soaring extended lift, an arabesque, a turn, then resuming the stepping, with Moncion making similarly deliberate steps around her; and eventually leaving in the manner in which she entered. Nothing like it has ever been seen before; and one can say of it what W. J. Turner said of the Overture to *Figaro*—that "its effect upon the mind is out of all proportion to its impingement on the senses": in its simplicity and quiet it has a sustained tension which builds up a final impact as overwhelming as that of the progression of melody in the Andante of Mozart's Concerto K.467. *(189)*

And on the other hand, overwhelming again in its different powerfully dynamic style, the *pas de deux* of McBride and Villella in *Rubies*—"the goddamnedest *pas de deux* ever!", the young critic Harris Green exclaimed, characterizing correctly the intricate involvement of the two dancers in the seeming ultimate in newly imagined inflection of their bodies by sharp, perverse, grotesque thrusts, twists and bends, all contrived to work with, and heighten the effect of, Stravinsky's powerfully sculptured melody, and all fascinating and exciting to see. Again one must say there has been nothing like it before. *(192–193)*

But this is what one has had to say for forty years. The *pas de deux* of Apollo and Terpsichore in *Apollo*, the seduction *pas de deux* in *The Prodigal Son*, the *Hand of Fate pas de deux* in *Cotillon*, the three Themes and the *Sanguinic Variation* in *The Four Temperaments*, the second movements of *Concerto Barocco*, *Symphony in C*, *Symphonie Concertante* (this one a *pas de trois*), the *pas de deux* in the Haieff *Divertimento*, *Theme and Variations*, *Metamorphoses*, *Agon*, *Episodes*, *Liebeslieder Walzer*, *Bugaku*—about each of these one had to say nothing like it had been seen before. And it is not only about the *pas de deux* in these ballets that one had to say this.

It is not, of course, that distinctive, beautiful, witty, moving ballets haven't been created by other choreographers in those forty years: Massine's *Le Beau Danube*, *Gaîté Parisienne* and *Capriccio Espagnol*, Lichine's *Graduation Ball*, Tudor's *Lilac Garden*, Ashton's *Façade* and *A Wedding Bouquet*, Lew Christensen's *Filling Station*, Loring's *Billy the Kid*, de Mille's *Three Virgins and a Devil* and *Tally-Ho* (now *Frail Quarry*), Herbert Ross's *Caprichos*, Robbins's *Fancy Free*, *Afternoon of a Faun* and *Les Noces*. It is rather that no one else has exhibited even in one work imaginative invention of the magnitude Balanchine has achieved in the unending succession of his ballets.

"I began to move people to music," Balanchine said once of his beginning as a choreographer; and moving people to music is of course what every choreographer does. It is what Ashton—whom Clive Barnes chooses to place with Balanchine as the other of the two great choreographers of our time—did when he made his dance ballet *Symphonic Variations*: he moved the six dancers to the music of Franck's piece for piano and orchestra. But the feeble and inane and boring things one saw those dancers of the Royal Ballet do in *Symphonic Variations* last spring, as against the things one saw the dancers do in Balanchine's *Jewels*, made it clear that moving dancers to music is not the same operation with Balanchine as it is with Ashton. With Ashton there is the music, there are the dancers, and he thinks up what seem to him effective movements for the dancers to make to the music, taking into account what he knows this dancer does and that one does not do well. On the other hand, Balanchine's quoted statement, "I always tailor my work for a person, for a body that moves," as amplified by what others have reported in conversation, indicates that he has with a dancer's body the kind of intuitive perception that some people have with an unknown person's handwriting. These people perceive in the handwriting the personal characteristics of the unknown writer; Balanchine perceives in the body its characteristics and possibilities in dance movement; and these set his imagination in operation to produce new invention—movements which achieve the twofold result of adding to the meaning and effect of the music they are done to, at the same time as they realize those characteristics and possibilities of the dancer in the fascinating new dance character presented to our eyes on the stage. Nor is this something Balanchine does only with his principal dancers—with Paul and Moncion in the *pas de deux* of *Emeralds*, with McBride and Villella in the *pas de deux* of *Rubies* and in *Tarantella*, with Farrell in her extraordinary solo with shepherdess's staff in the first act of *Don Quixote*. He did it in the second act of *Don Quixote* with a boy in the *corps*, John Prinz, in whom he perceived the possibilities of the dance character he made of Prinz in the *Pas de Deux Mauresque* in folk-dance style with Schorer. *(180)*

With this as Balanchine's manner of creative

operation, and with *Jewels* and the other marvels as what this operation produces, one realizes what uncomprehending nonsense Clive Barnes wrote (his "Declaration of Love" in the program of the New York State Theater prompted the thought that with Mr. Barnes's love Balanchine needed no enemies) when he concluded an appreciation of the company's achievements last December with the statement that in female dancers "the company lacks strength at the top" because of its stress on youth that "is getting more and more damaging as time continues." Specifically, with Kent absent, the company's only experienced older dancers were Hayden and Verdy; and young Paul, McBride and Farrell "are not yet mature enough to lead a ballet company." The statement was applicable to the kind of company the New York City Ballet is not: one whose repertory includes the great classics—*Giselle, The Sleeping Beauty, Swan Lake*—to which its experienced older leading dancers impart an effect that its inexperienced young dancers cannot impart (though I must point out that Paul and Farrell are impressively effective in Balanchine's second act of *Swan Lake*). It is not applicable to the New York City Ballet, whose repertory is largely the works Balanchine has tailored for the particular capacities and styles of his dancers—today the capacities and styles of Paul, Farrell and McBride in addition to Verdy and Hayden. Maturity has no relevance in this situation: Balanchine wants precisely what Paul and Farrell can do, and what they do perfectly and with marvelous effect, right now. (A difficulty arises sometimes when what he tailored for one dancer must be danced by another: *Tarantella* lost a great deal when Prinz danced in place of Villella; *Liebeslieder Walzer* did when Leland danced in place of Verdy; but on the other hand Mazzo did superbly in place of Paul in this ballet and in *Emeralds*.)

But this was not the first piece of uncomprehending nonsense from Mr. Barnes; and it was not the last. In a later piece about the differences between the Royal Ballet and the New York City Ballet and the reasons for them, Mr. Barnes chattered on about everything but the all-important essential: that the Royal Ballet does not have, and the New York City Ballet does have, the towering creative genius in the arts today producing its repertory.

Whatever the Balanchine eye has seen—American show dancing, modern dance, Scotch dancing, Japanese dancing—has turned up in his ballets. In 1936 he demonstrated in *On Your Toes* that he could use the American show idiom more effectively than most Americans; and last spring he demonstrated that he could go back to that idiom of thirty years ago and use it again with delightful effect in a new version of the famous *Slaughter on Tenth Avenue* in that show. In certain ways it was even better this time because he had not only Farrell dancing the Strip-Tease Girl but members of the New York City Ballet *corps* doing movements he couldn't ask the "boys and girls" of *On Your Toes* to do. But Mitchell's style in this kind of dancing was not as effective as Ray Bolger's in the part of the Hoofer. (200)

To the program that included the première of this piece Balanchine added the only performance of *Requiem Canticles*, an arrangement of movement to Stravinsky's recent piece with that title, in memory of Martin Luther King. There have been occasions when music by Stravinsky or Webern that was expressively communicative for Balanchine was noncommunicative for me but the movements he contrived to go with it were fascinating to look at. But this time the movements of the white-veiled figures in changing formations, now holding candelabra, now placing them on the stage and stepping among them, now raising them in homage to the Negro in purple and silver who was lifted high above them, while at intervals a single unveiled female dancer moved among them across the stage—the first time pausing here and there in an *arabesque*, the last time a figure of mourning—all this, which undoubtedly represented deep feeling for the occasion in Balanchine, presented to the eye nothing that I found moving or that even had the distinctive impress of his mind to make it interesting.

The other new repertory piece was young

Clifford's *Stravinsky: Symphony in C*, whose choreography exhibited a liveliness related to his quick, sharp, light-footed, but contained ebullience as a dancer. His best invention, in fact, was the lively activity in the fast movements of the Stravinsky piece: the slow movements of the Larghetto were not very interesting. That lively activity in the fast movements showed that he had seen Balanchine's work; but it included original and effective details which revealed that he had an individual and inventive mind of his own. That someone might find it slight and uninteresting was certainly possible; but that this inoffensive piece should be characterized as "a choreographic monster" in almost a full *Times* column of excoriation— and this by a critic who had pronounced a real choreographic monstrosity, Butler's *Ceremony*, a great work, and to whom a moderately interesting first ballet by another young dancer, Feld's *Harbinger*, had signalized the explosive advent of a major choreographer—this was astoundingly excessive, and demonstrated the extreme of irresponsibility attained in the throwing of words around that is Mr. Barnes's operation as a critic.

Of major importance was Kent's return to enchant the eye again with the exquisite delicacy in *Scotch Symphony* and *Serenade* that exhibits impressive tensile strength in *Bugaku*, and to do this also in several new roles—Valse-Fantaisie in *Glinkiana, Pas de Deux and Divertissement*, the final Bach-Webern Ricercare in *Episodes*. Verdy, appearing in *Ballet Imperial* the first time here, enriched and pointed up the movements excitingly with the subtle inflections of phrase and rhythm and the accentuations of her highly individual style. Farrell was fascinating to watch doing the Siren's movements in *Prodigal Son* so effortlessly and beautifully; but I was disconcerted by her face, to which not a speck of make-up had been applied to change it into the face of the Siren. In addition to the Paul roles in *Emeralds* and *Liebeslieder Walzer* Mazzo took on Concerto Op. 24 in *Episodes*, giving it an impress of her own in a superb performance, and was charming in the second *Pas de Trois* of *Agon*. And Schorer, not a satisfying replacement for Sumner in the *pas de trois* with Leland and Prinz in *Emeralds*, op-

erated impressively with Villella in the third movement of *Brahms-Schönberg Quartet*.

I might not have been disconcerted by Farrell's innocent face in *Prodigal Son* if I hadn't remembered what Yvonne Mounsey had been made to look like. And quite possibly I would be affected as others have been by Villella's performance, and in particular his miming of the Prodigal's anguish, in the scenes after his despoilment, if I didn't retain the image of Moncion in those scenes: in the first, the long progression of movement with a continuity and tension unbroken from the moment he began to sink to the ground to the moment when he dragged himself into the wings; in both, the impassive face that worked so powerfully as a dramatic mask. But in *Bugaku* it is the image of Villella's own early performances that keeps me from accepting what he does now. Discussing Kent's performance in this ballet, in a superb article for *Partisan Review* on the company's dancers, Robert Garis speaks of how unemphatically she achieves the breath-taking security of her difficult balances and extensions; and Villella was similarly unemphatic in what he did in the early performances, executing his movements with a quiet elegance that gave him a princely dignity and grace. And having seen them done that way, my eye now rejects the italicizing that makes them heavy, violent, angry—and out of key with what Kent continues to do.

After Balanchine's version of *The Nutcracker* —his wonderful realization of a 19th-century Christmas party and of the imagined world of a dreaming child—it would have been difficult to accept "a child's vision distorted by Freudian spectacles," as someone characterized the new Nureyev version presented by the Royal Ballet, even if this distorted vision had been realized interestingly on the stage. But it was not: for example, the strange idea of having Herr Drosselmeyer, mimed by Nureyev, turn into the Prince of Clara's dream, danced by Nureyev, didn't justify itself by anything done by Drosselmeyer that would account for his becoming the Prince in Clara's dream, or even by an effective miming of Drosselmeyer by Nureyev. And what was true of the changed dramatic action was true of some of the new dances—notably the comedy skit in the place of the *Danse Arabe*. But the *pas de trois* in place of the *Danse des Mirlitons* was fine, as was the climactic *pas de deux* of Clara and her Prince. The few good dances were the only successes of Nureyev the choregrapher; and they were enhanced by the performances—among them the excellent one of the *pas de trois* by Carole Hill, Lesley Collier and Wayne Sleep, and the dazzling one of the *pas de deux* by Merle Park and Nureyev.

His other offering as a choreographer was an effective staging of Act 4 of Petipa's *La Bayadère*, which the Kirov Ballet did here a few years ago. What made it excitingly effective the night I saw it was the performance: the beautifully precise execution of the famous slow entrance of the *corps* at the beginning, the excellent dancing of the lesser soloists, Monica Mason, Georgina Parkinson and Deanne Bergsma, all framing what was central—the bravura dancing of Nureyev, overwhelming one with its visible contained power; and the dancing of Fonteyn, exhibiting not the slightest lessening of the beauty of bodily configuration in movement and pose that she achieved with her quiet elegance.

Postscript 1970 In the fall of 1969 Mr. Barnes, not one to allow a contradiction of a pontifical pronouncement of his to go unanswered, repeated his nonsense about the New York City Ballet's mistaken stress on youth. Melissa Hayden's twentieth year with the company provided the occasion for a Barnesian fantasy about an imagined Hayden who from the first had seemed "born to be a straightforward classic ballerina," who in fact "became a great ballerina, as did Margot Fonteyn, the hard and gradual way," and who, if the New York City Ballet were "organized to have a Queen Bee prima ballerina at its head . . . would be [its] Queen Bee." The company was "dominated by youth—but Melissa Hayden is its greatest dancer. Youth is not an important quality in ballet . . . a good mature dancer is almost certainly better than a good teen-age dancer of the all too sudden moment." But the actual Hayden one saw on the stage was not the company's only mature dancer: it had also Kent and Verdy, who

exhibited in classical dancing the exquisite fluidity, elegance and distinguished style that the actual Hayden didn't have. Also, if Balanchine had concentrated his attention on the young dancers—Mimi Paul, Suzanne Farrell, and now Gelsey Kirkland—it was not just because they were young but because they too had extraordinary elegance and individual style in classical dancing; and the performances in classical roles by these young dancers with elegance and style were excitingly beautiful experiences that one was right in preferring to the technically proficient but stylistically crude and at times hammed-up performances of the mature dancer without them. And finally, these young dancers with their elegance and style had nothing to learn from the mature dancer without them; whereas Villella, talking about Verdy once, had spoken of how the younger dancers had learned by watching her; and when Balanchine, in the fall of 1968, had wanted to teach Prinz how to dance with a ballerina in a classical *pas de deux*, it had been Verdy, not Hayden, whom he had chosen for Prinz to learn to dance with in *La Source*. On the stage of the New York State Theater, as against Mr. Barnes's writing, it was Verdy who exhibited the matured art in classical dancing that made her the company's greatest dancer and the peer of Fonteyn.

Spring 1969 Not announced in the New York City Ballet's advance prospectus and schedule last fall, and slipped into three programs of a November week-end, was a new Balanchine *pas de deux* to music from Delibes's *La Source*. I was fortunate to be able to watch most of the pre-season rehearsals at which Balanchine devised the dance movements that as usual were beautifully suited both to the charmingly melodious dance music and to the particular dancers he was using—on the one hand the experienced Verdy, on the other hand the gifted young Prinz, for whom the piece was to serve in addition as material with which to learn increased elegance of style as soloist and skill as partner in a classical *pas de deux*. (This meant that I too learned something about what elegance of style in classical dancing and skill as a partner in a classical *pas de deux* involved; and the learning included the fascinating experience of seeing the details of elegant movement and skillful partnering demonstrated by the extraordinary practitioner of ballet movement and master of elegant style in this movement that Balanchine is himself. For years I have watched him do a movement he devised for a dancer more beautifully than the dancer for whom it was devised.) But I was unable to see the unpredictably scheduled last rehearsals of the two weeks before the first performance. And so there was on that occasion the surprise and pleasure of seeing Prinz execute with assurance and ease what I had last seen him still working at. But what was overwhelming was to see the movements Verdy had done with her exquisite perfection at rehearsals now done with additional excitingly beautiful inflections of toe and hand and subtleties of rhythm and accent—the idiosyncratic breath-taking elegances of style that distinguish her performance in the Tchaikovsky *Pas de Deux* or the first movement of *Symphony in C* from those of other fine dancers, and made *Allegro Brillante* and *Ballet Imperial* look like different works when she appeared in them after those others.

The new *La Source pas de deux* was unusual in structure: instead of the customary sequence of initial supported adagio, brilliant solo for each dancer, and brilliant coda for the two, it offered first solos by Prinz and Verdy, then their supported adagio, again a solo by each, and then a final waltz by the two. Even with a couple of brief musical interludes (which broke continuity) the sequence was so taxing that at the third performance Balanchine made a cut in the final waltz; and I expect to see changes when it is done again.

As special in his way as Verdy in hers was the young Danish dancer Peter Martins, who had made a few guest appearances with the company the previous year and was allowed by the Royal Danish Ballet to spend the entire season with it this year. What was special—in the first movement of *Symphony in C* with Verdy, in *Diamonds* and *Liebeslieder Walzer* with Farrell, in *The Nutcracker* with Farrell, then with

Kent, and in *Apollo*—was the quiet, unassertive manner of the operation that was at all times extraordinary, whether in the physical and the personal grace of his attentive and secure partnering, or in the elegant precision of his unstraining execution of brilliant technical feats (made possible by reserves of physical strength). With the beauty of movement there was the golden-haired beauty of physical appearance; and together they gave an impression of beauty of spirit that ennobled the performances. *(194, 139–140)*

Substituting for Hayden, who in the *Jota Aragonesa* of *Glinkiana* had participated in its parodying of Spanish style, Farrell danced in straight ballet style which had no relation to the parodistic context. But her clarity and suppleness and ease produced the most beautiful *Sanguinic Variation* I can recall, in *The Four Temperaments* which also offered Sumner's superb Third Theme, and in which Moncion was powerful in presence and movement, but not phlegmatic, in the *Phlegmatic Variation*, Clifford was sharp and vivid, but not melancholy, in the *Melancholic Variation*, and Renée Estopinal was rather bland in the *Choleric Variation*.

I found the Fracci-Bruhn *Giselle*, in American Ballet Theater's season at the Brooklyn Academy of Music, even more impressive and affecting than two years ago. Fracci seemed to have added projective force to her exquisite dancing and expressive acting, and Bruhn to have increased the grandeur of his powerfully sculptured movements in the air, the authority and force of presence that enabled him to achieve so much with so little in his miming. I speak of the Fracci-Bruhn *Giselle*, because I imagine it is in its essentials a constant which in non-essentials is adapted to the various productions in which it is presented. This time it was the new Ballet Theater production that was first shown at Lincoln Center last summer; and reading Clive Barnes's review of it at that time I was struck by the fact that although he had looked forward to it because it would eliminate the Berman scenery and costumes of the old one, he did not write a word about the new Oliver Smith scenery and Peter Hall costumes. And when, in December, I saw how mediocre and tasteless they were, this didn't explain why Mr. Barnes hadn't described invented excellences, as he had done in the case of Smith's scenery for *Swan Lake*. But he did, last summer, write his approval of David Blair's new staging; and my opinion is that it was a mistake for Blair to clutter up the early part of the first act with new details to make more realistic and plausible a dramatic situation which is basically so unbelievable—that the better procedure is to treat the action as the excuse it is for the dancing, and to cut it down to the absolute essentials required to connect one dance with the next. But I compliment Blair for one innovation: having the Prince's party resume the hunt, from which it is recalled by Hilarion's blowing of Albrecht's horn. *(197)*

Fracci was charming, and Bruhn revealed that his dramatic gift extended to comedy, in the first two acts of *Coppélia;* and their climactic classical *pas de deux* in the last act was breath-taking. This addition to Ballet Theater's repertory was staged well by Enrique Martinez, with adequate scenery and costumes by William Pitkin.

What effect these two classics had with other principals than Fracci and Bruhn I cannot report. But I did see Michael Smuin's new *Gartenfest,* which offered a no more than competent fitting of ballet movements to a minor Mozart piece. And I saw Smuin's excellent performance in the title role of *Billy the Kid,* with Koesun's lovely performance in the *pas de deux* that is the high point of this American classic.

For lack of space I must defer comment on a highly important book, Edwin Denby's *Looking at the Dance,* the collection of his reviews and articles published in 1948 and now reissued,* except to say that it takes its place beside the theater reviews in Stark Young's *Immortal Shadows* and the reviews of music in Bernard Shaw's *Music in London* as the great and unique classic in its field, with its writing that is like theirs in its accuracy of critical perception and its discipline, and that is not only as illuminating today as twenty years ago, but

*Looking at the Dance, by Edwin Denby. Horizon Press.

provides today the necessary corrective to other writing that it did then. (Someone quoted to me recently a line in a routine of the entertainer Phyllis Diller about the food she had had in a Japanese restaurant, which seems to me to provide the suitable term for Clive Barnes's writing: "It was the *chic*-est garbage!")

The sustained perceptive observation and comment in Robert Garis's marvelous article on the great dancers of the New York City Ballet in a recent issue of *Partisan Review* is something no one should miss.

Summer 1969 I was able to see only one program of the Harkness Ballet, with three new works. Benjamin Harkavy's *Grand Pas Espagnol* offered, with music by Moszkowski, a feeble use of Spanish style that made the dancers look embarrassingly foolish; Rudi von Dantzig's *Moments,* unlike Balanchine's *Episodes,* presented nothing of interest in its movements to go with the fragmentary and, for me, meaningless Webern music; Butler's *After Eden,* to music by Lee Hoiby, was yet another of the assemblages of straining contortions that he devises in endless profusion for the hapless dancers. The program ended with a piece originally in the repertory of the New York City Ballet, Bolender's *Souvenirs,* to engaging early music by Barber— its humorous points much too heavily italicized in the performance it got this time. To judge from this one program, the Harkness Ballet is still what Clive Barnes described in one of his rare moments of accurate perception: "a company of splendid dancers in search of a splendid ballet"—such splendid dancers as Elizabeth Carroll, Helgi Tomasson and Lawrence Rhodes, whom one regrets seeing in the mostly feeble or awful ballets of the company's repertory.

Balanchine's emergency method of dealing with the excessive physical demands which the six consecutive numbers of the new *pas de deux, La Source,* made on Verdy and Prinz was to end the work abruptly about half-way through the concluding waltz, which was disconcerting to both ear and eye. I expected him to try other methods; and when the piece was given a few weeks later it was combined with three numbers from the earlier *Pas de Deux and Divertissement* danced by Schorer and a group of girls. One of these gave Verdy and Prinz a rest before their second solos and waltz; but this wasn't enough to enable them to do the entire waltz and then the finale of the earlier ballet; and so the waltz still had the damaging cut.*

The other new works of the winter season were d'Amboise's *Tchaikovsky Suite*, to the Suite No. 2 for orchestra, and Clifford's *Fantasies*, to Vaughan Williams's *Fantasia on a Theme of Thomas Tallis*. It is inevitable that d'Amboise should, as a choreographer, think in the language of Balanchine he learned as a dancer; and all one can ask is that he achieve something good of his own with that language. This time he has done so—not all the time, but in the outer fast movements of the work, and especially the first, with its exciting invention superbly contrived for the powers of a satanic-looking Prinz and for the lovely style of Morris. (It isn't only the general Balanchine language that he uses here, but the peasant-style arm movements of Prinz in Balanchine's wonderful *Pas de Deux Mauresque* in *Don Quixote*.) The finale also is good, though a little arch and cute. But what d'Amboise contrives for the slow middle movement—danced by Kent and Moncion in alternation with Mazzo and Blum—is less effective and convincing.

Clifford, in *Fantasies*, uses the Balanchine idiom in a way that Balanchine usually does not—which is to say, in a ballet with an idea. It is an idea of the kind Tudor is concerned with—the contrast between dream and reality in love; and Clifford's skillful invention for the two couples in his piece—Mazzo and Ludlow, Leland and Blum—includes Tudor-like details; but the result is a much more interesting piece than those Tudor has done since *Lilac Garden*.

Then there were the earlier Balanchine works with new dancers: *Divertimento No. 15*, with Farrell (in the absence of Hayden) adding her seemingly effortless flow of supple movement to the beautiful contributions of Morris,

Schorer, Sumner, Leland and Blum—the result being realizations of the variation movement and the Adagio that had one spellbound; *Allegro Brillante*, given a new look by Kent's exquisitely delicate movements; *Swan Lake*, with Peter Martins not only a superb partner for McBride but moving one with his dramatic expressiveness; *Ballet Imperial*, with Martins again a superb partner for dazzling Verdy, and executing his feats of virtuosity with his contained power and elegance. And though I had seen *Firebird* made exciting by Verdy's extraordinary make-up and performance several times before, there were this year what looked like new details—new plungings of arms, new stabbings of legs, new intensities in other movements—that were evidence not just of her remarkable powers of technique, style and imagination, but of her unending work to produce their continuing development.

Fall 1969 Several years ago, when it looked as if Violette Verdy would be making her home in London, she made a number of appearances with the Royal Ballet. If she had stayed in London and become a full-time member of the company, I think there would have been recognition by press and public there of the style that was as excitingly individual as Margot Fonteyn's, the technique that was as impressively brilliant, elegant and secure, the authority that was as regal; and recognition of the total Verdy operation as that of a dancer of the same magnitude as Fonteyn—which is to say, of one of the greatest dancers of our time. What was recognized in London would have been reported here; and this would have led the American press and public, when she appeared here with the Royal Ballet, to give her the attention and response Fonteyn gets, or if she returned to the New York City Ballet, to give her the superlatives and roars of approval that go to Melissa Hayden.

I am impelled to these observations by Verdy's performances last spring, beginning with the *Giselle* with Villella in Boston, where they had done the work together for the first time a year earlier. This time they operated, individ-

---

*Balanchine finally omitted the entire waltz.

ually and together, even more beautifully and effectively; and Verdy had me wondering at times whether I really *was* seeing the marvels I thought I was seeing. One such marvel was the slow movement around Albrecht, in Act 2, with which Giselle makes him aware of her incorporeal presence, and in which one saw the exquisite changing configuration of Verdy's pointed toes, legs, torso, head, arms and hands completed in breathtaking fashion by her fingers—those Verdy fingers that seem to be activated by intelligences of their own which keep their movements in constant fascinating relation with those of the rest of her body. (It was a shock, after this, to see Fonteyn's lovely movement, at the same point in *Giselle*, end in an extended hand whose fingers were motionless.) And in addition to such marvels of dancing there were those of Verdy's acting, of which my memory recalls most vividly the utter desolation on the face she raised after her collapse at the disclosure of Albrecht's deception. *(201–209)*

This year again the Boston Ballet provided Verdy's and Villella's great performances with an admirable context: the strongly danced Myrtha of Anamarie Sarazin, the believable Hilarion of Warren Lynch, the acceptable first-act *pas de deux* of Robin Adair and David Drummond, the excellent Wilis of the *corps*. But Balanchine's *Pas de Dix* demands virtuoso-caliber technique and stamina which not even the two principal dancers in the Boston Ballet's performance had. One discovers that while Balanchine's ballets are what ballet companies throughout the country need to win the interest of the public, they are enormously difficult works which most of these companies are unable to perform well enough for the public to become interested.

With the New York City Ballet, later, Verdy was given her first opportunity to dance in Balanchine's *Raymonda Variations*, and demonstrated that she was the one who should have danced in it from the beginning. For, as in other instances—*Allegro Brillante, Ballet Imperial,* Tchaikovsky *Pas de Deux*—the idiosyncratic inflections and accentuations of her style gave the movements a new look that was enchanting. They did the same thing in the second-act *divertissement* of Balanchine's *A Midsummer Night's Dream* a few nights after Kent had danced in it with her exquisite delicacy. And also in *Swan Lake*, in which Verdy's performance this time attained new heights in response to the superb partnering of Peter Martins and the embodiment of Prince Siegfried that was made extraordinary not only by his princely physical beauty, the intensity of his ardor and, at the end, of his grief, but by the joyous, delighted fascination with which he gazed at Odette in their early encounters—a dramatic stroke I cannot recall seeing in any previous performance.

In addition Martins danced for the first time in *Divertimento No. 15*, adding to its beauty and effect throughout with his unassertive grace, but especially in his second-movement variation with the unstraining, elegant execution of its bravura feats. And his single performance in *Apollo* calls for mention because it was even more beautiful and moving than his previous ones, and because in spite of this it was his only one of the season. Why this was so, and why Balanchine had the season's other *Apollos* disfigured by the monstrous embodiment of d'Amboise's distorted idea of what a Greek god should look and move like, I can't imagine. Nor, I might add, why there has been no *Apollo* with Villella for several years; and none with Ludlow, whose performance, taught to him by Lew Christensen, had the extra value of its accuracy in addition to its beauty.

If Villella were unwise enough to give Balanchine an ultimatum on the issue of *Apollo*, and, when Balanchine didn't yield on the issue, were to leave the company, Balanchine would have to put another dancer into Villella's role in *Rubies*, and this dancer presumably would be able to do the steps. But since these steps were contrived for Villella's individual capacities and style as a dancer, and even his personal characteristics,° another dancer, though he had the technique and stamina to do the steps, would

° It is amazing how Balanchine, seemingly unaware of anything in Villella but a body with capacities for dance movement, should reveal the extraordinary perceptions of Villella as a person that one sees in *Tarantella* and *Rubies*.

not give them the appearance and effect they had when Villella did them. And a reviewer who wrote that this dancer's performance was preferable to Villella's would be someone with eyes that managed not to see what was happening on the stage, and to see instead what, for some reason, he wanted to see happening there.

In the actual situation it was Farrell who unwisely gave Balanchine the ultimatum (on behalf of her husband, Mejia) and left the company, and who had to be replaced by other dancers—in *Diamonds* by Mazzo, in *Liebeslieder Walzer* by Karol von Aroldingen, in the second movement of *Symphony in C* by Mazzo or Kent. And it was concerning these dancers' performances that Clive Barnes wrote what he wanted to believe about them. He "rather preferred" Mazzo in *Diamonds* for her "quieter qualities... pleasingly secretive passion... and, most of all, a touching vulnerability—she is the kind of girl any decent man would offer his subway seat to." He implied similar preference in the statement that in *Symphony in C* Mazzo was "exceptional," and that, "avoiding the stylistic mannerisms of her predecessor—who here had an overfondess for kissing her knee—she was elegance itself." And he did so again in the statement that the European dancers in the New York City Ballet "always seem to have had a particular sensibility for 'Liebeslieder Walzer,'" a ballet which created a European world of vanished sentiment; and that von Aroldingen, "yet another European-born dancer... immediately revealed a natural feeling for the ballet" and "was absolutely enchanting, dancing with just that sense of deliquescence the ballet demands." (By implication Farrell, as an American who lacked the European's natural feeling for this ballet, had danced it less well; and it followed that since all the girls who had appeared in it except Verdy, and all the boys except Martins this year, had been Americans, the work hadn't ever been danced properly.)

Actually *Diamonds* was made by Balanchine for Farrell's tall body and her style of large movement, neither of which Mazzo has; and although she danced it beautifully, anyone who had seen Farrell's performance could see that Mazzo's was a lovely miniature which didn't produce the effect of Farrell's grandly sweeping movements. And in *Symphony in C* too, originally made for tall Tanaquil Le Clercq, those movements of Farrell's—including the tremendous extended *arabesque penché en pointe* that Mr. Barnes referred to as "kissing her knee"—were more impressive than Kent's exquisite smaller-scaled performance, which I saw, and presumably than Mazzo's, which I did not see. As for the Farrell role in *Liebeslieder Walzer*—originally made for tall Diana Adams, and given the stamp of Farrell's idiosyncratic style—though von Aroldingen was fairly tall and equipped to produce an approximation of Farrell's performance, anyone who had seen Farrell could see that von Aroldingen did achieve only an attractive approximation of what Farrell's extraordinary powers made breath-taking, and occasionally was unable to achieve even this adequate approximation. Thus, in one of the most striking details of the work Farrell, her hands held in support by her kneeling partner, bent over him in an *arabesque* on her flat foot, then rose on its pointed toe effortlessly, her other leg pointing straight up, and held that position for an instant before coming down. When she did this one was conscious only of the stunning climactic force of what one saw; but when von Aroldingen managed to get up on her pointed toe and came right down again, one not only saw a movement with no climactic force, but was aware of how difficult even this ineffective movement was for her.

To the admiration for Balanchine he professes constantly Mr. Barnes adds constant correction and instruction; and he ended his report on *Liebeslieder Walzer* and von Aroldingen with a paragraph about the "two strange flaws" in the work. One was that the boys at one point arrange chairs in a diagonal line for the girls to sit on, which "would be perfectly appropriate in a Lichine or Massine ballet-bouffe," but is strange in what Mr. Barnes characterized as the naturalistic choreography of *Liebeslieder Walzer*. The other was that "in the first duet between Miss Verdy and Mr. Magallanes it is the man who is constantly putting his hand across his face, in a gesture more easily identified as one of coquetry rather than rapture. It should surely be the girl doing this." So it should if it were a gesture of coquetry; but it isn't. The Verdy-Magallanes duet he referred to is not their first, but a later one in the succession of pieces for two or three or more dancers that are not just dances but danced dramatic episodes in which one sees the relations of the dancers change. Verdy in particular begins by dancing gaily and flirtatiously with Magallanes and the others; but the later slow duet Mr. Barnes referred to is one of dark estrangement, which she exhibits in the face she turns away from Magallanes, and he exhibits, at one point near the end, in the hiding of his face from her with his hand. It is beyond belief that anyone looking at them here should see coquetry in what they do; but Mr. Barnes managed it, demonstrating again that he is a dance critic who lacks the first essential of being able to see correctly what is presented to his eye. Moreover the steps of Verdy's and Magallanes's feet in this duet are those one might have seen in a nineteenth-century Viennese ballroom; but not the movements of the rest of their bodies that make it a dance of estrangement: these were produced by Balanchine's imaginative use of his idiosyncratic dance vocabulary, and make the choreography of the piece not naturalistic but fantastic. This is true of the other danced dramatic episodes of the work, whether serious or gay, in which the basic waltz steps are blended with imaginative Balanchine movements (most clearly true of the dances in the second part, in which the 19th century ball dresses and high-heeled shoes of the first part are replaced by ballet skirts and toe shoes); as it was true, let me add, of the danced episodes and games in Balanchine's great 1932 ballet, *Cotillon*, which Mr. Barnes didn't see (not that it would have made a difference if he had seen it). *Cotillon* had a delightful bit of *fantaisie Balanchine* in which the men stood behind the gilt chairs they had placed together for Riabouchinska to recline on languorously as though on a luxurious sofa and receive their homage; *Liebeslieder Walzer* has the episode which begins with the men placing chairs in a diagonal line for the girls to sit on and swing an arm gracefully from side to side. And Mr. Barnes's faulting Balanchine for this non-naturalistic detail was another instance of his inability to see correctly what is presented to his eye—to see that the detail is a manifestation of the *fantaisie Balanchine* operating from beginning to end of the work. *(160)*

These comments on dancers and choreography were only minor instances last spring of the Barnes operation, in which—unable to see what is actually happening on the stage, and thus, in effect, not tied down to it—Mr. Barnes is free to let what an editor I know characterized aptly as his rat's-nest mind produce his irresponsible chatter about imagined happenings. The major instance was his review of Jerome Robbins's new ballet, *Dances at a Gathering*. "Genius is simple, only talent proffers complications," was his opening statement about the work he wanted to have seen: the work that was "one of the most significant evenings in the American theater since O'Neill"; the work that left the answer no longer in doubt to the question "who—when the time eventually comes, in say 40 years, for Balanchine to retire—could possibly succeed him." It was a work whose choreographic invention had "something of [the] dazzling, virtuoso ease" of Balanchine, and whose "pattern of feeling [and] gestural language . . . to some extent adapted from Balanchine" were evident when "the dancers glance at one another with a loving awareness," and presumably when "they gesture to one another with the affection of friends, and they share life together"; a work that had also, indeed, "the feeling for the community, life and the earth" of Tudor's *Dark Elegies*, its "ultimate triumph" being perhaps that "it presents, with complete conviction, people walking and holding hands. People not hiding behind character, but being themselves" —like "three girls walking with innocence and tenderness under a warm night sky"; a work that in this feeling captured "Chopin's feel . . . for that peasant assurance of the earth beneath him and the sky above" in his music; a work that exhibited in other ways, if not Balanchine's "mandarin musical taste," then the "musicality . . . down to his eyebrows" that enabled Robbins to "choreograph not the musical beat of a score but its inner logic," to "hear the second voice, caress the internal rhythm."

My eye, on the other hand, sees the operation of genius in the unending flow and variety of excitingly beautiful and intricate movement that Balanchine's manipulation of his richly developed personal ballet vocabulary produces in the hour-long series of pieces to Brahms's *Liebeslieder Walzer*; and it saw mere talent operating even in the best that Robbins produced for the hour-long series of Chopin pieces. Thus it saw only the moderately attractive use of a limited conventional ballet vocabulary in a few pieces; and in others it saw the attempt to push beyond those limits, the straining for novelty and effect, produce details as outlandish and unattractive as the one in which McBride, her body extended in the air in a lift, drew her legs up into a squatting position, or the one in which Mazzo cycled in the air as she was carried across the stage. My eye saw Robbins's gift for comedy in the amusing piece in which Kent kept on dancing charmingly and hopefully as one boy after another showed interest and began to walk beside her, but then lost interest and drifted off; it saw the perceptive Robbins eye in the étude, to the Etude Op. 25 No. 4, made of Verdy's striking manner of pointing up the movements a choreographer gives her to do. But it saw in some pieces the Robbins gift for applause-getting show-biz tricks and stunts, the gift also for show-biz tear-jerking folksiness in that piece in which the three girls sauntered across the stage, their hands clasped behind their backs and their faces turned up to the sky; and it saw the Robbins addiction to attempts at profoundly meaningful simplicity in the final piece in which the dancers stood motionless facing the audience, their eyes following something that moved across the sky. In the pattern of feeling and gestural language of the folksy and pseudo-profound episodes my eye saw nothing adapted from Balanchine, and nothing related to Chopin's music, in which my ear heard no feeling for earth and sky. What my eye and ear did note instead was the misfit of Robbins's choreography and the B-minor Scherzo, most glaring at the return of the stormy opening section, and the amazing lack of sensitivity to the character of the closing section of the very first piece, the Mazurka Op. 63 No. 3: to this music of quiet retrospective reflection and summation Robbins had Villella do one of his high-powered crescendos of spins and leaps around the stage.

The few good pieces would have made an attractive 15 or 20-minute work; but with the numerous poor ones added to make it a Big Work and a Big Event for Mr. Barnes, it was, for me, a big bore. And not only for me: my guest at one of the performances, an experienced actor and director who once exclaimed after a new Balanchine work: "The fact is, the important things happening in the theater nowadays are being done right here," exclaimed now with a laugh after the Robbins work: "I thought it would never end! I haven't seen anything like that since the stage shows that were sent around to the big movie theaters years ago!" But as he said this the audience was roaring its enthusiastic approval of the Robbins work.* Robbins is not, then, the man who when Balanchine retires could provide the company with ballets continuing where Balanchine's left off, but rather the man who could provide it with the kind of entertainment miscellanies the public enjoys more than Balanchine's ballets.

The successful Robbins ballets for me have been the ones in which his powers have served the gift—which is to say, the sharply perceptive eye and mind—for comedy that I mentioned earlier: *Fancy Free*, the Mack Sennett ballet in *High-Button Shoes*, the sleepwalking ballet in *Look, Ma, I'm Dancin', Afternoon of a Faun*. They don't include *Interplay*, which is, for me, as unsuccessful in its strenuous attempt at humorous cleverness as the Morton Gould music it goes with. Leonard Bernstein's *Prelude, Fugue and Riffs* is an attempt at something much, much more sophisticated than the Gould piece, with results in which the pretentiousness is equalled by the awfulness. And Clifford's choreography for it last spring was in something

*In 1966 a friend, after about fifteen minutes of *Liebeslieder Walzer*, heard a bored member of the new subscription audience that had displaced the ballet-lovers who had supported the company until then sigh and exclaim: "Enough already!" Evidently the subscription audiences that were bored in 1966 have acquired interest but not taste and discrimination.

very much like the excessively clever style of *Interplay*, made even worse by the additional cuteness and archness.

With the transfer of Mazzo to *Diamonds*, the Mimi Paul role she had danced in *Emeralds* was assigned to Kent, who danced it exquisitely, but without the effect of the pointed style of Paul, which Mazzo had reproduced. On the other hand it was a pleasure to see Kent's lovely Terpsichore again, after several years, in the *Apollo* with Martins, which had Morris's excellent Polyhymnia and von Aroldingen's new and good Calliope. And though Mazzo didn't look like a queen she danced Titania in *A Midsummer Night's Dream* beautifully, and acted convincingly in the angry confrontation with Oberon and delightfully in the humorous scene with Bottom. Von Aroldingen, the new Helena, and Leland, the new Hermia, performed well (because I was watching them with special attention I also saw with new awareness what they were dancing—Balanchine's extraordinary adaptation of ballet idiom to imaginative purpose in now the solo of Hermia's frightened search for Lysander, now the *pas de deux* of Demetrius's violent rejection of Helena, now the *pas de deux* of her bewildered resistance to the ardor of Lysander, now the *pas de trois* of Lysander wooing Helena and rejecting Hermia); and Morris was a superb new Hippolyta. And I must mention the excellent Third Theme of Carol Sumner and Michael Steele and *Choleric Variation* of Gloria Govrin in a *Four Temperaments* in which Rapp's was the first satisfactory *Phlegmatic Variation* since Bolender's.

The Royal Ballet's opening program offered two new works of Frederick Ashton, *Enigma Variations*, a setting of the Elgar score, and *Jazz Calendar*, a setting of an elaborately uninteresting piece by Richard Rodney Bennett. It pleases Mr. Barnes to write about an imagined Ashton who is Balanchine's equal in his use of the choreographic medium and in the feeling for music he exhibits in that use. And one wishes Ashton really were the master of a ballet vocabulary and style as richly developed as Balanchine's and really could, like Balanchine, produce with it movement which not only was exciting in itself but was like a line of counterpoint in the way it completed the music and added to its meaning; for then there would be additional ballets as exciting to see as Balanchine's. But in reality Ashton has a limited conventional ballet vocabulary with which he produces bland sequences that at best are agreeable, but most often are boring, to look at, and that do no more than conform to the beat and character of the music. This was to be seen last spring in his new *pas de deux* for Florimund and the awakened Aurora at the end of Act 2 of *The Sleeping Beauty*, the music of which was the entr'acte Balanchine used in 1945 for a *pas de deux* for Danilova and Franklin. I retain only the image of Franklin walking backward out of the wings, leading a regal Danilova on her points; but I remember that what followed was an enthralling sequence of grand classical movement which enlarged the music it flowed out of; whereas in the Ashton *pas de deux* last spring—"one of the greatest of all Ashton pas de deux," said Mr. Barnes—one saw an attempt to give a new look to the few old lifts and turns and leaps, and thus to give to the sequences of movement an appearance of the life they didn't have—a pretense of producing something that actually produced nothing.

Ashton has a more modest view of himself—or at least had it in 1949, when a friend reported him as wondering what, after seeing so much of Balanchine's work, America would think of *his* babblings. But that was being a little too modest; for the babblings included two superb comic pieces, *Façade* and *A Wedding Bouquet*. And comedy still seems to be what he is best at: almost the only good things in the new works last spring were the comic bits for the eccentrics among the friends of Elgar one saw in *Enigma Variations*, and the one in *Thursday*, among the night-club-style pieces in *Jazz Calendar*. Most of the other attempts to show in movement what Elgar tells us about a friend in one of the variations were unsuccessful. Ashton could realize the "dance-like lightness" of "Dorabella" in a charmingly sprightly dance that communicated her gaiety, though not her pensiveness; he could have "B.G.N.," an amateur cellist, play the cello; but his visual dem-

onstration of "Winifred"'s "gracious personality" that "is sedately shown" in the music was
uninteresting; and his visual representation of
the deep friendship between Elgar and "Nimrod" had "Nimrod" placing a hand on Elgar's
shoulder and looking long and meaningfully
into his eyes, then the two beginning a Tudor-
like joint prance around the stage, and at the
end Elgar's wife joining them in a final solemn
exchange of glances. And while the other
danced portraits were not as bad as that, they
weren't good. All were performed well—in particular "Dorabella" by Antoinette Sibley, and
the eccentrics by Alexander Grant, Brian Shaw
and Wayne Sleep. And Grant was excellent
in *Jazz Calendar's Thursday*. Julia Trevelyan
Oman's Victorian set and costumes for *Enigma
Variations* were charming; Derek Jarman's sets
and costumes for *Jazz Calendar* were what one
would see in night-club sketches.

Postscript 1970 Robbins's setting of four additional Chopin Nocturnes, titled *In the Night*,
for the New York City Ballet provided an occasion for Clive Barnes—not, as I observed
earlier, one to ignore contradiction of his
pronouncements—to proclaim again what had
been contradicted: "Robbins is a genius."
This was in a Sunday article, *Jerome Robbins,
Choreographer*, in which Mr. Barnes wrote:

> Robbins was born to be our leading choreog-
> rapher one day. He shouted greatness almost
> with diffidence.... For a time it appeared that
> he was prepared to accept the secondary role
> of theater director—interpreting other men's
> work—and desert the primary, creative role of
> choreographer.... But I suspect that Robbins
> has...made his real creative commitment.
> Robbins is a choreographer. This is probably
> quite important for the well-being of Robbins. It
> may be absolutely vital for the well-being of
> American dance and, for that matter, world
> dance.

For the new piece showed that "what Robbins
is doing now is to explore the whole possibilities of choreography." One could see this
being done by other choreographers—by young
Eliot Feld [thus, in passing, the over-estimation

of Feld was reaffirmed], by Balanchine and
Ashton, both over 60 [their equality also was
reaffirmed]. "But Balanchine and Ashton, while
still extraordinarily fertile, are probably not
going far from where they have been before. It
is Robbins who is searching out all around
him"—for example in partnering: in the new
piece "Robbins has devised some extraordinarily ecstatic pas de deux." And reaffirmed also
was the special musical character of the Robbins
operation—the way the dances came straight
out of what was happening in the music.

But the actual three *pas de deux* of *In the
Night* that one saw on the stage reaffirmed the
truth about Robbins as a choreographer of
classical ballet: his limited talent for it, evident
in his limited vocabulary and imagination,
which he attempts to transcend with the straining ingenuity that achieves now this spectacular
acrobatic detail, now that one—e.g. the sensational lift in which Verdy was held upside down
—devised for its striking effect with no regard
for its lack of basis in the music. The lyrical
first two *pas de deux* lent themselves to being
made attractive by the personal styles of Mazzo
and Verdy in their dancing with Blum and Martins; the violent third one seemed to embody
an idea of Robbins the choreographic deep
thinker about humankind, in its danced conflict
between McBride and Moncion with now one,
now the other rushing off the stage and almost
immediately returning, and with its conclusion
as awful as anything in Robbins's *Facsimile*:
McBride, after such a return, walking slowly
across the stage to where Moncion stood, looking at him intently, then beginning to touch him
from face down to leg, ending on her knees before him in abasement. And after that, with the
fourth Nocturne, a Robbins coda in which the
three couples exhibited human togetherness.

The Robbins piece was shown up as the pretentious rubbish it was, a few days later, by the
completely unself-conscious and unpretentious
operation of the actual genius whose unending
exploration of the possibilities of choreography
is of world importance—Balanchine's in *Who
Cares?*, his setting of 17 of Gershwin's lovely
songs for musical shows of the 20s and early

30s. Balanchine had seen Gershwin's *Funny Face* in London, and other musicals there, so that he had become familiar with the genre and its dance style even before he came here, and was able to use that style with assured mastery in his dances for *On Your Toes, Babes in Arms* and *The Boys from Syracuse*—to mention only the early ones I saw. The plots of the Gershwin musicals, devised to provide occasions for someone like Fred Astaire to sing a song and go into a dance with it, would be unbearable today; but the Gershwin songs and the dances that were done with them—which can be seen in the Astaire films *Shall We Dance?* and *A Damsel in Distress*—still delight the ear and eye. And Balanchine's new ballet offered a succession of the songs with his exciting elaborations of all the kinds of movements in the dances originally done with them, in numbers for large and small ensembles and for soloists alone, in couples and in groups. The elaborations included classical ballet movements; and for *The Man I Love* Balanchine devised as original and beautiful a classical supported adagio as those he had made for music by Delibes and Glinka.

Do I have to add that Mr. Barnes, "looking at Balanchine's Broadway work"—which is to say, looking at what he had seen of it, "the deplorably vulgar" *Slaughter on Tenth Avenue* and the contributions to the films *The Goldwyn Follies* and *Star-Spangled Rhythm*, but not the Broadway-style dances Balanchine provided for the early musicals in addition to his innovative choreographies like the burlesque of *Scheherazade* and *Slaughter on Tenth Avenue* for *On Your Toes*—felt able to say that "this is not his medium" and that while Balanchine "was an innovator, a pioneer in musicals, he was not, perhaps, a masterly creator in this field." This was confirmed for Mr. Barnes by *Who Cares?*—by the "fussily trivial" choreography of "the ensembles and duets in a kind of bland Broadway style," and on the other hand by the solos and classical *pas de deux* that were good because in them Balanchine was "working in his own style." And though Gershwin "had considerable melodic invention . . . and many of his melodies have deservedly passed into our folk heritage," Mr. Barnes "would question whether he is worth a ballet in our national repertory."

Verdy, speaking in reply to questions at a meeting of Dance Society, thought—in reply to the first question—that a Balanchine dancer was one who could do what Balanchine wanted. The music he was working with gave him ideas of movements, of these movements in a time, a shape; what he asked you to do might seem impossible for you to do, but it was a challenge and you must attempt it; and when you succeeded it turned out to have been thought out precisely for what you could do.

Asked about the difference in working with Robbins in *Dances at a Gathering,* she pointed out that unlike Balanchine, Robbins—returning to the company after many years—wasn't acquainted with most of the dancers he had to work with, and therefore had to do a great deal of experimenting with them to find out what he could do with them. Something he tried with one dancer in one Chopin piece suggested following it with something else done by another dancer in another piece; what this dancer did suggested trying him together with someone in another piece, or trying him in something originally devised for someone else. And his way of working out her single solo was to dance it himself while she watched and imitated his movements behind him; then, when he told her to dance it, he kept stopping her after a phrase in order to try by dancing himself something new this phrase had suggested to him—a different thrust of the arm, an additional syncopation. For this experimentation he had to have all the dancers present all the time; and with the other rehearsing they had to do for the company's large repertory this created great difficulties for them.

One important difference between Balanchine and Robbins was that Balanchine, after completing the essential architecture of his ballet, left the detailed finishing of the movements to the dancers, whereas Robbins controlled their every slightest movement. And another important difference was that Balanchine worked only in terms of classical ballet, whereas Robbins brought in all his experience outside of classical ballet, his sense, from his Broadway experience, for audience reaction, and even psychoanalytic ideas. So for a dancer who had been doing only pure classical ballet with Balanchine, working with Robbins was a fascinating, exotic, almost naughty experience—like having a little fling. For herself she could say that the experience had given her a new realization of Balanchine's greatness; but she had to add that Robbins was the only choreographer with a creative drive similar to Balanchine's; and in this statement, as in the others, she revealed a recognition of his impressive gifts.*

Asked what—as someone who had danced a great deal with Villella—she would say about him, as against what she could say about dancing with Peter Martins, Verdy answered that

*But I am sure this extraordinarily perceptive and intelligent person recognized also what understandably she left unsaid: that in this art, as in every other, value depends not only on what gifts the artist possesses, but on what use he makes of them—in which Robbins can be faulted for his lapses of taste, his show-biz cleverness, slickness, cornyness and pretentiousness.

her long experience with Villella had taught her to respect and admire his intelligence, his honesty, his intense desire, when he performed, to give everything he had, his real suffering when he failed to achieve what he expected of himself; and for her there was no question of his greatness. In their work together she felt a "provocation" between them that almost always produced moments in which they achieved something extraordinary. It was a relation she would describe—and here she smiled winningly—as "loving competition: I *submit*—but compete; he is *gallant*—but competes also." Martins, on the other hand, was still in the process of revealing himself; and feeling safe with the technical background provided by the school of the Royal Danish Ballet, he was free to explore what Balanchine could give him. Her experience with him had been too limited for her to know much about him; but she could say she had found him a wonderful partner. And there was physically so much of him—here she smiled again—that at whatever point she had felt apprehensive, she had found a bit of Peter Martins there to make her secure.

PHOTOGRAPHS

Alexandra Danilova in Act I of *Coppélia*
(Ballet Russe de Monte Carlo) (Photos:
Fred Fehl).

Danilova and Frederic Franklin in last Act of *Coppélia* (Photos: Fehl).

Alicia Markova in *Pas de Quatre*
(Fehl).

Above: Markova and Hugh Laing in *Romeo and Juliet* (Fehl). Right: Yurek Lazovsky in *Petrushka* (Anon.).

Theme and Variations: Comparatively simple example of a favorite Balanchine contrivance, in which dancers clasping hands twist around each other or under each other's arms, in an intertwining involvement of their linked bodies.

Above: Alicia Alonso in *Swan Lake* (Fehl). Right: Igor Youskevitch in *Theme and Variations* (Ballet Theater) (Fehl). Facing page: *Theme and Variations* with Violette Verdy (New York City Ballet) (Martha Swope).

Top: *Theme and Variations*: Finale with Verdy and Edward Villella (Swope). Bottom and facing page: *Symphony in C*: Second Movement with Tanaquil LeClercq and Francisco Moncion (Ballet Society) (Peter Campbell).

Facing page: *Symphony in C*: Second Movement with Mimi Paul and Conrad Ludlow (top), Suzanne Farrell and Ludlow (bottom) (Swope). Right: *Orpheus* with Nicholas Magallanes and Moncion (Swope); Below: with Maria Tallchief and Magallanes (Fehl).

The Four Temperaments: Third Theme with Suki Schorer and Roland Vazquez (above), Paul and Frank Ohman (below) (below left, Fehl; others, Swope).

The Four Temperaments: Melancholic Variation with Richard Rapp (Swope).

Facing page top: *The Four Temperaments*: *Sanguinic Variation* with Melissa Hayden and Jacques d'Amboise (Swope); facing page bottom and this page: *Phlegmatic Variation* with Arthur Mitchell (Fehl).

Concerto Barocco: First Movement with Hayden (far left) and Farrell (Fehl).

Left: *Concerto Barocco*: Second Movement with Marie-Jeanne and William Dollar in the American Ballet's 1941 première (Schulman photos reproduced from *Dance Index* of February-March 1945).

Facing page: *Concerto Barocco*: Second Movement with Hayden and Ludlow (Swope).

Concerto Barocco: Second Movement with Farrell and Ludlow (left) (Swope), Hayden and Ludlow (below) (Fehl).

Concerto Barocco: Second Movement: These two photographs taken at different performances show two successive moments in a Balanchine involvement of dancers linked by clasped hands: the girl on the right in the upper photograph—her left hand clasped by that of the girl in the center, her right clasping that of the principal dancer on the left—twists under their arms to arrive at a point on the left of the principal dancer in the lower photograph.

Above, one moment (the only one photographed) in another such involvement—this one much more complicated, and amusing in both its complication and eventually (in the later moments not photographed) its resolution into simplicity.

Concerto Barocco: Second Movement with Farrell and Ludlow (Swope).

129

Above, at a climactic moment near the end of the movement the boy
repeatedly thrusts the girl's extended body in a slide away from him,
then pulls her up into the position shown in this photograph. (A photograph of the slide was not to be found.)

Left: Margot Fonteyn in Act II of *Swan Lake*. Below: *Billy the Kid* with John Kriza and Janet Reed (Fehl).

Facing page top: *Concerto Barocco*: Second Movement with Patricia McBride and Ludlow (Swope); bottom: Third Movement with Hayden and Farrell (Fehl).

Firebird with Verdy and Moncion (top left, Fehl; others, Swope).

134

Apollo with André Eglevsky, Tallchief, Diana Adams and LeClercq (Fehl).

Facing page: *Apollo* with Lew Christensen, Marie-Jeanne, Marjorie Moore and Olga Suarez in the American Ballet's 1941 production (Schulmann photos reproduced from *Dance Index* of February-March, 1945).

Facing page top: *Apollo* with d'Amboise, Patricia Wilde and Jillana (Swope); bottom left: with Ludlow and Nancy Johnson; bottom right: with Sally Bailey and Christine Bering (San Francisco Ballet, 1956) (Anon.).

Right: *Apollo* with Ludlow, Jillana, Allegra Kent and Wilde (New York City Ballet) (Fehl); below: with Villella, McBride and Schorer (Swope).

Facing page: *Apollo* with Villella, Schorer, McBride and Carol Sumner (Fehl). Right: *Apollo* with Peter Martins, Farrell, Marnee Morris and Karol von Aroldingen (Swope).

Apollo: Another Balanchine involvement of dancers linked by clasped hands, in which Terpischore moves on points around Apollo and the other two muses.

"Those large-spanned, soarings leaps...around the muses
... that express his wonder and delight." (page 44)

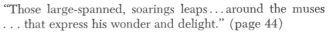

Apollo with Martins (Swope). Facing page top left: *Prodigal
Son* with Moncion and Yvonne Mounsey beginning the seduc-
tion pas de deux; bottom left: Moncion in the scene after the
Prodigal's despoilment; right: *Bourrée Fantasque* with Le-
Clercq and Jerome Robbins (Fehl).

141

This page and facing page top: *Le Baisér de la Fée* with LeClercq and Magallanes (Fehl).

Swan Lake with Kent and Ludlow (Fehl).

Swan Lake with Verdy and Villella (Swope).

Facing page: *Les Sylphides* with Markova and Erik Bruhn (Fehl). Above: *Filling Station* with d'Amboise and Reed. Right: *Afternoon of a Faun* with LeClercq and Moncion (Fehl).

Facing page: *The Nutcracker* with Verdy as
Dewdrop, Tallchief and Bruhn as the Sugar
Plum Fairy and her Cavalier (Fehl). Above:
Divertimento No. 15: Adagio with Wilde and
Bruhn (Fehl); right: Paul and Mitchell (Swope).

Left: *Agon: Pas de Trois II* with Hayden, Jonathan Watts and Roy Tobias; above and facing page top: *Pas de Deux* with Mitchell and Adams, Mitchell and Farrell; facing page bottom: Coda (Fehl).

Episodes: Symphony Opus 21 with Verdy and Watts (Fehl).

Episodes: Concerto Opus 24 with Kent and Magallanes (Swope).

Above left: *Episodes*: Concerto
Opus 24 with Kent and Magallanes
(Swope); above right: Five Pieces
Opus 10 with d'Amboise (Swope);
left: Variations Opus 30 with Paul
Taylor (Fehl).

Facing page: *Episodes*: Concerto Opus 24
with Kay Mazzo and Magallanes (Swope).

Above: *La Sonnambula*: top left with Kent and Bruhn (Fehl), others with Verdy and Magallanes (Anon.).
Below: *The Figure in the Carpet* (**Swope**).

Facing page: *Liebeslieder Walzer*: Part I with Verdy, Ludlow and Magallanes (top), Verdy and Magallanes (bottom) (top and bottom left, Swope; right, Fehl).

Above: *The Figure in the Carpet*: The Prince and Princesses of Lorraine with Schorer, Susan Borree and Villella (Swope). Right: *Donizetti Variations* with Verdy and Villella (Fehl).

Liebeslieder Walzer: Part I with Verdy and Magallanes, Adams and Bill Carter, McBride and Watts, Jillana and Ludlow (above), Adams and Carter (left) (Swope).

Liebeslieder Walzer: Part I with
Farrell and Kent Stowell (Swope).

161

Facing page top: *Liebeslieder Walzer*: Part I with McBride and Ohman, Farrell and Stowell, Verdy and Magallanes, Paul and Ludlow; bottom: Part II with Jillana and Ludlow, Adams and Carter, Verdy and Magallanes, McBride and Watts (Fehl). Right and below: *Liebeslieder Walzer*: Part II with Verdy and Magallanes (right, Swope; below, Fehl).

Sequence 3

Sequences and single movements from film copy of Bell Telephone
Hour telecast of Tchaikovsky *Pas de Deux* with Verdy and Villella
(telecast produced by Robert Drew Associates). It should be realized that a single frame of a film cannot be as sharp and clear as a
still photograph. In addition, regrettably, these photographs reveal
evidence of deterioration in the film.

Supported adagio, continued,
single movement.

Solo

Sequence 5

Solo: "... *passé*, *passé*, hold ..."   (page 75 of text)

Coda

A *Midsummer Night's Dream* with
Villella (above), Farrell (right)
(Fehl).

Bugaku with Kent and Villella (Fehl).

Bugaku with Kent and Villella (Fehl).

This page and facing page top: *Bugaku* with Kent and Villella (left and facing page, Fehl; below, Swope). Facing page bottom: *Movements* with Farrell and d'Amboise (Fehl).

Left: *Tarantella* with Villella (Swope).

Below: *Les Noces* with Sallie Wilson and William Glassman (Fehl). Facing page top: *Les Noces* with Glassman and Erin Martin (rear center), Veronika Mlakar and Wilson (front); bottom: Glassman and Martin (Jack Mitchell).

Rudolf Nureyev and Fonteyn
in *Swan Lake* (Fehl).

This page and facing page bottom: *Don Quixote*: Act II, *Pas de Deux Mauresque* with Schorer and John Prinz (Swope).

Above: *Don Quixote*: Act II with
Farrell and Balanchine (Fehl).

Don Quixote: Act III with Farrell
and Ludlow (Swope).

Emeralds: The photographs of Verdy supported by Ludlow show three successive moments in the continuous progression in which the dancers' exchanges of hands make possible the leverages for the turns and other movements that take Verdy from the moment in the first photograph to the one in the second, and from this to the one in the third.

Jewels: I, *Emeralds* with Verdy and Ludlow (Swope).

Jewels: Emeralds with Paul (Swope).

Jewels: Emeralds with Verdy (Swope).

Jewels: Emeralds with Paul and Moncion (Swope).

"...Paul enters, held and escorted by Moncion with great ceremony, and makes delicate step after step on pointed toe to the *moderato* beats of the still Fauré music—at one point...interrupting her stepping for...an arabesque, a turn...." (page 95).

Jewels: II, *Rubies*: First Movement with Neary (Swope).

Jewels: Rubies: Second Movement with McBride and Villella.

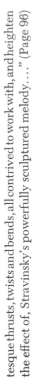

" . . . 'the goddamnedest pas de deux ever!' . . . the seeming ultimate in newly imagined inflection of their bodies by sharp, perverse, grotesque thrusts, twists and bends, all contrived to work with, and heighten the effect of, Stravinsky's powerfully sculptured melody. . . ." (Page 96)

Left and facing page: *Jewels*: III, *Diamonds* with Farrell and d'Amboise (Swope).

Diamonds with Farrell and Martins (Swope).

Facing page top: *Konservatoriet* performed by Royal Danish Ballet (Fehl); bottom: *Variations* (Swope). Right: *Giselle* with Bruhn and Carla Fracci. Below: *Glinkiana* with Verdy and Paul Mejia (Fehl).

"Some dancers are good only in certain things: they are lyric dancers, or dramatic dancers, or romantic dancers, or *demi-caractère* dancers. But Verdy is such a rounded dancer that I can see her doing any role." (page 76)

197

Giselle: Boston Ballet's 1968 production with Verdy and Villella; left: Act I (Frank Derbas); below: Act II (André de Ribère); facing page: Act II (top, Derbas; bottom, de Ribère).

Pithoprakta with Farrell and Mitchell (Swope). Mitchell making motions of support in the adagio with Farrell in which he actually is not touching and supporting her at all.

Slaughter on Tenth Avenue with Farrell (Fehl).

This and the following pages give single movements
and sequences from the film made by Gerald Fitzgerald of the Boston Ballet's 1969 production of *Giselle*
with Verdy and Villella.

from Act I

Act II: (Left to right) Moments in the sequence in which Giselle makes the kneeling Albrecht aware of her incorporeal presence.

Giselle: Act II, continued.

Giselle: Act II, continued.

Giselle: Act II, continued.

Balanchine in rehearsal with Adams and Mitchell (top), Verdy (bottom) (Swope).

"For years I have watched him do a movement he devised for a dancer more beautifully than the dancer for whom it was devised." (page 100)

INDEXES

INDEX OF WORKS AND DANCERS*

*Numbers in bold type indicate pages with photographs.

ACKNOWLEDGMENTS

I am indebted to

Martha Swope, for her extraordinarily generous help — given out of a feeling of comradeship in a common objective — without which the section of photographs would have been impossible.

Peter Campbell, Frank Derbas and André de Ribère, for generously making their photographs available to me.

Violette Verdy, Yurek Lazovsky and Conrad Ludlow, for the loan of photographs by unknown photographers; Miss Verdy again, for the loan of Gerald Fitzgerald's film of the Boston Ballet *Giselle*, and Mr. Fitzgerald, for his help to Miss Verdy in the use of frames from it.

Edward Villella, for the loan of his film copy of the Bell Telephone Hour Tchaikovsky *Pas de Deux*; and American Telephone and Telegraph Company and N. W. Ayer and Son Inc., for their permission to use frames from it.

The staff of the Dance Collection in the New York Public Library's Library and Museum of the Performing Arts, where I found Peter Campbell's photographs, and also several taken in London of Francisco Moncion and Yvonne Mounsey in the seduction *pas de deux* of *Prodigal Son* which I was unable to use because of difficulties with the photographer.

The New York City Ballet, for the loan of several photographs and help in obtaining others.

Dance Index, for permission to reproduce the Schulmann photographs.

William H. Youngren, for his help in the selection of the text.

Oxford University Press, for its permission to include passages from a few reviews previously reprinted in *Music Observed*.

The staff of Horizon Press, for the thought and time and work that were given to the planning and making of the book.